Leadville

U * S * A

Leadville

U * S * A

> ED B. LARSH & ROBERT NICHOLS <

> FOREWORD BY LORIN HOLLANDER <

Johnson Books: Boulder

Library of Congress Cataloging-in-Publication Data
    Larsh, Edward B.
        Leadville, U.S.A.: an intimate history of a Colorado
mining town / Ed Larsh & Robert Nichols.
            p.   cm.
        Includes bibliographical references and index.
        ISBN 1-55566-097-5
        1. Leadville (Colo.)–History.   I. Nichols, Robert, 1944–   II. Title.
F784.L4L37   1992
978.8'46–dc20   92-25236
                                                                              CIP

Cover Photograph: Leadville looking west to Mount Massive
Cover Design: Bob Schram/Bookends
Frontispiece: John Minor Larsh family, circa 1895

Printed in the United States of America by
Johnson Printing Company
1880 South 57th Court
Boulder, Colorado 80301

Contents

Foreword

There has always been considerable debate among those who study the paradigms in which history is written about whether the *subjective* telling and recording of the memories of those who lived in a particular period has the same historical credibility as does the *objective* writing of history. The question posed is whether the memories of the people about whom a historical record is created—often available through the memories of their children—are a credible source about what happened in a time long past.

No one would argue that there have been self-serving accounts of historical events and the crucial people involved that have little value as a historical document. Nor would anyone argue that the rigorous objective science of historical detective work is of less importance, or lacks the credentials in its own right to search for an understanding of past events and experiences. It is, however, the balance of the objective and subjective paradigms of history that allows us to more closely feel and touch the essence of what subjective or objective histories often lack in and of themselves—a grasp of the human drama. We discover that we are studying the lives of real people, flesh and blood, body and soul, with dreams and fantasies, successes and failures, shadows and utterly complex personalities—that knowledge often does not shine through when only an analytical approach is utilized.

The Sufis, a mystical Moslem sect, admonish that "all wisdom will be yours when you learn the difference between the *contents* and the *container*." In music we have seen this distinction lost when creativity is polarized into the realm of engineers, who play fast and brilliantly, but without warmth and compassion, without the heart and soul of the poet. In history, the distinction is between those who accept only writings of historians who survey their domain from a distant, objective position, and those who tell it as they remember it from the subjective state of their own recollections. It is surprising that the objectivists do not readily admit that they often base their own overviews and conclusions on just such personal recollections of people. Indeed, some of the greatest history is available only through the testimonies and remembrances of those who lived through the experience.

Ed Larsh has recorded the oral history of a small town in the Colorado Rockies as told through his ancestors and his neighbors. Larsh shares his memories as a grandchild, and speaks to us about the research he has done into the memories of his neighbors and friends. The work he has created out of these memories and recollections is at once beautiful and wildly hilarious, often totally unbelievable but true, and poignant beyond the limits of all but those with an overflowing heart and soul. He shows us that history is alive because it is about people who lived. The historical names were human beings, who without an Ed Larsh would have left us no account of their existence save the civil notices of birth and transition and their tombstones.

In *Leadville U.S.A.* we embark on an epic journey overflowing with rich and dramatic characters so much like ourselves that we empathize and become them. We understand what they must have felt as they lived lives which required strength and fortitude to survive. They did it while always keeping alive their song, their dance, their craft, and their intuitive understanding of the central importance of the family. Although many were gamblers, prostitutes, and eccentrics, they displayed more humanity and compassion, more insight and intuitive greatness, than do most members of our present society.

Ed Larsh and Robert Nichols have not only written an oral history, but they also give this form of history a new and vital meaning.

They illuminate how the oral tradition can be a revelation with bold dimensions, history with a deeply humane vision that renders the oral retelling of history a necessary and irreplaceable component of the historical record, and one that alone brings to life the heart and soul of the people about whom we are studying. In one grand drama, oral history sweeps us into the lives of families about whom we learn to care, love and understand, and into a life and time which teaches us lessons about ourselves that we couldn't learn in any other way.

This is a great work of history, in part because it is also a great work of art. Its accomplishment is that it places the entire realm of the subjective mode of retelling the past on a new plane. In doing so, it illuminates the reasons for many of our problems and everyday stresses. We are given a glimpse into what we have lost in living and what we must regain in order to be complete human beings, imbued with the dignity, compassion and creative cultural involvement that gives us the right to consider ourselves special as living creatures.

Ed Larsh and Robert Nichols open our minds to an archive of oral historical records that tell the stories of those who lived in earlier times and who left us their experiences, not as was surmised from the distance of years, but as was recollected by those who were there at the moment of unfolding—real, deeply human, and alive. *Leadville U.S.A.* is a book to treasure.

Lorin Hollander

Jane Ann Larsh
1930–1992

That Jane courageously lived with cancer for fourteen years showed a tenacious spirit in a life dedicated to helping others. In the sixties before Jane and I left the pebbled beaches of Carmel by the Sea for Africa and the Peace Corps, she camped in a tent on Mount Massive near Leadville. She helped search for corner posts on hundred-year-old unfulfilled dreams of delinquent mining claims. She climbed twelve fourteen-thousand-foot Colorado peaks and plunged into the purity of an icy pool every morning to "the sound of mountain water." She was very much alive.

In early fall of 1992, the disease had gone to the liver. From our writing desk—every day—in summer and winter, we had watched the Canadian geese, our eagles, and Jane's dog, Sophie, with Mount Sopris as a divide to the ethereal beauty of the universe. From our deck—every day—we listened to the symphony of the river. It seemed to be both transient and eternal. In such a magical place, it was impossible to believe that one would ever die; our senses all said otherwise. We felt alive, creative, together, and very fortunate.

On September 6, our daughter, Skye, helped me carry her ashes to the top of Mount Sopris. From the snows of Mount Sopris can be seen the snows of Mount Massive. Jane edited every line that Robert and I wrote. She had become fascinated with Leadville's history. History, especially oral history, connects rivers, mountains, clouds, and the Kingdom of God. Jane Ann O'Herren Larsh lives on in this book—it is dedicated to her in both her memory and her presence.

Preface: Staking Our Claim

The land and the time and the people: the intersection of opportunity and personality that creates an event. The history of humanity is that of cultures built by the integration of commerce, beliefs, geography, and individuals. In Leadville, there was the commerce of precious metals, the belief in El Dorado, the geography of the Rocky Mountains, and thousands of individuals who created the amalgam of the city's human character.

It is tempting to be polemical—to affirm that there were black and white scenarios, clear-cut patterns of development leading from past to present. But 130 years of Leadville's "chicken and feathers" history is enough to convince one otherwise.

Writing factual essays on the past (history, if you will) is not easy. Contemplating the mass of "objective" data, Carlyle's "great dust-heap" of history, and the grand theories constructed to explain them, we sometimes fail to see what is significant in the supposedly non-essential details. But the details are where the life was—and is. To avoid being statistical or encyclopedic, all of which has been done before for Leadville as well as for the whole West, we need to bring to our writing the human truths we have learned ourselves the hard way, by living. With those in mind we will, we hope, be able to recognize and tease out the human truths that lie inert in the raw material of our story.

What has been most interesting in our examination of the community of Leadville has been the project of reconstruction, our attempt to "back map" the daily lives of the real people. We discover that the real people of the West are not those depicted by John Wayne. They are more like our grandparents and great-grandparents who wore much smaller Stetsons. They are the aunts and uncles of family legend more than those of the myths of the mighty of sword or bankroll. They are the people who had grand-children who asked questions like "How come?"

The grandchildren of those who chose to stay in Henry County, Iowa, or Preble County, Ohio, in 1875 probably view the world more conservatively than the grandchildren of those who, in the same year, sought the openness of the High Plains and then continued westward and upward against the flow of waters—into the Rocky Mountains. There was something, perhaps, about the uncertainty and adversity of life in the mountains that broadened the mind.

If you fly across Colorado today in a smooth arc from, say, Des Moines to Disneyland, you will realize that the word "Mountains" in Rocky Mountains is not on the same level of generality as the "Plains" in High Plains. The plains are pretty much plains for hun-dreds of miles; the mountains are in reality a succession of massive ridges or ranges, each with its own character. First is the Front Range, dominated by Mount Evans in the center, Pikes Peak to the south, and Longs Peak to the north. Then, you pass over the Mos-quito Range and soon the Sawatch swelling from the Mount of the Holy Cross on south to Mount Princeton. The roll call of ranges continues as you fly southwest, but stop for a moment to realize that nestled down there between the cresting waves of this great rock sea is the town of Leadville. You will begin to realize the hard-ship of going west in the nineteenth century. Your perspective is radically different from those who journeyed to the middle of the Rocky Mountains in the summer of 1877. You are looking down; they were looking up.

In 1860, from the settlement called Denver at the confluence of Cherry Creek and the South Platte River, it took Augusta and Horace Tabor three months to reach California Gulch, about seventy-five miles as the crow or airliner flies. It would have been far easier for them to have veered south along the relatively gentle terrain on the east side of the Front Range, perhaps settling in

Rocky Ford to become melon magnates instead of the royalty of a silver boom. How much of their decision to struggle to the higher lands was based upon dreams or a sense of adventure or upon simple gold fever is impossible to say. But it is clear that they didn't take the easiest route to their future.

Just getting there, going against the grain of nature, was not enough to qualify one as a contributing member of the community. The journey was difficult but not as demanding as the dues you had to pay once you arrived. Because of the rapid development of Leadville, traditions were formed quickly. The values of a single cycle of seasons established norms for a generation. But you had to stay there long enough to know these values by living them. In his essay, "The Book and the Great Community," Wallace Stegner writes:

> Except as we belong to a tradition and a community—and perhaps except as we bear some constructive hostility to those bonds—we are nothing. We have no language, no history, no lore, no legend, no myth, no custom, no religion, no art, no species memory. But the moment our built-in emotions of fear and aggression are modulated to the need of companionship and mating and protection of the young, we have begun to form, in the most rudimentary way, the community of men, for which another name is the Kingdom of God. We are both bound and emancipated by that membership. It is probably bad anthropology, but I like to think that some of the hand prints painted in ochre on Utah cliffs were made by primitive men and women making an assertion of their simultaneous and joined identity. And if their sons, escaping in anger from the harsh domination of the family and the tribe, should dip their own palms in ochre and press their own marks on a cliff to demonstrate that their hand and their strength is greater than their father's, so be it. Maybe it is bigger. But it is well to have daddy's hand print there for a beginning and a gage.

The "hand print" of such people of sufficient courage (or perhaps abandon) and perseverance (or perhaps stubbornness) to make their way to Leadville and then to establish a community there is indelibly imprinted upon the character of its history as well as its future.

The myth of Sisyphus can be a most depressing way to characterize the meaning of life, but it is appropriate for a hard life in the midst of the Rocky Mountains, and there is more than one way to interpret it. According to the story, Sisyphus was damned to struggle throughout eternity rolling a large stone up a steep hill only to slip just as the peak was almost attained. The stone rolled back down, and Sisyphus started again in an endless cycle of futility.

The people of Leadville have rolled a rock or two toward impossible summits, only to be flattened as the boulders of failure came rumbling back down to the bottom again. But rather than wallow in the disillusionment of a lost El Dorado, our mountain Sisyphus managed to salvage and even relish the richness and worth of the climb. This is perhaps the final truth of the myth. You will find satisfaction in life if you value the climb for itself, but if you value it solely for the attained goal, you are doomed to perpetual frustration.

The people who struggled and still struggle against the grain may find more of a real El Dorado than those who actually know the fleeting wealth of gold and silver. This may be the message of Leadville and its communal peers around the nation. We need to listen; we need to see and not just look; we need to learn what it is that we need to learn, and then learn it.

Ed B. Larsh
Robert Nichols

Introduction

All four of my grandparents arrived in Leadville long before the twentieth century. My paternal grandfather, John Minor Larsh, came over Mosquito Pass late in the summer of 1877. At that time, Colorado had been a state for only one year, and Leadville was still called Oro City. Like many early settlers, his family arrived in phases. First came his brother Charles, who traveled there with his best friend, Lewis Lamb, in 1876. John followed their lead a year later, and finally, after another year, another brother and three sisters made their way west from the conservative and economically distressed plains to the risk and promise of the rugged Rocky Mountains. Along with his family came his wife-to-be, Rachel Edwards. His sister Mamie, my great-aunt, became the first school teacher officially employed by what is now the Leadville School District. His sister Edie, also my great-aunt, became a prostitute.

Between 1880 and 1892, eight children were born to John and Rachel, my father, Edward Larsh, being the youngest of them. He was born in a cabin at 230 West Second Street, less than a block-and-a-half from the infamous Pioneer Bar and the rowdy times on State Street. After graduating from the sixth grade at Central School in 1904, he went to work as a printer's devil at the *Leadville Herald Democrat*, where he began a lifelong career in printing and newspaper work.

As a kid during the Great Depression of the 1930s, I listened to the Leadville stories told by my aunts and uncles and by my parents. I knew the old people who had survived the early days to tran-

scend epochs and tell their tales first-hand. Later I read historical
and mythical writings about the lives of H. A. W. Tabor, David Moffat, David May, Meyer Guggenheim, John Cleveland Osgood, and
others and found such accounts to be of a different kind than
those of an oral and personal tradition. Nowhere in the chronicles
of the times or the historical literature is there mention of Rachel
Larsh and how she raised eight children in a small wooden house
without electricity or running water. Nowhere is there mention of
the heroes and heroines who, confronting the rigors of an
extremely difficult economic and physical environment, maintained households abundant with love and self-respect.

   In this work Robert Nichols and I endeavor to correct this over-
sight and present elements of a personally encountered and thus
more universal history. All that we write actually happened and,
whenever possible, actual names are used—to protect the innocent from obscurity or oblivion. In fact and figure, date and data,
we have striven for accuracy, though statistical perfection has not
been our highest criterion of excellence. Among the most thoroughly documented lives and events of this era there is considerable inconsistency in the source material. In the "soft" history of
families and personal legends even less precision is possible.

   Surely there will be purists who will judge us in violation of certain precepts of style and historical convention, particularly in the
use of narrative and dialogue in our attempt to breathe life and
sense of being into lives which have been relegated to single-lined
entries in courthouse records and sparse data chipped into the
granite of gravestones.

   But they will have missed the point—a very important point.
An issue much larger than the glorification of my simple family or
my small hometown is being expressed here. Our approximation
of an era is intended to be more humanly accurate than historically verifiable. And only if the descendants of the so-called "little
people" who have been the essence of the unwritten reality of history—the children and grandchildren of men who toiled lifetimes
in twelve-hour shifts in mines and smelters to provide the basic
needs of decent existence, the heirs of women who were the heart

and strength of families and the ethos that created a continuing community from the sprawl of an expendable mining camp—only if such people decide that we have missed the mark will we consider this work a failure.

In doing research, we read extensively, but we listened even more extensively. We've been to the libraries, the courthouses, the graveyards, and the newspaper morgues. But of greater importance, we have listened to the recollected truth of generations. Robert and I have taken notes and worked out contradictions and chronologies, but also, I clearly remember the talk at Friday-night taffy pulls in my mom's kitchen when my dad would tell us stories of his father, John Larsh the gambler, and of his mother, Rachel Larsh, who was the soul of a fine family.

The history of Leadville as a socio-economic phenomenon could be written in an objective style by any good scholar. *Leadville U.S.A.*, from the uncommon perspective of common people, could only be written in a personal style. You, the reader, must know who my Aunt Mindy was if you are to appreciate what my Aunt Mindy and all the other "Aunt Mindys" of the American West did.

I have always greatly admired the first paragraph of Steinbeck's *Cannery Row:*

> Cannery Row in Monterey in California is a poem, a stink, a grating noise, a quality of light, a tone, a habit, a nostalgia, a dream. Cannery Row is the gathered and scattered, tin and iron and rust and splintered wood, chipped pavement and weedy lots and junk heaps, sardine canneries of corrugated iron, honky tonks, restaurants and whore houses, and little crowded groceries, and laboratories and flophouses. Its inhabitants are, as the man once said, "whores, pimps, gamblers, and sons of bitches," by which he meant Everybody. Had the man looked through another peephole he might have said, "Saints and angels and martyrs and holy men," and he would have meant the same thing.

Looking through the swinging doors of the Pioneer Bar in Leadville on any night back in the 1880s, you would have seen exactly the same kind of people, the only difference being that some of them would have been my relatives.

Larsh gambling room at 230 West Second Street,
Leadville, Colorado, circa 1890.

Part 1

Getting There: The Pioneers

*Left to right, top to bottom: Rachel Larsh, Edith Larsh,
John Minor Larsh, Mamie Larsh, Minda A. Lamb*

1

From Deadwood to Fairplay

As you enter the town of Fairplay from the south, the mountains to the north and west are splendid in the clarity of clean air and a cloudless day. Patches of snow cling tenaciously to the high rock faces of the Continental Divide, and beneath the summer sun the streams of South Park rush with chilled mountain waters. Last night's cool air invigorates the bright sunlight. The wooden buildings cast long shadows to the west. Fairplay seems to sleep while the rest of the world spins out of control.

It seems as if half of the fine old town of Fairplay is boarded up, and the other half is for sale. Looking past the half-dozen or so pedestrians scattered along the sidewalks, past the trickle of traffic coming down the highway from Hoosier Pass, past the rooftops of abandoned gift shops and diners, you see the timeless rocks and seasoned snowfields that edge the blue sky.

The mountains have been here through vast epochs of geological time. In the relatively brief sojourn of humankind on this sphere of rock and sea and fertile soil, it would seem that greed and corruption and violence have dominated the time of our habitation. Such can be the mental and emotional burden of those who ponder more than the demands of their own comfort or survival and consider the grand purposes of our species. But such despair does not befit the West.

Fairplay is not a dead town, nor is it dying. It is a mountain town, and it has known many phases of boom and bust. The grocery store thrives, as does the hardware store next door to it and the Brown Burrow Cafe down the street. Out on the highway the J-Bar-J Lounge has quarters stacked on the pool table, the juke box blasting amplified, raucous sounds. A couple of convenience store/gas stations are doing okay, and the Rocky Top Cafe (a.k.a. "The Dinky Diner") crowds the hungry into its Lilliputian confines every breakfast, lunch, and dinner. The new Mustard Seed Restaurant will soon need a maitre d' to sort out the hungry who clamor for its delectable sustenance. Over on Main Street, there are successful purveyors of antiques, collectibles, and junk, and the Park Bar packs them in every afternoon for a seventy-five-cent-draught happy hour. Prunes, the famous burro preserved in statuary on one of the side streets, ignores it all in timeless indifference.

It's a mountain town. It's tougher than hard times.

At the end of Main Street is a historical exhibit, South Park City—a block of history, an assemblage of buildings with furnishings, goods, and ghosts intact.

Gasping for a breath of hope amid the congestive crises of a world of cocaine crack, chemical warfare, degrading welfare, and couch-potato indifference, it is difficult to express positive belief in the potential of the human spirit. Never, it seems, has our magnificent species been in such jeopardy of either a "bang or a whimper."

This is why we ask you to join us and journey together across Mosquito Pass to the town of Leadville—because, throughout the history of this town, difficulty has not spawned defeat. The people of Leadville have found the courage and persistence essential to survival, qualities that would serve us well whether we dwell in the tenements of New York, the tract houses of suburbia, or the Rockies of Colorado. Look upon this journey as a resource in the inevitable struggle of thinking people against despair.

We begin in the dining room of the Fairplay Hotel, which has served road-weary travelers and locals for well over a century. The hotel has been renovated only to the extent that basic necessities of modern living are apparent. Save the presence of a few light switches, the sound of a radio playing, and the proximity of a microwave oven, it is similar to the accommodations provided since the hotel opened in 1873. The uncarpeted, wooden floors creak as waitresses move about. The walls are a light pink, trimmed with dark molding. The high ceiling is supported by polished timbers, and the windows along the south wall are large and edged by ruffled curtains. All that is lacking in the ambiance of rustic formality are the long-dead players of its century of scenes. The coffee is excellent.

John Minor Larsh, my grandfather, passed through Fairplay sometime late in the summer of 1877. It is likely he spent at least a night in one of the rooms here. He probably ate breakfast in this dining room before he embarked upon foot or horseback on the trek across Mosquito Pass. The toll road traversed by ore wagons and stages of the Spottswood McClellan Coach Line would not be open for another two years. Though an easier wagon route over Weston Pass, miles to the south, was open at the time, John chose to take the more arduous and direct route to Leadville.

Regardless of the specific roads, rivers, tracks, or trails taken, the migration to Leadville was radically upstream and upslope. The character of those who braved such an unorthodox migration was a crucial element in determining the nature of the communities they established.

But John was dealing with more than just the difficulty of the environment during his brief stay at the Fairplay Hotel. Just days earlier he had paid Henry Boyer—carpenter, furniture maker, and mortician—thirty dollars for a pine wood coffin and a plot of ground in the cemetery at Georgetown, Colorado.

In early 1877, when John Larsh made his way from his home in Illinois to St. Louis and up the Missouri River to Fort Pierre, South Dakota, and then on to the town of Deadwood, everywhere—in conversations overheard in general stores, in rumors spread about the decks of riverboats and along wagon-rutted trails, in wistful dreams of flatland farmers, and in boasts of young and old—was spoken the magnificent word "west." West was not a direction or a region; it was a concept and the concept was an obsession.

West was the bank of the river. West was the taste of the wind. West to Deadwood was west of St. Joe. West was where the land was still wild and open for the taking, and the gold in glimmering mountains abounded for harvest. West was where a clever young man, a gambler by trade, could seek riches, romance, adventure— all the elements of a life rescued from the furrows of Illinois and freed to know the rich abandon of risk.

John had heard of the boom towns, the all-night saloons, the no-limit gambling, and the pans and pouches filled with gold. He had heard the tales of fortune's gifts and fortune's reversals. And he was ready. Apprenticeship was over, and it was time to ply his craft. He had trained with a master, a guru of gambling, an old man who had played the gold fields of California and the river-boats of the Mississippi and who had settled down for his last years in Deadwood, South Dakota. You can quit the game, but it's hard to put down the cards. The old man, Mac was his name, took a liking to John and spent evenings with him shuffling the deck and teaching the tricks that had supported him for decades.

John was immediately fascinated with gambling and quickly developed the dexterity needed to deal a card from the bottom of a deck and the quickness of eye to read its reflection in a well-placed "shiner," a silver dollar polished to a mirror's clarity. But soon John learned that the tricks, the marked cards, the sleight of hand were only a partial means of obtaining the advantage necessary to succeed in a profession where luck could turn upon the best of the double dealers. People like Mac and John were not the crooks they would seem to be. At a table of greed and deceit, to be an honest player was to be a fool. It was a condition of the territory— unspoken and bitterly contested when exposed—that legerdemain, as well as wit and luck, was an element of a game of chance.

Winning in such a league was as much a mental matter as it was skill and good fortune. Mac had a term for it that had originated on Mississippi riverboats. When you knew the cards and the art of deception, when you had mastered the complex and subtle nuances of a poker face, when you knew the psychology of the sting and could manipulate an entire table of winners and losers and quietly walk away with most of the cash, then you had gained "the river's edge." You were in control.

No amount of instruction or practice could give a gambler "the river's edge." It was a quintessential amalgam of knowledge, experience, intuition, and confidence that could play for one hand or gamble for a dozen years. Mac told John he would know when he had it and, for damn sure, know when it was gone.

John was a natural. He had a quick and resourceful mind, exceptionally fine motor skills, and an uncanny knack for reading the moods and emotions subtly expressed by the human face. In other words, he could count cards and bluff, he could cheat, and he knew when it was time to fold, flee, or be shot. He had a vision, albeit one built upon hearsay and exaggeration, of a vast and exciting world awaiting him to the west and, thanks to Mac, he had a skill that might pay his passage and build him a life.

When John Larsh left Illinois he didn't know it, but he was heading for Leadville. Larsh family lore concerning grandfather John and two young ladies of Deadwood is probably somewhat sentimentalized, but there are enough facts to justify a bit of romantic license.

Emma Miller was a delicate and petite young woman who had arrived in Deadwood with her closest friend, Rachel Edwards in April 1877. They were accompanied on their journey from St. Louis by Rachel's father, a fur trader from Quebec. He had left the two women to the security of a decent boarding house and headed off to establish business in the territory toward Wyoming. John made the acquaintance of the two ladies soon after his arrival.

Deadwood was booming with Black Hills gold and all the enterprises associated with the riches and ruin of mineral prosperity. With its dance halls and casinos and wide-open gaming tables, Deadwood seemed to be the perfect proving ground John had been seeking when he left the Midwest. Over a period of months, he gradually improved his skills. He progressed from a level reliant upon the sporadic quirks of the fates to that of a consistent dependence upon competence. He began realizing the emergence of a true gift. Even without the advantage of an inside track with the casino operators, he was breaking even.

By midsummer he was becoming restless, ready to take his talents farther west to new territories where the house tables were not staked out by established gamblers. His brother Charles had moved on to Colorado, and it seemed a good plan for John.

Gambling was a serious pursuit for those who chose it as a profession and, unlike many who spent their evenings in such environs of iniquity, John did not become a drunk. And though he liked the dance hall girls who, with wiles and willingness, lured the gold from prospectors' pockets, his desire was for more than the ease and immediacy of their purchased or gratuitous favors.

He was a lonely young man of twenty-five, and he wanted a wife to venture west with him. He wanted to be a gambler, but he also wanted to live a full and respectable life. He was becoming a man of the West, but he carried with him some of the values of his Illinois childhood.

Emma and Rachel—lovely, proper, demure, and conveniently unchaperoned—were the delightful companions of his daylight hours in Deadwood. Alone, either would have likely been reluctant to converse so easily with such a questionable individual as the charming young gambler, but there were safety and propriety in numbers.

Romance, love, and friendship were intermingled in the light conversations of their afternoon walks. Often John talked of his plan to leave Deadwood on the stage for Cheyenne and then find his way on to Denver and west into the Rockies.

June had passed and July was passing and summer was the only sane season to breach the Rockies. No family recollections about their relationship speak of the bitterness of a love triangle, and tradition has it that sometime in July, John asked Rachel to marry him and head west. Though she loved him, she turned him down, probably because he was a gambler and because her father would surely have disapproved. But she did love him. Years later she told her grandchildren how hard it was to let him go.

But go he did—with Emma instead. She had no such qualms about his profession. Within days they were married and on their way to Cheyenne and points beyond.

The four-day coach ride to Cheyenne, either in actual measure or as judged by the calendar of experience, was said to take up to twelve days. John, in great spirits for the promise of the future, was not discouraged by such a prospect. But Emma grew more and more tired as the miles and days dropped behind in wake of dust.

Their exact route to Denver and then up into the mountains is not known. It is likely they took a stage to the gold town of Central City and from there another stage down Virginia Gulch to Idaho Springs and on to Georgetown. Central City would have posed a similar problem to that of Deadwood in that it was already controlled by established gamblers. By contrast, Georgetown was exhibiting the character of a family oriented community even in the heyday of its silver mining. Leadville's gold days of the 1860s were long gone, and it was experiencing the beginning of a silver boom. It was a logical choice to push on to a region less developed and, thus, less closed to a new player.

These were the wild times of the mountain West, times of gun-play and gambling, gold strikes and armed camps of claim jumpers, the stuff of Hollywood movies and western novels. There is truth to the gun fights, the overnight fortunes, and the prostitutes with hearts of gold. But there is also the truth of death by the violence of nature and death by the insidious work of nature's diseases. Smallpox was as rampant in the rowdy, rugged camps of miners as it was in the settled community of Georgetown. Mainly it killed the children. But it also killed Emma Larsh. On August 10, 1877, she was buried in the cemetery at Georgetown.

The coffee probably wasn't as good at the Fairplay Hotel back then as it is this bright morning, but there is an excellent possibility that John Larsh, alone and somber with grief, sat here and sipped what fare there was and thought of the mountain pass to the west and of the town that lay beyond it. It would be surprising if he didn't also look back a little wistfully on the last big gathering of the Larsh family, Christmas 1875 in Illinois, and wonder if he had made the right decision.

2

Christmas Dinner 1875: The Farm in Illinois

John Minor Larsh held the wooden bucket beneath the spout of the pump and steadily moved the cast metal handle up and down. It was midwestern, bitter cold—damp and chilling beneath the steel-gray sky of late December. Inside the farmhouse, beyond the translucence of steamed windows in the large kitchen, warmed by the crackling blaze of the open-hearth fireplace, he could hear the laughter and industry of a room filled with three generations— young girls, their mothers, and a matriarchal grandmother—all busy with the creation of Christmas dinner. Outside, beyond the black wood barn, he could hear the sound of men and their different, deeper and more guttural laughter punctuated with single shots of rifle fire as they competed with black powder rounds and shared generous swallows from jugs of hard cider.

The fallow fields surrounding the house and the barn were dark with the moisture of frost. In creases of sunless shadow were drifts of snow clinging to the plow-turned earth. John set down the full bucket and stared beyond the cleared acreage and over the stark, dark clustered oak trees of the winter-bare woods that lined the fields. It was Christmas Day 1875, and his brother Charles and friend Lewis Lamb were talking of heading west with the spring thaw.

His reverie was broken by a tap on the window and his mother's voice asking, "Johnny, where's that bucket of water?"

John's father, Lewis Larsh had the responsibility of keeping the flame of this branch of the L'Archeveque family. His kinsmen had emigrated from France to Quebec and then, long before the Revolutionary War, had changed their name to Larsh and moved down the rivers and lakes to the virginal heartland of the North American continent.

The direct lineage of Lewis went back to Colonel Paul Larsh, the son of Charles Larsh and Sarah Swearingen. In 1806 Colonel Larsh married Mercy Minor, daughter of General John Minor of Revolutionary War fame. Paul and Mercy Larsh had a total of twelve children, most of whom settled in Ohio, Indiana, and Illinois, establishing a tradition of farming and large families.

Two of the sons, Lewis Larsh (my great-grandfather) and his elder brother Newton (who had the distinction of being the first white child born in Preble County, Ohio), staked a claim to fertile farm land on the border of Ohio and Indiana near a town with the improbable name of Eldorado. They cleared the trees, planted corn, built their own houses, and began raising their families. Newton had only three children. Lewis had seven children in Preble County and then moved on to a farm in Peoria County, Illinois, where he and his wife Mary had eight more children. The eighth child born to Lewis and Mary Larsh was John Minor Larsh. Back home in Preble County, Ohio, Newton and his wife Eleanor had a son whom they, too, named John Minor Larsh after grandfather John Minor. My wife, Jane, and I spent a week in Illinois, Indiana, and Ohio, straightening out this genealogical duplicity. Newton's John Minor Larsh became a farmer in the Midwest, and Lewis's John Minor Larsh became a gambler in Leadville, Colorado.

The two John Minor Larshes were cousins, kin by blood, but they were not of kindred spirit. For our purposes, it is probably more significant to know where they were buried than where they were born.

John Minor Larsh of Preble County, Ohio, was born to Newton and Eleanor in the white frame house that sat on the earth of the family farm. Throughout his life he worked that same land, nurturing season upon season of growth and harvest from its dark soil. And when his time was over, he was buried in it.

John Minor Larsh of Peoria, Illinois, was born to Lewis and Mary and to a similar fate—the agrarian legacy that came to the children of the Midwest. But he defied it and left home to wander west and spend his days in the gambling halls of mining towns. When his time was spent, he was buried in the Evergreen Cemetery in Leadville, Colorado.

Change is as frightening as it is exciting, as sad as it is promising. When the midlands of the country were desperate in the grips of the economic depression of the 1870s and families were large and farmlands scarce, change was critical to survival. Family roots planted in the rich soil of the emerging nation were torn up by the truths of fiscal reality. In September 1873, bank failures and the ensuing financial panic plunged the nation into an economic turmoil that lasted for five years. There were twelve surviving children in Lewis Larsh's family of Peoria, and in such troubled times, who could know what profit or loss might come from each year's harvest?

Some would stay by the hearth and tend the fields; others would know the trauma and insecurity, the enlightenment and adventure of change and seek new worlds. Theirs was a time when the great systems of communication and transportation that would link the diverse regions of the nation were still in their infancy. A family severed in 1875 was a family rarely united again.

As the Larsh family gathered around the large kitchen table that Christmas afternoon, a pall of impending change hovered above the delectable ambiance of the aromatic feast, the ruddy-faced gaiety of cider, and the heart-songs warmed by familial touch and love. Lewis stood up and looked at his family. The kitchen was full, with the little ones spilling over into the next room. In 1875 on farms in Illinois, tradition mattered, family mattered, and love endured.

Though the times were desperate about them, and the uncertainty of a world mired in economic struggle bore heavily upon the simple economy of their farm, no deprivation was apparent in the spread of their Christmas feast. No child or uncle was chided that day for "elbows on the table"—there was no room for elbows on the table. It was crowded with turkey, ham and roast beef, freshly baked, butter-crusted breads, great bowls of mashed potatoes and "boats" of dark gravy, pickled beans, and deep red beets. It was a summer's harvest brought forth in the dead of winter, having been canned and dilled and dried and hung and cellar stored, then exhumed from the lightless silence of spider webs and boiled and baked and seasoned and served in steaming rhapsody of nurture and flavor.

Lewis knew that his son Charles was going to venture west in the spring and that his good friend, Lewis Lamb, was planning to accompany him. He also knew that John Minor, as well as Mindy and Mamie, were also thinking of risking the unknown if Charles reported anything promising.

Family tradition mandated that special occasions such as Christmas were to be celebrated not only with feasting but also with festivities. Each family member came prepared to perform for the pleasure of the group—songs, poems, dances, tricks of magic, recitations, complimentary toasts, and other performances were very much in order and shared with all.

Lewis began this Christmas festivity with a toast to his family, and especially to his faithful and loving wife, the mother of his children. He talked of new frontiers, of umbilical cords and apron strings; he talked of the legacy of the adventuresome L'Archeveques. He spoke of being your brother's keeper and of the importance of home and family, whether it be in Preble County, Peoria, or Eldorado.

The laughter turned from nostalgia to the realism of imminent change. Papa Larsh gave the limelight to Charles who moved around the table, raised his glass and announced, "It's true that I am taking my jewelry business to the West, but I plan to return. My home is here with you. Leroy and William are older than I, but they have families of their own. I will go—but I will return home. Raise your glasses, I toast our home and each of you!"

John Minor, a twenty-four-year-old adventurer, spoke next. He was hesitant, for he, too, was leaving the nest, but his spirit was not with the soil on which he had been nurtured but with the western drive to the new frontier. He couldn't compete with the learned Mamie or the intense Mindy, and he certainly couldn't sing like Edith.

John looked at his father and said, "Mom and Dad, I guess we all know that some of us are headed in the general direction of west, across the wide Missouri. One of the things I most remember about this loving home has to be the evenings that we gathered around Edie and sang together, so Edie, how about you playing, and we will all sing one of our favorites, a tune that somehow seems to fit the situation."

Edie went to the piano as John Minor carried the first verse in a voice that trembled with emotion:

Oh, Shenadoah, I love your daughter,
Hi-oh, you rolling river,
I'll take her cross the rolling water,
Ah-hah, I'm bound away cross the wide Mizzoura.

Mindy, who always struck the serious chord, moved slowly around the table. She knew without posturing how to be dramatic. As she reached the head of the table, she looked into the eyes of each person in the room and then quietly said, "If Lewis Lamb writes to me from beyond the wide Missouri River, and says, 'Come west and marry me,' I will. But I'll come back here too, to this house. Mama, you asked me long ago to take care of little Edith, to help her find her way. I'll do that, Mama; I haven't forgotten. I would like to recite a poem by William Wordsworth . . ." And looking only at Edie, she began:

She was a phantom of delight
When first she gleamed upon my sight;
A lovely apparition, sent
To be a moment's ornament;
Her eyes as stars of twilight fair;
Like twilight's, too, her dusky hair;
From May-time and the cheerful dawn;
A dancing shape, an image gay,
To haunt, to startle, and waylay . . .

Before Mindy sat down, the lithe and beautiful fifteen-year-old Edie was moving, not to the head of the table but back to the piano.

Without looking at anyone in particular she said, "If Lewis asks Mindy to marry him, and if Mindy insists on watching after me, she won't have to come to Peoria to keep her promise because I'll be with her. I want to marry a 'roving gambler,' not an Illinois farmer."

Edie looked at her devoted mother, winked and began to sing and play:

I am a roving gambler, I've gambled all around,
Whenever I meet with a deck of cards I lay my money down.
I had not been in Washington many more weeks than three,
Till I fell in love with a pretty little girl and she fell in love with me.
She took me in her parlor, she cooled me with her fan,
She whispered low in her Mother's ears, 'I love this gambling man'. . .

When we conjure such a medley of sensation from a past long lost, we must recollect our own joys, fears, and humanity and travel with them into the invisible abyss of the past. From documents we know that the Larshes' last formal assemblage as a complete family occurred on December 25, 1875. In the spring of 1876, brother Charles and his childhood friend, Lewis Lamb, departed the Midwest and headed for Deadwood, South Dakota. Soon thereafter, John followed as did his sisters Mamie, Mindy, and Edith. From oral history we know that well into the twentieth century Mamie and Mindy Larsh were still talking about that Christmas feast and the loss of familial ceremony.

One of the purposes of Jane's and my trip to the Midwest in the fall of 1991 was to check out the concept of "home" and the farms of Ohio, Indiana, and Illinois. We went to Eldorado, Ohio, searching for answers to questions. What was it that made six members of a family of fourteen leave the cornfields and the rolling hills that straddle Indiana, Illinois, and Ohio? Why did they shirk their traditional obligation? Three young men, three young women, all unmarried brothers and sisters leaving home to become adventurers. Why?

I have seen the farms where each was born and raised, and one thing seems very clear—if there is to be adventure, it must start by leaving home. In going back to those roots, we move back not only into history but back into the cultural bread basket, back into the acceptable law-abiding behavior of the conformist, and then we become aware that the conservatism of the present is partially explained by those who chose a less intrepid path in 1875.

The juxtaposition of the six that ventured forth with those that stayed behind indicates a conflict, a dilemma that resides in all of us. Risk takers make history. They contribute, ultimately, to the antithesis of the standard. Their history is not for the pious. The risk takers challenge; they break the laws; they flaunt the codes; they question authority.

Those who left the "old country," whether it was County Cork, the County of Preble in Ohio, or the rigidity of parochial true believers, did so while realizing the risk. That is the reason that not everyone is an adventurer. Those who stay behind fear change more than the quiet rot of daily desperation, something not true for those pioneer Leadville gamblers.

Seeing the farm, meeting the good solid, respectable folk, who are my non-adventuring counterparts, the people who inherited the last throes of the Agrarian Age, I developed a few other territorial beliefs. The risk taker is within us and competes for our patronage with the conforming social person we are programmed to become. The lifestyles are incompatible. The excitement and challenge of one we dream about, even desire; the other we are conditioned to accommodate. We were born to explore and yet, in order to survive, we build an inhibiting cage of laws, rules, and traditions from which we stare with yearning.

The risk takers, the gamblers, are defined by their attitude toward the game we all play. They knowingly come to the plate with two strikes against them. First, they already carry the stigma of being breakers of the social and conventional law. Second, they choose the unknown, not just face it when forced to as most do. But, ironically, the gambler's life is not a straight line; it is more like an ellipse. It eventually comes back around to the universal laws. The unknown becomes the known.

What I was looking for in the Midwest was evidence that as a mature grandson of John Minor Larsh (a young man who knew the wheel was fixed but still played), I also am an adventurer. If that be true, then there is real hope—for me and for the world.

Charles Larsh, in the early days of Leadville, lived in Alma, Colorado, as a jeweler. He would walk from Alma to Leadville on the trail that comes down into Birdseye Gulch. One late summer afternoon in 1880, while on this trek he stumbled over a quartz rock containing three ounces of pure wire gold. Larshes have been looking for the source of that find ever since. On our trip to find my roots in the Midwest, Jane and I saw Charlie's gravestone, evidence that he did, in fact, round many bases and return home. His brother John would not be content until he found a new one.

3

Commitment to El Dorado

Clouds gather to the west, building to the almost daily afternoon storm, but the sky above is still blue and the sunlight brilliant. On Mosquito Pass—13,110 feet above the level of the distant sea—the air is cold, and the wind coming across the pass is raw and strong.

Beside the road at the crest of the pass is a stone monument commemorating Father Dyer, an itinerant preacher who delivered the mail and the "word" over this route on snowshoes in the 1860s. I don't know how many souls he saved among the miners, but I'm sure the dedication and fortitude he demonstrated just by getting there assured him a respectful audience for his message.

In any encounter with the past, we are reminded of basic conditions of existence that would challenge the most hardy of our own generations. Even in the relative mildness of a summer day these mountains are harsh and forbidding. There is little air to breathe, and what there is of it is in the form of cold, fierce rushes of wind that blast you with painful showers of fine gravel. You have to wonder how this man on his "snowshoes for Christ" could have braved these cruel reaches in weather much more severe.

The entire Sawatch Range, from the Mount of the Holy Cross to the north, Mount Massive to the west, and Mount Elbert to the south—a wall of 14,000-foot peaks—confronts the traveler who stops to rest at the crest of Mosquito Pass. Below, in a deep and immense sweep, are coniferous forests and mirror lakes, deep canyons and green mountain meadows. And directly down the incredible slope, in stark contrast to the surrounding arboreal sea, is the rugged stone and timbered island of Leadville, looking like a child's creation of "Monopoly" pieces set up in a box of black sand.

After John Larsh finished his coffee at the Fairplay Hotel, he made his way up this pass, probably pausing at this very spot and gazing at the same peaks and forests and the same sheer mountainside falling to the town beneath him.

Mosquito Pass was the route taken by many in the days before the train connected Leadville to the rest of the world in 1880. It wasn't the only way to Leadville, but it was the most dramatic. In those days, both realistically and metaphorically, those who dared to head on down the west side of the mountain must have been sharply aware of the commitment they were making.

At least John Larsh had seen a few mountains before he ventured this far. Imagine what gold-crazed kids right off the farms of Iowa or Minnesota must have felt when they crawled up this hair-raising trail and then, peering over the other side, realized their destination was another ten twisting miles and three thousand feet straight down the edge of the top of the world. There were likely some who wished they had settled for the golden tassels atop a stalk of corn or a golden sunset seen between the ears of a mule at the end of a good day of plowing.

The town that John Larsh viewed was considerably smaller than the sprawl we see today, but the settlement was clearly established by then, and he must have had some sense of a vision realized when he first saw it. Even if the town was undeniably ugly, it was unlikely he had ever seen a town in a more spectacular location.

Leadville was and is a town that was never meant to be, a place inhabited by people who, for most of its unique history, never intended to stay. It is an economic phenomenon sprawled across a bed of rock so cantankerous it can take blasting powder, persistence bordering on fanaticism, and an afternoon's hard labor to plant a petunia. It is a diverse cluster of humanity huddled on a 10,000-foot high plateau at the foot of mountains that are immense and magnificent to the cursory examination of tourists but as forbidding as they are beautiful in the seasoned view of year-round residents.

Leadville, not unlike the gentler lowlands of our nation, has four seasons. There is, of course, winter—a time of deep snows, howling winds, and bitter cold that spans the months from mid-October until sometime in late May. Then around Memorial Day, with a generous application of wishful thinking, one may, with a subtle and somewhat desperate awareness, perceive the slight lessening of the ferocity of winter. This is optimistically referred to as spring. Summer arrives with the solstice, but as many who have known the metamorphosis of turning years in Leadville have said, "Don't bet the mother lode that you can picnic before the end of June." July has warmth, but it is a rare year when it doesn't snow up on Johnny Hill sometime in August.

Autumn is the most amazing season of Leadville. More remarkable than the intensity and duration of winter, the hint of spring, and the blessed respite of the short summer is the exhilaration that stirs the spirit when frost touches the crystalline morning air—a time when the early snows lie fresh upon the Sawatch peaks, and the crisp nights tell of the certain cycling toward the challenge of winter.

Perhaps herein lies a suggestion of the spirit that drives this community of hearty souls dwelling amongst the rock and rubble of nature and the scattered remnants of scores of busted schemes. For any who have borne the full course of Leadville's seasons, it would seem that autumn should be a time of dread—the final bastion of tolerable climate before the burden of a frigid truth. But not so. For most, autumn is the best of times. It is a time of anticipation of far more than just another meteorological assault; it is a season of mental and material preparation for yet another challenge. Rather than a time of trepidation, it is a season of excitement and expectation. Once one has endured the trial of a full cycle of seasons in this town, the demands of fortune and philosophy are put in a less commanding perspective.

Throughout its history, from 1860, when gold was discovered in nearby California Gulch, through the silver years of the 1870s and

1880s, and on into the gold and molybdenum decades of the twentieth century, Leadville has been in existence ostensibly for metallurgical purposes. If the early settlers had been looking for a good location for a town, they would have built their settlement farther down the valley where clear Rocky Mountain streams cascade and large meadows flourish in summer's warmth, and winter's most vicious charges are kept at bay by sheltering hillsides.

Instead, Leadville sprouted on the base of a rock mountain where the surface can only with some exaggeration and goodwill be called "soil." But it was beneath this hostile ground that the minerals lay, and so upon it stands the town. Forget the aesthetic and human comforts—Leadville was a pinewood necessity planted in the proximity of geological bounty. People didn't come to this God-forsaken gravel pit to set up white picket-fenced, American-dream dwellings. They came to get rich and then to get the hell gone. El Dorado, the mythical city of fabulous riches, was the lure of Leadville.

By the thousands, first in the 1860s and again in the late 1870s, they came to the hard land to find their fortune with pick and shovel, an enterprising swindle, or a deck of cards. The people who came to Leadville were not just dreamers. They were of that rare ilk who risk acting on their dreams.

Commerce ruled the mining camp. Within a short time, the silver boom had accomplished the deforestation of this region that once was to have been named "Bough City" for the density of spruce trees surrounding it. But the demand for timbers for the mines and firewood for the struggle with December's chill proved a more important priority than the preservation of pristine groves of Christmas trees. They were there to extract material wealth, not to savor natural richness.

Mining claims measured 1500 feet by 300 feet, while lots for houses were a slim twenty-five feet wide by the distance from the board sidewalks to the muddy alleyways deep. People were secondary to commerce, and spatial relationships and the need for privacy were given little consideration in planning the town.

So why do we dedicate ourselves to the task of filling these pages with stories and characters from such a blatantly exploitative enterprise as Leadville, Colorado? What can be learned from its history of struggle and ever-failing dreams?

Except for a handful of mine owners, including some of American history's most infamous wheeler-dealers, nobody found the El Dorado they sought in Leadville. It didn't take long for the few enterprising giants to emerge as owners of the most productive claims and for the rest of the miners to end up working for them for two or three dollars a day—lousy pay even in a century when the dollar had some value.

For the most part, the common man or woman who came to Leadville for a chance at discovering great wealth either departed in economic ruin or remained for the dubious task of establishing a fully functioning community from the mud-stuck rubble of tent cities and crude cabins. But those who stayed discovered an entirely different El Dorado than that of glittering metal and mansions of stone.

Leadville became a settlement where people gathered to do extremely hard work for poor wages while suffering living conditions that were anywhere from marginal to miserable. Why did anyone put up with such difficulty? And why did anyone stay past the booms and endure the trials and hardships of economic calamity?

Many did leave, but not all. Throughout the Rocky Mountains are the rotted and rusted ruins of abandoned mining towns, snow crushed and wind scattered: Gothic, Waldorf, Geneva City, Douglas, and Independence. Muriel Sibell Wolle's book, *Stampede to Timberline*, lists dozens within just one state. But Leadville is not among them. Beyond the ghostly scrap iron and splintered timber of mines and mills and deserted dwellings that clutter the region, there is a population of flesh-and-blood Coloradans who boast both body and soul intact. For some strange reason, the early settlers and the generations they produced have loved the place. With all of its physical and economic hardships, Leadville is inhabited by people who choose to live nowhere else.

I've been grown and gone from this town for fifty years, and I still call it home. Present and former residents meet annually to just drive around and talk about who lived in what house and who owned the hardware store and the grocery stores and where the hangings and the shootings took place. The true Leadville people—the ones who stuck it out and were, in succeeding generations, there to enjoy and to suffer the rise and fall of well over a century of booms and crashes—are a hard-assed bunch, and they truly love their town. There are books detailing the facts and figures of Leadville, and biographies that chronicle and immortalize the lives of the Tabors and the Browns, but the true heroes of this town were its survivors, not its exploiters.

Baby Doe Tabor lived out the final thirty-six years of her life in poverty as hard as that of any miner. She would walk to town regularly from her run-down cabin up at the Matchless Mine. Often she would come into the newspaper office where my dad was a printer. She would talk with him, and whenever he could spare it, he would give her a quarter to help her out. But disaster came to her only after she and her husband had contributed most of their fortune, amassed from the blood and sweat of Leadville miners, to the economy of Denver and points east and had found themselves penniless following the silver devaluation of 1893. J. J. and Molly Brown, Horace and Baby Doe Tabor, and others led fascinating lives, but their stories have been told and mis-told often enough.

My grandfather made his way down Mosquito Pass in August 1877. He was never particularly famous, but he was, indeed, important and interesting in the way that people who struggle and survive always are. I would like to think that he can stand and speak for them all.

Details about his first year in Leadville are sketchy, but his circumstances were probably not much different from those of most of the early inhabitants. Many lived in communal tents or, if they were fortunate, crammed into small, primitive log cabins along with two or three other less than hygienic males. All we know with certainty is that he put up with hard times, but he stayed the winter, and by the end of the first year he had accumulated enough profit from the tables at the Pioneer Bar to build a two-room cabin on West Second Street. By that time, he believed the town and himself to be of sufficient worth to warrant sending for his three sisters, who by then had made their way to Deadwood. Also, he wrote to a pretty young lady there and asked once more if she would be his Colorado bride.

There are many colors to El Dorado gold.

4

Reunion at Georgetown

Life breaks everyone and afterward
some are stronger in the broken places.
—ERNEST HEMINGWAY

One late afternoon in 1878, the summer sun cast long shadows of peaks and pine trees and of a woman and a man upon a grassy flat above the flood plain of Clear Creek. Nearby, a buggy and a single horse stood motionless at a hitching post. The cold weight of a wrought iron cemetery gate, slightly ajar, separated the two figures.

John Larsh stood by a grave marked by a simple stone. In his left hand he gripped the brim of a black hat. Though it had been a rugged life for him the past year, a time of threat and wonder and risk among the burly, revolver-carrying dreamers and thieves of a mining camp, and though about him the slopes were scarred by the yellow-brown spill of mine tailings blasted from the bowels of the earth by men who were as tough as the hills themselves, the hand that clasped the hat dangling at his side was neither callused nor knotted. It was still delicate. Not delicate as the fine flesh of ladies and gentlemen of the pampered classes, but delicate as the meticulous hand of a skilled surgeon and delicate as are the lean and artful fingers of a classical musician.

Years later, when Rachel told her children the story of the visit to the Georgetown graveyard, it was still with a mixture of grief, happiness, and confusion. She had felt compassion for the shameless tears in John's eyes as he stood before the year-old grave of his first wife and had felt sorrow for the death of her friend. But it was also a day filled with the joy of being reunited with the man she loved after spending a long year of second thoughts and regret. So much had happened. Abandoning the approval and security of her father, she had joined John Larsh's sisters and headed for Colorado to marry a gambler. In a rush of short weeks she had packed a simple wardrobe and taken off to ride stages and trains, and now, finally, a small buggy that brought her to the grave of her best friend.

Though for reasons economic and domestic, John and Rachel did not marry until the following summer, it was the afternoon at the cemetery above the rushing waters of Clear Creek that she assumed responsibility for the strength of his survival.

In the year that had passed since he had buried Emma, scores of new markers had been laid in random patterns in the meadow. Grass had grown to cover the dirt he had shoveled on her grave. Time and nature's processes had cured the earth of the scar of her death but, more than he realized before confronting the stark and simple setting of her grave, no such healing had assuaged the sorrow in his heart. The rigors of his new life in Leadville had masked the depth of his mourning. The pain he felt as he looked at the plot was not the grief of emptiness. He had known her for such short months before she was gone. What he sensed was the frailty of all matters human and mortal before the impersonal might of nature. Before him lay Emma Larsh in seeming proof of the insignificance of a single life.

Human statistics, even when accurate, are seldom honest. The death toll of an earthquake in China, a tidal wave in Bangladesh; the body counts of battles and holiday weekends; the thousand-to-one odds against contracting a disease—there is no truth to a statistic until it is your child swept into the torrents of mud, your friend whose art and humor and youth are sealed in a body bag; your fevered mind that curses the sterile walls of a hospital room. Along the Oregon Trail, the Santa Fe Trail, the Mormon Trail are the scattered remnants of rock-pile monuments left stacked on shallow graves. The babies, the children, and the old folks lost to the strain, the young ones to injury and empidemic—each life as vital and fragile as any life dear to us this very moment.

John Larsh stood in the cemetery where the weeds and grasses and late summer wild flowers flourished as if there had never been a lovely young woman named Emma.

Such was the afternoon of the first day of reunion with the man Rachel intended to marry. This was her welcome to Colorado—a brief embrace at the Georgetown platform of the Colorado Central Railroad, a rushed check-in at the Barton House Hotel, and then a ride out of town in a rented buggy. Rachel knew it was her place to accompany him to the graveyard, but she also knew it was her place to get him out of it and on with their lives.

We wouldn't be so foolish as to assume that, without her assistance, John might have remained at the grave indefinitely in the grips of depression and loneliness. But it was true that Rachel's influence at that critical moment had significant sway on the pace of his recovery from grief. It was she who, in a gentle yet forceful voice, called him from the grave, knowing that life is the only salve for the losses of death. He closed the gate of the cemetery, and they rode back into town.

Rachel was a lovely woman, not slight or frail as Emma had been, but of a soft and sturdy flesh that was the stuff of future generations. Years later, when he spoke of them, John likened Emma to a flower and Rachel to a tree. After recovering from the punch she gave him for his clumsy poetry, he quickly explained away the bite of his metaphor and claimed he had complimented her strength to persevere through all the seasons of life—not just the gentle gifts of summer.

She had known it to be important that they pay their respects to Emma. She understood that reckoning with the past was necessary if regret were not to taint the riches and hope of the future. But she also knew when it was time for them to put the death of her friend and his first wife behind them. It was such intuitive and life-learned wisdom that was essential to the nature of Rachel and the strength of the Larsh family. John was a good man, but Rachel was one hell of a good woman.

I believe in the existence of ghosts—not the ghastly, chain-rattling variety that haunt movies and the dreams of those who have feasted too near bedtime. I mean the residue of the human spirit perceptible wherever we have passed—where men and women have touched the land, molded the clay, piled high the stones, and gathered in shelter; where we have uttered our prayers, sung our songs, shouted our rage, and wept our tears; where we have killed; where we have died. Among the artifacts of stone and cloth—the collective junk and treasure of a hundred thousand years—is the presence of those touching, breathing lives that were as close and real as our own.

A man named Henry Boyer lived in Georgetown, Colorado, from 1864 until 1913. He was a carpenter and also the local coffin maker. In 1875 he opened a furniture store and mortuary. Beginning in that year, he kept a careful record of the services he provided. I found his notebook in the Western History Collection at the Denver Public Library. *Henry Boyer's Burial Book* is a cardboard-bound ledger of decades of death. In a steady, practiced hand he entered the names of the dead, the cause of death if known, and the fee he charged.

As I carefully examined the document, a somber presence of life, love, and hope forever departed arose from the fragile pages. For most, the touch of Henry's pen on the lines of his notebook told all that written history would know of them. Their ghosts were about me as I read their names. There were so many children—simple entries, a last name followed by the word "child." And so much violence—landslides, avalanches, shootings, murders. And there was disease.

1877 August 10 / Mrs. Larsch / Small Pox / $30.00

Following the reunion at the cemetery of a man with a sad episode in his past and a woman with her husband-to-be, the couple returned to the hotel where Rachel spent the evening in the company of John's three sisters. Later that night, in the back room of Tommy Barnes's Pool Hall on Rose Street, John won a decent sum from the locals gathered for an evening of illicit gambling.

And the chill of darkness sank into the deep canyon.

It was quiet in the cemetery save the water on the rocks below and the wind in the pine trees high above on the mountainside. Emma Miller Larsh, she lies there still.

May she rest in peace.

5

The Community of Leadville 1878–79

If you pray for rain, you pray for mud.
—AFRICAN PROVERB

In the 1870s, a man named Pratt came to the emerging city of Denver and contemplated what was to be his life's work. With some considered observation, he deemed his role in the entrepreneurial scheme of the West to be of a more cerebral than brawny variety. Instead of heading into the Rockies with gold pan, pick, shovel, and dream, he talked prospecting with a few hard rock veterans and then wrote a paperback, how-to manual on the art of gold and silver mining. His guides sold as fast as he could get them printed. The booklet proved to be more of a gold mine than those who purchased it would ever know.

For Leadville's newly arriving gold- and silver-seekers in 1878, it soon became painfully obvious, even for those thoroughly versed in the wisdom and technique of Pratt's book, that riches were rare and seldom came to those who were not in possession of extensive know-how and a bundle of money to back it up. Most of the placer or stream gold of the 1860 boom had played out by then, and the money was in deep-rock silver mining. If you didn't have the engineering expertise and the financing for a major operation excavating deep shafts and tunnels and operating complex machinery, instead of becoming an instant millionaire, you were likely to become a long-term, $2.50-a-day employee of H. A. W. Tabor or one of his Denver or New York banker buddies.

John Minor Larsh, like Mr. Pratt, did not seek his fortune "way down in the mine." He determined that his niche in the community was to provide diversion for the rock-weary miners with games of chance down at the Pioneer Bar. It was consistent with a miner's mentality that many had a love of gambling, and they were seldom excessively bitter about departing the rowdy confines of that establishment with considerably less jingle in their pocket than when they had arrived. There were nights when the fates were with them, and those were the nights they remembered the best. The city of Las Vegas was built upon that exact quirk of selective memory.

In the early days, John Larsh was also something of a real estate developer. While establishing his game at the Pioneer, between 1878 and 1879, he also built two log cabins along West Second Street. He, his three sisters, and his fiancée eventually lived in one of them, and he sold the other. The abundance of canvas-walled cabins was rapidly being replaced by less transient structures.

So it was that Leadville, rather than being a temporary inconvenience to be endured while one scooped up one's fair share of plentiful wealth, was to become, in its early days, the permanent home of a population consisting largely of hard working, poorly paid men, the capitalists and crooks who victimized them, and the hookers—victims themselves—who served them all.

With prosperity, even if it was less than equitably distributed, there came first the semblance and then, through painful evolution, the reality of civilization. Historians equate civilization with the development of cities and ordered commerce. Before 1879 Leadville had been less than "civil" and considerably less than "ordered." Indeed, well into the 1880s, neither law nor order had much precedence over chaos. In a society where citizens commonly carried guns, drank whiskey, and stole from one another, disputes were often resolved by rapid violence rather than by longer processes of litigation.

In the long run, however, order must prevail if money is to be made. Drunks and murderers don't make good employees and, besides, the common good is most often served by reasonable restriction. By 1878 Leadville had a city council, a mayor—not too surprisingly, H. A. W. Tabor—and a city marshal. In fact, during a two-month period of that year, as a result of well-heeded threats and a barroom murder, Leadville went through two marshals before the appointment of a third, Martin Duggan, who proved himself to be ruthless and corrupt enough to keep the job until he resigned in April of 1880.

It was still a rough town, one of the roughest in the West, but the subtle forces of culture, society, and religion were persistently eroding the rowdy terrain. Fancy hotels and a nationally renowned opera house were built in 1879; a community of mining supervisors and engineers and their wives and families was established at the north end of town in an upscale residential area grandly called Capitol Hill; and preachers had gathered sufficient flocks from both saloons and pockets of decency to justify the construction of permanent places of worship. Probably most significant, though, was the fact that miners (and even a rare gambler) were establishing families. With the influence of such values as are necessary for the proper rearing of children—to a great extent as imposed by the wit, wisdom, and whippings of motherhood—the wild town was beginning to settle.

Civil authority, as is yet the case in most urban areas, concentrated on dealing with tactical problems rather than strategic issues. City planners created a grid pattern for streets and required all buildings to be numbered but made no allowance for existing and future excavations within that pattern. Wells and test holes for mines can yet be encountered in alleyways and backyards throughout the town, not to mention the labyrinth of tunnels that honeycomb beneath every block of the east side. (Much to the consternation of my mother, the outside toilet behind our home on West Sixth Street was conveniently, if somewhat precariously, perched over a test hole that disappeared deep into the earth.)

The process of rendering order from the forces of chaos is neither simple nor quick to realize. Simple concepts and good intentions are seldom sufficient for significant change. For example, during the years before the wonder of concrete and asphalt paving, Leadville, as a town of ore wagon traffic and an annual two-to-three-month flow of spring run-off, had somehow to deal with a perennial dilemma: What does a government do to remedy the serious threat to order and domestic tranquillity posed by the dreaded curse of mud?

It is interesting that of the numerous fonts of misery the early people confronted in Leadville—the cold, the altitude, the blinding snows; the challenge of toil and the pittance of reward; the isolation from vistas and persons familiar and secure; and the constant presence of mortal danger—tales of aggravation with the mire of spring-soaked streets are prominent in the collective memory of generations hence. Rachel Larsh was at times less than fond of the raw climate and rustic abode that had become her destiny to endure, but she really *hated* the mud.

The urbanization of the wilds, as with most efforts at imposing human concepts on the timeless and indifferent processes of nature, is seldom as successful in producing true progress as it is at creating excessive complication.

What could be done about the mud?

A. The strategic solution for Leadville in the nineteenth century was to expend large sums of money and considerable effort in the creation of a massive ground-water drainage system.

B. The tactical solution for Leadville in the nineteenth century was to dump slag from the southside smelters on the swampy boulevards.

As long as there are the altruistically visionary, the pragmatically fearless, and the criminally greedy, there will be city councils to address matters of civic concern. Political expedience is often more a factor in making decisions than is long-range vision. In Leadville of the late 1870s the quick fix was the easiest choice to make. The mire of May was buried beneath the slag, but by July the eyes and throats and noses of Leadville were choked by clouds of slag dust rolling up in the wake of wagon wheels in the bustling city.

But the inroads of civilization were being paved by the emerging communal instincts of the common people. There were still plenty of shootings and hangings and whorehouse brawls as this decade came to an end, but the basic decency of the general population was gradually starting to dominate the culture.

Leadville, like any historical phenomenon, had its milestone events and its designated personalities. Knowing a little of them will help us know the world in which the miners and shopkeepers lived their private and artful lives.

In 1878 the city's mayor, Horace Tabor, was a man who exhibited elements of all three of the above mentioned perspectives of government. He had the vision to foresee the creation of a fantastic city of commerce and culture, the courage to commission architects and craftsmen to enact the vision, and the cunning to make damn sure he "owned" a major portion of the whole system.

The word "legend" comes from the Middle English term *legende*, meaning a collection of stories about the lives of saints. The current meaning of the word seems to have defined the gap between the fiction of the church and the reality of the common person. It acknowledges the myth while it magnifies the subject. Horace Tabor was a Leadville man, and now he is a Leadville legend. The centuries tend to create marble statues out of human flesh. Homer had no eyes and Thomas Jefferson was thirty feet tall. There is no patina of Athenian political corruption on the bust of Socrates. We can still salvage some flesh for Horace Tabor and his family, though we must act fast if we are to succeed in the race against canonization.

From 1877 to 1880, the changes in Leadville were so spectacular that it gained worldwide notoriety as an incredible boom town. In this short span, the explosion of population and activity dwarfed the previous booms at Central City, Georgetown, and Silverton. The life of the Tabor family parallels the developments of the town that was successively named Oro, Oro City, and finally, in 1879, Leadville. They were there when it all started and still there seventeen years later to reap the harvest of its greatest days.

Horace Tabor and his wife Augusta arrived in the region shortly after the first discovery of gold along California Gulch in 1860. Following a short and unsuccessful attempt at farming on the grasslands of Kansas, the Tabors opted to abandon their fields to the scorching sun, the grasshoppers, the drought, and the rattlesnakes—Augusta never did get over having to share her cabin with such dangerous house guests. They decided to start over in Colorado.

Horace Tabor was not an educated man. Judging from the few existing examples of his writing, it is quite likely that he was borderline illiterate. However, he was a very shrewd businessman and throughout most of his life demonstrated a genius for making profitable alliances and acquisitions. Although he manipulated fortunes with some of the most renowned capitalists of the nineteenth century, probably the most beneficial alliance he ever negotiated was his marriage to Augusta.

The couple opened a small grocery store on the bank of the stream that ran through the California Gulch tent city called Oro. In addition to providing supplies and clothing for the miners, Augusta quickly earned a reputation for compassion and decency in a society of rugged men. She was one of the few "nonprofessional" women in the whole camp. There is an anonymous Leadville saying that simplifies the demographics of the population inhabiting the area when the Tabors arrived that summer: "First came the men who worked in the mine, then came the girls who worked on the line."

Perhaps representing a link to a gentler past, Augusta—as storekeeper, nurse, counselor, and cook—was immensely popular among the men who crowded the narrow gulch working sluice boxes. Over five thousand prospectors were already there and, following a winter that was but a holding pattern of survival while awaiting the spring, that number had doubled by July of the next summer. Business must have been good for the Tabor grocery store. Augusta tended to the logistical, medicinal, and psychological needs of the camp while Horace made daily rounds to the sluice boxes being constructed along the stream at an exponential rate. While a family enterprise such as a grocery store can afford one a good living, it has seldom proved the route to world-class riches. Horace knew this and early on began investing in the luck and labor of others.

For fifty to a hundred dollars worth of equipment and supplies, he would grubstake a prospector and, in doing so, lay claim to up to fifty percent of whatever was discovered. The odds of hitting it big were not exactly favorable, but the stakes weren't too high either. By gambling upon the good fortune and honesty of an occasional hard-up miner, he created the prospect for a cut of some serious money.

With ten thousand eager shovelers mucking the gravel of a short stretch of creek bed and the adjoining rock formations each day that summer, it is not surprising that the surface gold was "worked out" by October of 1861. In a rush even more impressive than that of Oro's creation, ninety percent of its population enacted the spectacle of its abandonment in a matter of weeks. The tent town fell, and the dreamers moved on to other El Dorados. Canvas saloons were folded; wagons were loaded with tables, chairs, and dance hall queens; and the whole operation rolled out of town.

The currency in Oro, as it was in many mining towns well into the twentieth century, was often gold dust. In lieu of calculators, clerks and bartenders used balance scales to take payment and make change for goods and services provided. The story is told that over two thousand dollars worth of gold was extracted from a few wheelbarrow loads of dirt excavated from what had been the floor of one of Oro's gambling halls. Gamblers may have had steady hands, but drunken miners apparently didn't.

The following year brought word of a new strike over Mosquito Pass north of the town of Fairplay. Horace walked over the mountain trail to the north of Birdseye Gulch early in the fall of 1862 and acquired a cabin. The snow was well on its way by time he returned for Augusta and their five-year-old son, Nathaniel Maxcy. The three of them and a hired mule skinner struggled over Mosquito Pass, a route that at the time was just a trail, to start another grocery store in the gold camp called Buckskin Joe.

As an emerging politician, Horace arranged for his appointment as postmaster, while Augusta managed the new grocery business. Also, in his first elected office, he became a member of the school board. Though no one can fault his ambition or sense of civic responsibility, it would seem these positions were not particularly appropriate for a man who had seldom been known to read or write.

In the 1960s, there was a bank robber named Willy Sutton. Upon his capture, some early practitioner of the art of "in-depth" reporting asked him the probing question, "Willy, why do you rob banks?" His reply was a classic answer to a dumb question. He said, "Because that's where the money is."

Horace Tabor and Willy Sutton both knew that simple truth and when, in 1868, word came that "the mother lode" had been discovered back near California Gulch at a place called Printer Boy Hill, Horace, Augusta, and Maxcy loaded up the grocery store in the wagon and moved back over Mosquito Pass to the new town now called Oro City.

Such opportunistic flexibility was necessary in those times. When one considers the complex migratory patterns of the upwardly mobile, middle-class family of America today, it would seem that Horace and his family and whole entourages of miners, merchants, and camp-town groupies were just a bit ahead of the times back in the 1800s. Even the town of Oro City was soon moved when the epicenter of mineral excavation shifted down the gulch from the Printer Boy Mine to the location of the current incarnation of the city officially dubbed "Leadville."

Horace Tabor grew with the communities he inhabited. He was postmaster of Oro City and then Leadville, and years later, after all else had failed him, he was postmaster of the city of Denver. His political calling, though never so profound as his commercial endeavors, led to his being mayor of Leadville and lieutenant governor of Colorado. He even served a thirty-day, temporary appointment as United States senator in 1883.

But the main thing he was by 1878 was rich. Cashing in on one of his grub-stake deals with a couple of miners named August Rische and George Hook, he and a banker associate, David Moffat, eventually took total possession of "The Little Pittsburgh Mine." Horace Tabor was on his way to amassing one of the largest and most fleeting fortunes in the history of the U.S.A.

Placer claims were not the source of the revived economy. The days of one-man, pick-and-shovel, stream-bed operations were over. Precious minerals were deep in the earth, and the stakes required for mining them were higher than most men could pay. It became an age of bankers, mining engineers, and armies of underpaid laborers; and Horace Tabor was a master at orchestrating such elements for his own profit.

Silver had replaced gold as the lure of Leadville, and the boom it created made the earlier rush of 1860–61 seem minor by comparison. In May 1879, the population of Leadville was estimated to be 1500. At the end of the summer of 1880, over 30,000 congregated there, making Leadville the second largest city in the state after Denver.

Tabor's art and luck held out. Horace was on a roll from the time he grubstaked Rische and Hook in 1878 until the final collapse of his silver prosperity in 1893. He had the luck, and he had the vision to make him seem invincible. Such was the state of the Tabor fortune in 1879. Horace had prosperity, political status, and no hint that the good times would not last forever. Legends are made of material such as this.

But whatever happened to good old, hard-working, literate Augusta? You've heard the story—in the summer of 1880 Horace dumped her for a pretty divorcée from Central City named Baby Doe.

6

From This Porch You Can See the Old Country

The house in which I grew up is at 520 West Sixth Street. The wooden sidewalks are still visible. At a quick glance, the forms and patterns of the town appear similar to the views of my childhood. The house is now the property of a defunct local radio station, and the lot is landscaped with large and ugly receiving dishes designed to scan the skies. Here I spent the first eighteen years of my life until catastrophic world events scattered almost everyone I knew.

If it were tied to real estate values in any economy of the western world other than that of Leadville, the house would be worth a great deal of money for its location. It is literally on top, with a panoramic view of the Mosquito Range to the east and the Sawatch Range from Mount Massive to Mount Yale to the west. Below is the placer cut of California Gulch and most of the town of Leadville in historical and contemporary tatter and artful array.

For our present purposes, we will reclaim the front porch for a while, and I'll give you a tour—a cultural and timeless look at the west side of the town called Leadville.

Looking out across the Sixth Street hill down to where the Colorado Midland Railroad had a large wooden barn that stood until the summer of 1934, you are looking across twenty-five square blocks of eastern Europe. This is where the Bohunks lived. The cultural gap was even greater than the dimension of the neighborhood.

The eastern Europeans who came to Leadville in the nineteenth century were from what was then Austria-Hungary. The Austro-Hungarian Empire included at one time or another countries we know as Austria, Hungary, Czechoslovakia, and parts of Yugoslavia. The latter, until recently, included Serbia, Croatia, Bosnia, Herzogovina, Montenegro, Slovenia, and part of Macedonia. Leadville settlers were from Slavic parts of Austria-Hungary, principally Slovenia. To refer to their descendants, as they themselves occasionally do, as "Austrian," may not be correct on the scale of world history, but it is accurate on the scale of Leadville history. "Bohunk" is a term that covers all eventualities. Some would even say that Mozart was a Bohunk; no one would deny that Dvořák certainly was.

In the spring, the Slovenian ladies would come in groups of two or three to pick dandelions on the Sixth Street hill. They wore long black dresses and heavy, hand-woven sweaters. On their feet were large, rugged shoes and tied around their heads were gypsy-bright scarves called *babushkas*. They carried gunny sacks from Frank Zaitz's Mercantile Company. With the bags full of dandelions, they would make their way back down the hill and disappear into the wooden labyrinth of neatly appointed houses and sheds, dirt streets and alleyways. In the winter, the same ladies made *potica*, a baked delicacy, the aroma of which could make a Bohunk of a Shanty Irish.

Frank Zaitz, Sr., was the unofficial mayor of the west side—mayor, borough chieftain, patriarch. Francis Stalzer told me a story of an Austrian woman who had been living in Leadville for several years and was applying for United States citizenship. She had done an adequate job answering questions about the history and government of her new country until she was asked a final question. The examiner queried, "Who is the president of the United States?" The aspiring American confidently replied, "Frank Zaitz." Had the immigration officer been another Austrian from Leadville, he probably would have agreed. Frank Zaitz was an important man in the community.

In 1934, as an eleven-year-old kid, I sat on this porch and looked down past the baseball field to where a long line of cars was emerging from behind the baseball grandstands on Leiter Avenue. From this vantage point I could see the cars in serpentine solemnity make their turn and head up Sixth Street. They passed our house, then crested the hill and drove along the Midland Railroad right-of-way where steel rails had given way to a corduroy road of cinders with indentations where each tie had been removed. The processional's destination was not the Carlton tunnel and the western slope beyond Mount Massive. It was the Catholic Cemetery.

Looking over the somber scene, I could see the roof of the Frank Zaitz Mercantile Company far across at 520 West Chestnut Street and the steeple of St. Joseph's Catholic Church, a block closer on Second Street. On every side street cars were backed up, patiently waiting to join the funeral procession. According to the *Herald Democrat,* the continuous line was four miles long.

Frank Zaitz, Sr., wasn't dead. The assemblage I witnessed slowly proceeding past my house was in honor of his son, Frank, Jr., who had been killed in an automobile accident on Battle Mountain. He had missed a corner on one of the scariest early highways in Colorado. At that time it was a one-lane, twisting, nightmare of a road connecting Red Cliff and Minturn, traversing ridges and ledges high above the headwaters of the Eagle River.

Mrs. Marian ("Poppy") Smith, the curator at the Healy House Museum in Leadville, worked for Frank Zaitz, Sr. Poppy read and answered all of Zaitz's mail. She told us, "He came by his property honestly, and everything he touched turned to money. After Frank, Jr.'s death, the father would look at his home from the mercantile store window and cry, saying over and over that his life was through." Two years after his son's death, Frank, Sr., died at age sixty-eight and brought to an end an epoch of international capitalism as resplendent with the "American Dream" as it was oppressive with despotic reality.

Frank Zaitz could not read or write English, but he could communicate quite effectively with both sides of the industrial world—both the old and the new. He would not have recognized the term, "global economy," but this man, who was born in tiny Korinj

Village in Yugoslavia in 1868, made a major difference in a mining town in the mountains of Colorado by understanding the significance of the concept.

His great-granddaughter heard him referred to as the "Godfather of the Leadville Mafia." Though neither the designation nor the organization was technically correct, there were important similarities. He was the man to deal with when you had a problem, and his system was powerful. In examining his life, it would be erroneous to look at it as either a matter of "the good that evil men do" or the "evil that good men do." One thing is for sure though, from the day he began his business in 1894 until the present, Leadville has had the imprint of Frank Zaitz all over it.

Conrad Beurman and his young wife Emma, my maternal grandparents, moved to Pueblo, Colorado, in 1890. They left Pennsylvania for the West, where he was promised a job as a blacksmith at the Colorado Fuel and Ironworks. My mother, Lillian, was born to them in Pueblo in 1894. When she was about ten years old, the family moved to Leadville where Conrad took a job as head blacksmith on the night shift at the Arkansas Smelter down in the west end of the community in an area called Stringtown; it was owned by CF&I and Meyer Guggenheim. The Beurmans moved into a house at 312 West Chestnut Street, directly between the Central School and the Zaitz house. Conrad blacksmithed for twelve hours a night and seven nights a week. Working with hammer and bellows, anvil and glowing coals, he bent, cast, and welded the iron and steel tools and machinery of the smelter. For thirty years he worked the night shift, and for thirty years he brought home a paycheck to his family. With the rigor of his craft and the hours and the days demanded of him, it seemed that while he worked just blocks away and slept in the same house, his children grew up without him. In the first decades of the twentieth century, only a fool would have given up such a steady job.

Conrad was paid in money. Most of his neighbors were not; their paychecks went directly to credit against their debts and to their benefactor, Frank Zaitz. They were part of the separate socioeconomic system born of the coalition of the Frank Zaitz Mercantile Company and the American Smelter & Refining Company.

Most of the workers at the smelter were immigrants from the Austro-Hungarian Empire who were recruited by Zaitz. The system worked roughly like this: Zaitz established a network that gave people from his European homeland an opportunity to come to America. He would arrange for the financing to bring laborers and their families to Leadville and upon their arrival provide them with housing, jobs at the smelter, and a general store where they could spend what they earned. For the most part, they formed a core of hard-working, inexpensive, and very dependable labor for the industrial enterprise of the city with Frank Zaitz the patrone of it all. Guggenheim employed them at the smelter, and Zaitz made sure that they and their families were never hungry or without warmth and clothing. The Mercantile sold provisions for food, coal for fuel, grapes for wine, and dry goods for clothes. To round off this mini-nation with its own "president," its own toiling masses, and it's own currency, there was St. Joseph's Catholic Church for the soul and the Slovenian Lodge for social activities, the nostalgic strains of "old country" music, and the security of ethnic homogeneity in an alien world.

This early global system has been interpreted as generosity. Some would assess the situation in a somewhat different light and start singing the last lines of Tennessee Ernie Ford's biggest hit: "St. Peter, don't call me cuz I can't go, I owe my soul to the company store."

To say Frank Zaitz was a good businessman is a gross understatement. He knew how to manipulate the system, and he had a Midas touch. Over the years, he developed far-flung enterprises: the St. Louis Tunnel; Coal Mines at Cameo near Grand Junction; the Coors Beer distributorship from Leadville west to Salt Lake City, Utah; various mines, including the Emmet and the Small Hope; a connection with Empire Zinc; and also a substantial share of the Colorado Hotel and the hot springs swimming pool in Glenwood Springs.

One of the early sources of the fortune he amassed was a long-term contract with the Colorado Midland Railroad and the

American Smelter & Refining Company. He agreed to unload the mining cars that were bringing ore down from the mines to the smelters at a fee that, for the times, seemed ridiculously low.

The challenge was that during the winter the loads of ore would solidify in the rail cars before they got down to the smelter. Zaitz knew of a miner who was an expert in the use of dynamite. The story relayed to Helen Bowen Skala from her grandfather—a miner who knew both Frank Zaitz and the "Hercules" artist—was that Zaitz took the miner and the railroad car to the end of the track down at the AS&R yard in Stringtown. The car was full of ore from the Little Jonny Mine. It was February and the load was frozen solid. The miner, a fellow named Olaf, climbed up on top of the load, and after surveying the situation he yelled down to Zaitz, who was standing there in his three-piece suit and an overcoat, "Balls, it's cold!"

Zaitz had to agree. The cold was one of the major factors in the risk he was taking in contracting to unload the cars. Olaf went to work with dynamite and blasting caps. "Olaf," Zaitz yelled up to him, "if you can break loose this load of ore without damaging the rail car, I'll give you two dollars a day more than John Campion is paying you up on Johnny Hill." The gamble paid off. With a muffled "whump," the rail car shook and the load was free. Zaitz's ingenuity and Olaf's deft touch were all it took to launch an extremely successful business.

Olaf, according to Helen Skala, was so proficient with small charges of explosives that, applying the physics of explosion and implosion, he not only contributed to Frank Zaitz's fortune, he also developed a moonlighting avocation: instantly cleaning Leadville outhouses. Helen, with her Irish eyes twinkling, admitted she knew of no witnesses to the latter endeavor.

There is no doubt Frank Zaitz was a great businessman. To say he was a philanthropist . . . well, so was John D. Rockefeller. It depends on how you want to look at the situation. Without his assistance, hundreds of people would have never had the chance to escape the oppression and hard times of east-central Europe; with his help, hundreds were able to experience the oppression and hard times, and opportunity, of Leadville. It is more than a subtle difference. And if the opinions which most of the Leadville Austrians held of him is a measure of his worth—the man had saintly qualities.

Helen Skala tells of hearing stories from her dad of Bohunks arriving at the train depot. There were crowds of confused men and their families herded together on the platform. Dangling from a string tied through a button hole of each of their coats was a "bill of lading" that read:

> DELIVER TO: FRANK ZAITZ, SR.
> LEADVILLE, COLORADO, USA

Welcome to America!
Welcome to Leadville!

7

The Line of Sights

The line of sight from our porch takes you out across the Leadville
baseball field. The ball diamond was made possible when the
Colorado Midland Railroad folded, which accounts for the out-
field being black. It was there that the mighty steam engines
belched cinders as they prepared to head west, up the grade past
Turquoise Lake to Hagerman Pass.

Uncle Jim, my dad's brother, was a fireman on the Colorado Midland. Jim was shoveling coal on the hapless train that became snow-
bound up on Hagerman Pass for seventy-nine days in the big
snowstorm of 1899. He was more interested in the Industrial Workers
of the World than in steam boilers, so he became an organizer for
Eugene Debs. He traveled the West: San Francisco, Seattle, Portland,
coming home to Leadville long enough to have three children—
Little Jimmy, Marvin, and Eugenia. His wife died in 1918, leaving the
three children virtually penniless. They were farmed out up and
down Sixth Street to their aunts, uncles, and grandparents.

Marvin went to Rachel, his grandmother; Eugenia went to
Mamie, Jim and Dad's sister; and Little Jimmy was raised by my
mom and dad. Neither the times nor Jimmy were easy. He was
eleven years old when he moved in. Jimmy was strong-willed, defiant of authority, and quite confused by the anger and sorrow he
felt at the loss of his mother. He spent much of his childhood getting into one kind of fix or another, and it seemed unlikely he

would ever amount to anything. Mom told me Jimmy would refuse to take baths on Saturday nights as he was supposed to do. As an expression of gratitude to his aunt and uncle for taking him in, he would wait until the neighbors were visiting and then announce, "Boy, I sure am dirty. I haven't had a bath since my mother died. Uncle Eddie, do you think I could have a bath someday?"

Jake and Ethel Sandusky ran a jewelry store and a pawn shop next to Ryan's Pool Hall on Harrison Avenue. Jake came into the *Herald Democrat* one day and showed my dad a ring he said Marvin had pawned with him. "The kid claimed he found it lying in the street. I let him hock it for $5, but I thought you ought to know about it." The ring was a silver horseshoe with tiny rubies. Dad recognized it immediately. It had been given to him by his father, who had won it in a poker game up in Deadwood, South Dakota, back before he had come to Leadville. Marvin had taken it from a box Mom kept in the bedroom. Dad gave Sandusky the five bucks and asked him not to mention it to anyone—especially young Jimmy or Marvin.

Two years passed with constant difficulties, but Jimmy learned respect and moved on; Marvin eventually graduated from the eighth grade. On the night of his graduation Dad gave him a gift—the horseshoe ring. Nothing needed to be said about trust and the value of honesty. Jimmy is in his early eighties now. He retired a few years ago as the chief executive officer of a major engineering firm in Denver. Beyond eighth grade he was self-educated but, also, he had been Leadville-educated.

On down the hill at the corner of Sixth and Leiter was a house where a Mexican family lived. Cultural bias is as prevalent as is cultural diversity among the many shades of flesh, bents of belief, and enclaves of civilization that make up this world of mankind. It is bitterly inherent in human nature that pride in oneself often seems to require antagonism toward others. In the bedsheet bedlam of cross-burning terrorism throughout this country of ours, we have known the viciousness of such bigotry. But, sometimes it seems, while in its adult manifestation hatred is most dangerous, in its childhood display it is most cruel, most insidious.

Almost all of the Mexicans in the area lived down near the smelters at Stringtown. The Mascarenas family was an exception and lived near us. For fun, we would torment them. The thoughtless harm of our actions never occurred to me until years later. We would stand on the hill above their house and toss rocks onto the tin roof. It seemed like such good sport. Those rocks made a great racket, and it didn't take more than three or four hits before Mascarenases would start pouring out of the doors mad as hell, and then we young sportsmen would run.

And that wasn't the worst of it. What started as a bit of devilment and target practice evolved into a plot. When I recall the way we treated those people, I cringe. But when I think about it in as honest a light as is possible, it seems that our actions probably stemmed from less devious motivation than racial harassment. I think we might just have been some kids expressing a generic, competitive meanness not uncommon to children of all persuasions. The Mascarenas kids were not so much victims of racism as they were victims of demography.

What we did was not so much a matter of prejudice as it was basic, adolescent orneriness. Bud Nadon was the agitator, John Swenson the bait, and I the trap. It began with Bud lobbing a few well-chosen stones down on the resonant slope of the tin roof. In an instant three raging Mascarenases came roaring out of the side door, hollering and cussing in righteous (and justified) indignation. Swenson was waiting for them up on the high wooden sidewalk that hung from the slope of the hill on the north side of the street. He started running just as they were about to land on him. Looking back over his shoulder, he taunted them as he ran. The race was on, as was the fix. Pacing himself so as to give the pursuing furies the illusion of gaining on him, John lured them toward their doom. In the meantime, I hovered in the shadows beneath the sidewalk ready to spring the trap. I could hear the rhythm of running footsteps as Swenson approached and passed and then the charge of his would-be nemesis coming fast behind him. At just the right moment, I raised a loose plank and sent the indignant pursuers flying and crashing, a tangled mass of arms, legs, and rage, into the Sixth Street ditch. They never knew what hit them until we were long gone. What good, clean, American-boy fun!

What does it take for young kids to act in a diabolic and violent fashion against others solely because they are different? My parents weren't racists, just the opposite, and I'd like to believe that I'm not either. Is it that in the pack-like mentality of youth we seek security in expressing collective malice toward common prey, regardless of what particular elements of race, creed, or uniqueness set them apart from us? Sometimes simply living on a different street was a sufficient cause for war. Over on the east side of town, the Ninth Street Irish Catholics used to beat the hell out of the Sixth Street Irish Catholics whenever they had a chance. Try to call that an example of cultural bias.

What can be done to prevent such outrageous behavior from continuing? Maturity helps some outgrow such narrowness, but it takes education, exposure, and understanding to develop an appreciation of cultural differences. Years later I became good friends with Gus Ariolla, the creator of the great comic strip *Gordo*. One evening we were sitting down at Doc's Lab in Monterey reminiscing about childhood experiences, and I told him a few Leadville stories, including the story of the Mascarenas assault. He laughed in appreciation of the universal meanness of it all, and then this kind, intelligent, gracious gentleman, this dear friend, said to me, "Hell, Ed. If I had grown up in Leadville you probably would have kicked the shit out of me." What could I say?

I think now of Mr. and Mrs. Williams who lived in a nice little white house farther on down West Sixth Street. My mother befriended Mrs. Williams during the influenza epidemic of 1919. The family had moved out to Leadville from St. Louis and were avid Cardinal fans. In 1934 they took the train to St. Louis and brought a World Series souvenir back for me. I prized my ten-inch baseball bat with a small pennant showing Sportsman Park and the world champion Cardinals with Dizzy Dean and Pepper Martin.

After that I would often stop by the Williams house on my trips up and down Sixth Street. Mrs. Williams had a bowl of candy that she generously offered while we sat and talked baseball. The

Williamses were the only black family living in Leadville at that time. Their kindness and loneliness combined with our shared love of the great American sport of baseball always made me feel like a welcomed guest in their house. My good fortune in knowing these fine people might have begun the shift in thinking that gave me a broader perspective of the differences among people and the ethnic and racial parochialism typical of small towns. I wondered, even then, why they never visited us.

However, it was human contact of a different kind that really drove the message home. When I was fourteen, my brother Donald and I were on our way to the Liberty Bell Theater to see a movie when somebody tapped me on the shoulder. I turned around and a very big, out-of-town Mexican let me have it right in the nose. I remember leaning against the wall of Davis Drug there on Harrison Avenue, dazed, my nose broken, blood dripping down my shirt, and wondering, "Why me, what did I ever do to him?" The answer to this question took a while to figure out. The answer: Plenty!

Like many kids, I usually ran everywhere I went. On a cold winter night in 1936, I was tearing down Sixth Street toward Pine and, just as I passed the side of the Seabry's house, I hit a patch of ice and took a memorable fall. With no little difficulty I picked myself up, made my way on back to the Davis Drug Store, laid my obviously broken left arm on the counter, and announced to Mr. Nash, the pharmacist, that I could use some assistance.

Mr. Nash called my house by first going through Central, who then rang the line we shared with all of Leadville. My Aunt Mamie, who lived across the street, answered and said my mom and dad were at some kind of Moose function and wouldn't be home for a while. She said I'd better not wait around for my folks but that I should head on up and see Dr. McDonald.

It was less than three blocks from there to where Doc McDonald lived and had an office just above Poplar on East Seventh Street. I was feeling pretty brave but also a little queasy by the time I knocked on the door. Mrs. McDonald, whom we all called Helen, let me in and escorted me directly into a room with a black leather examining table. Doc studied my arm briefly and gave me a blast of ether that still lurks in my memory of things to avoid. My arm was in a cast when Mom and Dad arrived.

The practice of medicine was somewhat simpler in those days. Before the intervention of legions of lawyers, physicians were able to concentrate more on practice than malpractice and get on with the mystery and mechanics of the healing arts. Doc told me to keep the cast on for six weeks, and the arm should knit without deformity. The last thing he said as my parents negotiated the front door with their wobbly son supported between them was, "Eddieboy, now don't get the plaster wet."

We didn't have insurance. Method of payment was not a consideration when Dr. McDonald saw my arm. We didn't have to fill out any forms because there were no forms. He knew we would do the best we could to square our obligation, but even if he had no notion of the Larsh family's sense of fiscal responsibility, he would have done his best to relieve my suffering, to heal my bones—regardless of assurance or insurance on the collecting of his bill. He was the doctor. He had sworn an oath. I know it is much too simplistic, but a plan to have a doctor like Franklin McDonald in every town might avoid a lot of debate about universal health care.

Dr. Franklin McDonald provided a second generation of medical care for Leadville, following his father, Dr. R. J. McDonald, who began practice around the turn of the century. Franklin and Helen had two children. Their oldest child, Franklin, Jr. (we kids called him "Doc"), was born in 1920, which made him exactly the right or wrong age to enter what Studs Turkel ironically calls "The Good War." He enlisted early in the U.S. Army Air Corps. His plane disappeared somewhere between Guam and Mount Fuji, and he never made it back to Seventh Street. I didn't know that one of the planes our squadron was searching for in the foamy brine was piloted by Franklin, Jr., until long after we were home.

The top of the Tabor Opera House, which opened in 1879, is visible from up here on the front porch. Diagonally across Harrison

Avenue is the Silver Dollar Saloon, which commenced dispensing spirit and sustenance the same year. Both of these venerable establishments are still in business. Down the street about a half block on the corner of Third and Harrison was Ed's Printing House. In 1938, after over thirty years of employment as a printer for the *Herald Democrat*, my dad decided it was time to go to work for himself. After three years he was able to purchase the building on Harrison Avenue which, up until that time, had been used as a saloon. Dad replaced the swinging doors and moved the bar and the back bar into an adjacent room where Mom helped with the business, not by serving whiskey and brew but rather by sorting and proofreading printed materials produced from the fonts of type and the platen presses.

One day in 1942, a couple of lawyers came into the print shop and offered to be partners with Dad, not as printers but as saloon keepers. Camp Hale was being built out at Pando, and times were really good for the saloon business. As they explained it, after two or three years of doing business with the soldiers and construction people out at Camp Hale, he and Mom could probably retire to sunny California and never have to worry about another Leadville winter. All he would have to do was stock the bar with booze and beer and count the money. Dad told the lawyers he would have to discuss the idea with his wife.

To put it simply, my dad sold the barroom furnishings to a man from Stringtown. If you want to see the bar that used to be against the wall of Ed's Print Shop, you have to go down to a Mexican restaurant called the Grille near Zaitz Slovenian Hall in the 500-block of West Elm Street. Shortly after his business discussion with the lawyers he sold it for fifty bucks: ten dollars down and ten dollars a month for four months. As my dad put it, "I told Mama we could make a pile of money and retire, and all she said was, 'Not by selling whiskey to young boys, we won't,' and that was the end of it." I had enlisted in the Army Air Corps; my younger brother Donald was anxious to join the Marines. It was no time to question Mama's values concerning the treatment of servicemen.

Dad liked being a printer anyway.

8

A Sign of the Times

The first block of what becomes West Second Street is called State Street. There isn't much left of what this notorious block used to be. The Miner's Club and the Bucket of Blood saloons burned down in a big fire back in the forties. The gamblers and the whores had been officially run off the street and out of the cribs years before that. The Pastime Lounge is still in business, but even with the brightest of signs blazing in its windows, it hardly emits more than a dim glow into the darkness. Next to the Pastime, the Pioneer Bar now stands in isolated darkness. It once had an international glow.

The Pioneer wasn't just another place to buy liquor. With eighty-two drinking establishments operating in Leadville in 1880, there were plenty of places to get drunk, laid, and/or knocked in the head and robbed. But the Pioneer offered more than cheap whiskey, warm beer, and three-dollar pleasure. It survived for well over a century, not as just another tavern but as a tavern that was a social institution.

"Just bars" are as plentiful as street corners in many towns and often as indistinct in character as the choking clouds of shadowy smoke that fill them. They are places where a soul can get lost, sometimes for only an evening or sometimes forever. In cycles of dim light and boarded windows, "just bars" come and go. But bars that become social institutions serve higher purposes than simply being stations of delusion and regret. Such exceptional houses of spirit are creations of sound and motion and poignant human interaction.

Listen. It's a mild summer night, and the sounds of the Pioneer Bar greet us as we approach, walking on the wooden planks of the front sidewalk. We've just passed the "cribs" where, in a row of cabin-like structures resembling a cross between a cheap motel and a centerfold section, convivial ladies have encouraged our interest with humor and hints of flesh but, barely escaping the crude call of the Sirens, we have laughed and promised our business for another time.

There are blends of raucous laughter, the guttural utterance of work-callused men, and the shrill encouragement of the women who tease them, the melodious entreaties of a piano and a fiddle, and the song of a ruffled and gartered lady named Josephina. It all meets us as we shove through the swinging doors and enter a pall of cigar smoke, the aromatic essence of spilled beer and sweat, and the subtle clatter of poker chips, rolling dice, and spinning wheels of chance. Serious gambling took place in the back room; the atmosphere in there indicated that unwanted distractions could lead to dire consequences. A stairwell climbed the back wall, and an open hallway with a row of small doors suggested carnal knowledge.

The Pioneer was not just another bar, it was a State Street extravaganza. Over the years within its walls were joyous celebrations of weddings and whiskey-solemn wakes; gun fights, fist fights, and dog fights; countless debates on the character of politicians, the state of the economy, the price of gold and silver, and who was the current queen of the cribs. There were testimonials to the sacred purity of motherhood and the holy gifts of grog, the hush of tear-burnt moments in the sad and lovely songs of broken dreams, and even rare occasions when the members of the band, the lady on the stage, and all the voices in the house sounded the same refrain.

Stand up at the bar. Have a drink. Listen.

The Pioneer is dark and silent now. It has been since 1979, when not only the business closed but also, as if to secure the final and lasting certainty of its demise, the massive mahogany bar and back bar were sold to a Chinese gentleman named Fat and shipped to his "wild-west" restaurant, called Fat City, in Sacramento, California.

That bar was built to order by French artisans, shipped in sections across the Atlantic Ocean, railed to Denver, freighted through the Rockies, and assembled at the Pioneer to stand for over a hundred years—only to suffer the humiliation of becoming a prop in a West Coast tourist attraction. I thought about buying it myself when I heard it was for sale—or at least I gave it some consideration. But Jane's good sense once more prevailed, and we didn't go fourteen thousand dollars in hock for seventy-five feet of polished, hardwood memorabilia.

On a trip to San Francisco a few years ago, I stopped at Old Sacramento to see the bar's new location and I met Mr. Fat. I showed him the bullet hole in the back bar that was produced when Wyatt Earp proved he could shoot a marble from the top of a whiskey bottle. My dad said his father was there that night. This is the real romantic stuff of western history: bullet holes and Buntline Specials, a quiet and deadly man named Earp, and my grandfather watching the whole shooting show from a poker table.

I also told Mr. Fat that I had a personal interest in his transplanted relic in that, when my dad was six years old, he and a buddy of his would hang around the Pioneer until one of the bartenders would give them the okay to tap dance on the bar for tips. My dad, a respected printer and journalist, got his start in the competitive world of free enterprise with thumbtack taps on his shoes and a questionable sense of rhythm. However, his terpsichorean endeavors were short lived. As soon as his mom found out about it, he was quickly convinced that he should investigate other, more traditional sources of income. Rachel never did have much good to say about the Pioneer.

The old bar weathered a century of all-night elbows, spilled booze, the collision of bar fights, and even the shuffle and tap of juvenile vaudevillians. But even with its gun-slingers, gamblers, and upstairs bed chambers, the Pioneer was by no means the wildest place in Leadville. Actually, in the 1880s, it was a rather moderate tavern, falling somewhere between such dens of iniquity as Jeff Winney's Bar on Chestnut Street, famous for "Mickey Finns" and missing wallets, and the Harrison Avenue upper-class saloon called J. C. Blake & Co., where gentlemen partook of refreshment of spirit and played civil games of chance. A man who didn't know the territory could start an evening with a recreational drink at the wrong bar and wake up the next morning with a staggering headache and empty pockets. Part of the Pioneer's success came from a reputation for somewhat less risk in having a good time.

The population of Leadville, when it reached its peak in the early 1880s, has been estimated at between twenty and thirty thousand. Though no accurate census records exist, it is likely that upwards of seventy-five percent of those residing in the area were men. A few women came into the Pioneer with a man just to have a drink, but for the most part, in those days Leadville was a man's world. The majority of the women who frequented such establishments as the Pioneer were there for professional reasons. There were some female "beer jerkers" who drew draughts for the male bartenders, but most of the ladies wandered about encouraging customers to buy them drinks. Some of them were entertainers as well and would dance and sing on the raised wooden stage in the back corner of the barroom. Of course, most of them were willing to sell their favors for the right price, and the management took a good cut out of all the business they did.

Between the bars and the cribs, prostitution accounted for a fair portion of Leadville's illicit economy. The cribs were still in business in 1942 when I headed off to college and ended up flying around the South Pacific, and the Pioneer was still known for its upstairs accommodations as late as the 1960s. Vice has always been profitable and likely always will be, no matter what town you're talking about.

Not only did the Pioneer operate for over a century, but for its first sixty-eight years, it stayed open twenty-four hours a day. It never closed. From 1874 until 1942, the swinging doors of the place were never disgraced by a lock.

Even during the 1920s and the early 1930s, when Prohibition was in effect, the Pioneer continued to do a thriving business dispensing illegal drinks. Except on superficial levels, Leadville ignored Prohibition. It was pretty much "business as usual" in the Pioneer and other drinking houses in the city. A decent local distilling industry developed during that period, and law enforcement was seldom a problem. There are advantages to planting your town so high up on the mountain. The intrepid Treasury Department was unable to lock up the doors of the Pioneer, but the coercive forces of commerce succeeded where the government failed.

In 1942 the influence of the U.S. Army put an end to twenty-four-hour drinking in Leadville—not by act of authority but by indirect means. On a wide meadow on the western slope of Tennessee Pass, the military built Camp Hale, headquarters of the celebrated Tenth Mountain Division. While training the toughest outfit of mountain scalers, back country skiers, and outdoor survivalists in the nation, the army considered Leadville to be too rowdy for the troops and made it off limits. As an act of appeasement and in hopes of luring some of those twenty-one-dollar-a-month paychecks into the city, Leadville businessmen agreed that bars would close at 2:00 A.M. The ban was lifted, the soldiers permitted to invade, and the last of the wide-open towns in Colorado was tamed a bit. The sixty-eight-year era of a barroom door that swung freely in both directions without the intrusion of locks or laws came to an end.

This is not to say that society's imposition of a degree of restraint is necessarily bad; it just seems significant that even the most defiant of institutions can fall prey to the priorities of simple economics. The Pioneer and its various counterparts thumbed their collective noses at massive threats such as Elliot Ness and company, but docilely succumbed to the pressure of the dollar and the military police.

Perhaps patriotic zeal was a factor as well. It might have seemed in keeping with the war effort to take whatever actions were necessary to insure that "our boys" were not denied access to such precious Americana as rot-gut whiskey and three-dollar whores. In any case, sixty-eight years was an impressive run without a "last call for alcohol."

It wasn't until I was living in California in 1950, that I heard one of the best Pioneer Bar stories. While doing graduate work at

Stanford University in Palo Alto, I had a professor who claimed the values and tone of a neighborhood could be analyzed by reading the signs hung in restaurants, bars, and garages. You really don't have to be a sociologist to analyze the difference between an eating establishment displaying a sign that says, "Bare Feet Not Permitted" and another that warns "Valet Parking Only." Nevertheless, pursuant to an assignment in his class, I found myself sitting at the bar of a small Italian place in North Beach in San Francisco jotting down such pertinent raw data as "No Checks" and "Restroom in Rear" when a gray-haired gentleman sat down next to me and started talking. I immediately put my notebook away because I certainly didn't want to give a lengthy explanation of the nature of my project.

Before long the conversation came around to the "where're you from?" stage, and I told him my home had been a little town in Colorado called Leadville. The mention of the word "Leadville" brought an abrupt reaction in him. He eyed me more carefully than he had at first and then, with a perceptible note of awe and caution, inquired, "Did you say, 'Leadville, Colorado?'"

I replied that, indeed, I was from Leadville and asked if he had heard of it. His answer was a rather emotional affirmative. "Hell yes, I've heard of it. I've heard of it, I've been there, and, for damn sure, I'm never going back."

I couldn't leave that line alone. I bought us a round and said, "So tell me what you remember about Leadville."

Sometimes we have to travel great distances to gain an enlightened perspective of our own backyard. This is the story the gentleman told me.

"I was a traveling salesman in Leadville for the night. I found a room in a hotel called the Vendome. It was about two-thirty in the morning. I had been sleeping for a couple of hours when some rowdy son of a gun of a miner started raising hell with his lady-friend out in the hall and woke me up along with probably half the people sleeping at the Vendome Hotel that night. He finally shut up. I don't know whether he was invited into the lady's room or finally came to grips with his rejection and departed, but by then I was wide awake and decided to go out for a beer to settle my nerves.

"I had heard that the Pioneer Bar never closed and, following the clerk's directions, I walked down Harrison Avenue to State Street. Mind you, it all might have been different in the part of Leadville you grew up in, kid, but this was back in the thirties; and down there on State Street it was still a wild-assed, western town. Within the half block from the main street down to the Pioneer I had to refuse the services of two different hookers, both of whom were tough enough looking that I was damn polite in telling them, 'Thank you, no.'

"From the size of the crowd and the sounds inside, you would have thought it was eleven o'clock on a Saturday night instead of three in the morning in the middle of the week. I pushed open the swinging doors. There were only two seats left at the long bar.

"The bartender said to me, 'What will you have?' I ordered a beer and determined the best thing I could do was to stay as inconspicuous as possible and just kind of watch the show.

"There were two big guys with huge biceps arm-wrestling at a table over in a corner and, in the whole time I was in the place— likely close to an hour—neither of them budged an inch. They just sat there glaring at each other and occasionally nodding at a passing waitress to bring them shots of whiskey which they would down in a single swallow. Then they would slam the jiggers back down on the table with a boom and cut loose with an utterance that was a cross between the howl of a coyote and the growl of a mountain lion.

"Toward the rear of the place there was an upright piano played by a fellow who might have known a thousand songs but, for all I could tell, he only knew one tune. But that didn't keep a steady flow of customers from staggering back and singing along or giving him a slap on the back, tossing a quarter in his hat, and telling him what a fine musician he was.

"I was having a pretty good time. You know, it was back in the deepest years of the Depression, and as a traveling salesman I had seen a good bit of this country and had found most towns to be so hard hit as to be nothing short of desperate. But this Leadville of yours, it seemed to be thriving—at least it did the one night I was there.

"I had noticed there was a fellow sitting across the empty stool from me—a rugged looking miner who was drinking shots and beers and not saying a word. After a while a younger looking guy came in through the swinging doors and made his way into the tavern. He was kind of hesitant, you know, not real sure of himself. The fellow made a quick dash for the vacant seat between me and the miner.

"The bartender came over and frowned at his new customer and barked, 'Whaddaya have?'

"'I believe I'll have a dry martini, thank you.' Without even looking up from his beer, the silent miner swung his mighty right arm around and backhanded the young man, knocking him right off his stool and onto the floor where he just sat, too stunned to move. The miner looked across the now-empty stool and said to me, 'For Christ's sake! Nobody orders a dry martini in the Pioneer.'

"I gulped down the last of my beer, made a rapid exit from the bar, and cautiously sneaked back up to the main street and then to the Vendome Hotel. I have never been back to Leadville."

The fellow looked at me to see what kind of effect this seemingly bizarre story had on me. I thought of a lot of things, none more bizarre than the fact that I was currently sitting in a North Beach bar on a weekday checking out significant signs for a college professor from Palo Alto and had just heard a very plausible story about another town that was an essential part of my being.

I thought of Steinbeck's *Cannery Row* and the idea of people seeing just what they want to see. So, I decided to give this guy another Leadville story to add to his perception of my hometown. I told him that my granddad had been a professional gambler in the Pioneer in 1880 and that he had talked about a sign that used to hang above the back bar. It read:

WINE   WOMEN   SONG
THESE THREE ARE SUPPOSED TO MAKE LIFE PALATIAL, AND
WHILE NOTHING OF AN IMPROPER CHARACTER IS PERMITTED,
WE CAN FURNISH ALL THREE ANY NIGHT.

The story about signs and the Pioneer Bar that Leadville folks love to tell is about the fellow who gets into town late one night and decides to have himself a drink at one of the local bars. He takes a hotel room, and the clerk recommends he try the Pioneer.

An hour or so before he got there, a Denver man, out for a unique thrill, had convinced a prostitute to perform her services up on the roof of the Pioneer. It was twenty below zero, but, what the hell, ten bucks is ten bucks. While they were in the clasp of lust, a howling gust of mountain air caught the "lovers" and froze them solid, and then another Boreal blast blew them right off the roof. They landed on the sidewalk in front of the swinging doors.

In the meantime the first fellow finds his way to the Pioneer and goes on in. The bartender says, "What can I get you?"

"Oh, I'll have a beer," he answers. "And, by the way, did you know your sign fell down?"

Some days are better than others—so are some bars. As I was driving back to Palo Alto, I thought of telling the Pioneer sign story to my professor to see if he could deduce what type of dress code the establishment insisted on—I remember smiling all the way down El Camino Real.

9

The Larshes of Leadville: 1879

John Larsh's cabin on Second Street was crowded for the first year after the arrival of Rachel and John's three sisters. Each of the women occupied a corner of the bedroom, and he had his bed in the front room that served as kitchen, dining room, and parlor. During the daytime, John would catch some sleep in the back room while Mindy and Rachel heated water on the wood stove and did wash for ten men who lived at a boarding house a few blocks away.

Mamie occupied herself three days a week teaching reading and writing to six children in a small cabin on Chestnut Street. More so than most in Leadville at the time, she was concerned about children. She could see that with the influx of families some arrangements had to be made for formal education. The city council was busy with street maintenance and allocating funds to feed the swelling population of drunks, thieves, and murderers assembled at the city jail. Mayor Tabor was steadily lengthening his visits to Denver. And, though few would admit it, for the most part the miners' community priorities were more along the lines of cold beer, hot women, and payday than they were with the edification of an increasing population of school-aged citizens.

It was one thing to have a town built on vice and greed with the law in the hands of drunken bullies, but, with babies being born and families moving in with little children, a different understanding of responsibility was critical. Mamie knew she would be a part of that understanding and the system it required.

Edie had other concerns. She was the youngest of the Larsh sisters living in Leadville, and to a certain extent the most lonely. In an age when young girls often married in their teens, she had no inclination toward matrimony. She felt she had no place to go. She described herself as "nineteen going on ninety." Her marital status was not the result of the neglect experienced by the ill-tempered or homely. She was an attractive young woman, and when she danced and sang at the Pioneer Bar, there were few men who did not lay down their cards or set down their drinks and pay close attention. She loved music and, when she was performing, all the hardship and distraction of the world drifted away from her in the abandon of song. She wasn't just another singing barroom whore. Edie was a beautiful and talented lady of the night who worked in a bar. She made part of her living selling "love" in the rooms on the second floor; but for herself, the only love she had was for moments on a crude stage when she could escape the traps and tragedies and travesties of the world she perceived about her.

Mindy was the most reserved member of the family, far less inclined to outbursts of anger at socio-political inequities than Mamie, or to bawdy or heartbreaking stories than Edie. Though not lacking in warmth or friendliness, she was wont to keep her thoughts and feelings to herself. She possessed an inner strength that the others respected and an openness that allowed them access to her resources. When she did speak, all the other women, and John as well, would listen carefully. She seemed to live her life and judge her own actions by a standard she would not apply to any others. Mindy would have made a powerful missionary except that she expected no one to live by her demanding values but herself. While she had stated flatly that she would never enter the Pioneer Bar, there was no condemnation in her words of either John or Edie for their choices to do so.

The Larshes of Leadville were the transplanted faction of an Illinois family of fifteen children. In addition to the four members who shared the cabin, there was also Charles, an older brother who, along with a childhood friend and neighbor, Lewis Lamb, had begun the Larsh family emigration by moving to Deadwood,

South Dakota, in 1876. First John and then the rest had followed him to Deadwood and then to Leadville. Another brother named Art was also living in Leadville. In 1879 Charles was thirty-six, Mamie thirty-four, Mindy thirty-two, John twenty-eight, Art twenty-six, and Edie nineteen. With such a spread within the same household, Edie lived along with Mamie and Mindy who had changed her diapers back in Ohio.

The historical context in which they had grown up and were living included both the devastation of the American Civil War and, more recently, the economic depression of 1873–78. Such external duress had bonded them as a family, diverse in personality but unified in strength. And Rachel, though she was younger than Mamie or Mindy, was a natural maternal head of the household—listening to the social activism of Mamie, the silent heart of Mindy, and the bitter façade of Edie's hidden torments. She was essential to the bond of the family. But it was crowded in the Larsh cabin in 1879 and, until living conditions changed, there was no way she was going to consent to John's insistence that their engagement had been extended well past propriety and that it was time they married.

She had a plan, and one afternoon, following a particularly congested day of climbing over Larshes while trying to do her laundry work, she expressed it to the rest with the vehemence of one approaching the end of patience. Though Mindy said little of it, Rachel knew Mindy had been in love with Lewis Lamb since he and brother Charles had been childhood friends and that she had most likely followed him to Deadwood and then to Leadville intent on marriage. All of this matrimonial intention had been stalled by the economic realities of hard times. John wanted a nicer home for Rachel; Lewis wanted a sense of his own prosperity to share with Mindy; and, in the meantime, five adults were tripping over one another's feet every morning down on Second Street. It was not uncommon for so many people to inhabit such limited quarters in Leadville in 1879, but for Rachel it was not a tolerable environment in which to commence a marriage, much less to begin a family.

Cupid's arrows can be as subtle as a whiff of perfume or the chanced meeting of eyes, but they can also be as sharp as a woman's honest rage. In one piercing volley, Rachel scattered the bunch. She told Mamie that when they built her a school they damn well better build her a teacherage as well. She told Mindy that if she and Lewis were going to postpone their marriage until their ship came in, they'd better get to some town that had a harbor. And she told John there would be another room built on to the cabin before she would give another thought to being his wife. To give tautness to the draw of her Cupid's bow she punctuated her demands with a reference to her dear old father back in Quebec who could surely use her company in his declining years.

They all would be welcome in her house, and there would be room for Edie to stay until she found her own direction, but it was time to make some drastic changes. In terms John could clearly understand, she was calling his hand and he had better not have been bluffing.

On the afternoon of September 30, 1879, John and Rachel Larsh were wed at the courthouse in Leadville. Five minutes later the judge joined Lewis and Mindy Lamb in matrimonial bond— "in sickness and in health,'til death do you part."

10

Dinner at the Clarendon

Horace Tabor had bought the Chrysolite and the Matchless mines and was involved in most of the claims that were being prospected up and around Fryer Hill and all the way up Big Evans Gulch. He was becoming a well-known figure in the banking and political circles of Denver as well as Washington, D.C. By September 1879, he was spending most of his time in Denver and in the East, though his generosity toward the people of Leadville was being well touted. His public gas works was ready to light the streets; his business associate R. G. Dill had opened the Clarendon Hotel, and it was ready to wine, dine, and lodge the most demanding guest; the Tabor Opera House was just two months from commencing over a century of producing the nation's theatrical and musical extravaganzas.

The miners still made $2.50 to $3.00 a day, while those who toiled in the newly opened smelters on the south end of town were making as much as $5.00. Disquiet between mine management and the men who spent their days down in the holes was intensifying, portending an inevitable open conflict.

The saloons abounded in beer, wine, crime, women, and song.

In the meantime, private lives continued in the foreground, playing before the backdrop of such public affairs and commercial contingencies as Tabor triumphs and labor disputes. The Larsh family had two marriages to celebrate.

At the end of September at two miles high, the weather can do anything. The frost is on the ground every morning, and the aspen groves high on the slopes are nearly barren of their golden, autumn leaves. On any given day, dense white clouds can descend upon the town and fill the skies with snow. But also, during this time of the year, there can be brilliant, sun-bright, blue-skied mornings with the high peaks above the spruce of timberline glistening with the powdered sugar of light, crisp snow.

There is a time in late September in the high country when the final moments of the day's sun begin to take on a special quality. As twilight approaches, a sense of the suspension of time infuses the soul with intimations of a less transient reality than the self-destructing pace of death, taxes, and other concerns over which we have little control. When you step outside, regardless of where you are, in the frenzied heart of a city or the tranquil isolation of the forest, no matter what the day's weather might have been, you know that the great wobbling orb of our mother planet is listing away from the heat of the sun and change is coming.

There is little desperation in such light. Time to contemplate and prepare for the needs of January is ample. Days of the transitional slide of autumn are there to experience. The signs are clear, and we know their message even if our homes and cars and malls are climatized, and winter is nothing more than a season of higher utility bills. The lawns and leaves take on a different hue in those precious moments when the message is spoken. There is poignancy in these early autumn moments suspended in the timelessness of universal understanding. In unspoken truth, we are one with the migratory of birds and the hoarding drives of beasts, as we are one with the cumulative strata of ancestral essence and the cycles of our own lives.

The sun falls to the west and to the south, and for an immeasurable moment we might be reliving a parallel instant of our own childhood, transcending the laws of time to dwell within our unguarded perception. We might well be our own ancestors caught in the glow and carried to our awareness.

I can close my eyes and see the reflection of the setting sun as it burnt like raging flame in the momentary mirrors of the mine windows up on Johnny Hill. In the stillness of such a twilight, my mother, especially during the war, would walk out the back door toward the panorama of Mount Massive to catch the last embers of day upon the high peaks. I think of it as her way of prayer.

It was in the aura of the final daylight glow of such a day that John and Rachel Larsh departed their cabin on Second Street. It was the evening of the day of their marriage. No royal couple or "silver king" and "silver queen" had ever stepped from day into twilight in a more glorious light.

John, Rachel, Mamie, Edie, Mindy, and Lewis had lived their lives and were long departed by the time I was born in 1922. I missed them by a generation, but I feel as if I knew them. Leadville, like many isolated communities before the wonder and curse of satellite dishes and the stifling effects of the homogenized mediocrity they broadcast, was a community of storytellers. The long winter evenings were filled with the traces of people and events remembered or repeated from the traditions of the past. And they weren't just related as flat and lifeless figures and incidents. People took great pride in the creation of living detail to give dimension to the stories. My father, my mother, my aunts and uncles, the neighbors, and any who came to visit—when they told of the old times, the times of their youth, the stories of their parents and aunts and uncles—they not only spoke the truth of an oral tradition, they also resurrected the spark, the animation, the humanity of the characters that made the stories come alive. My father and his brothers and sisters brought Rachel alive for me as they did the others about whom I write. And it is good that I listened well, for now it comes to me to pass their story on to you. It is my time to be the story teller.

So it is that in the magical connection of the alpine glow of a mountain twilight we join the newlyweds as they go to dinner at the Clarendon Hotel. And though the decades have passed, in such an ethereal atmosphere, even in the present we can hear their laughter.

"Johnny, just look at the light out here. The world's aglow with this sunset. Even these shacks and the rutted street look like something out of a painting."

"Did I forget to tell you, Rachel?"

"Tell me what?"

"Oh, it's just another little benefit, that's all." He put his arm about his new wife and they walked the board sidewalk east toward Harrison Avenue.

"What are you telling me now, John Larsh?"

"Maybe I should have mentioned it before, but with all the rest it slipped my mind."

"Yes?"

"All the glory of nature glowing upon the likes of Leadville—it's not such a big thing."

"But it's so beautiful."

"Sure it is, but this is the way the world always looks to a Larsh—welcome to the family."

September 30, 1879, there had been two weddings of note, and on the autumn-chilled evening of that marvelous day, Larshes and Lambs stood on the high wooden sidewalk in front of the Clarendon Hotel, the newest and most lavish eating and sleeping establishment in the rapidly growing town.

The wedding party entered the hotel. As the Larshes—John and Rachel, Mamie, Edie, Charles, and Art—and the Lambs, Lewis and Mindy, were escorted across the main dining area to a private alcove they had reserved for their marriage banquet, the natural elegance of the occasion transcended matters of fashion and affluence. The ladies of the party with "best clothes" assembled from hope chests, bequests, and loans from friends, and hand-sewn innovations of necessity and art, carried themselves with a presence and a grace equal to any dining in the luxurious environs who were dressed in imported finery from the East.

It was a wonderful night of extravagance and festivity. Champagne glasses clinked in the poetry of heartfelt toasts to the brides and grooms, to the family assembled, and to the families far away.

Charlie was speaking about his migration from the flatlands. "So I tell my buddy Lou, I think I'll travel on out west to where the gold is. I'm a jeweler and what better place to be than squarely in the middle of a gold rush and a silver boom. And he says, what the hell, he'll just come along for the fun of it. How was I to know I would be leading a whole parade of Larshes out into this devilish notion of a promised land?"

"I don't know whether to call you 'Moses' or the 'Pied Piper,'" said John. "But there have been plenty of days I felt like calling you other things for luring me up on top of this damn mountain."

There was the laughter of good-natured agreement, for it was true that though most of the veterans of Leadville's various modes of assault harbored a caustic affection for the place, few were not more than ready to voice a hearty complaint about the region.

Mindy spoke up as she clasped her husband's hand, "I don't care about the mountain, or as you put it, Johnny, the 'damn mountain.' I'm glad Charlie and Lewis started all this. I might have never known Lewis otherwise."

Art lifted his glass and said, "And here's to Lewis and sweet Mindy and all the happiness to the both of them for finding and loving each other."

Champagne was poured, glasses clinked, and the blessing of the toast was enacted.

Edie smiled and said, "It's such a big country, and isn't it wonderful that so many of us are together so far from home?"

"I agree," said Mamie. "It's amazing how we've stuck together but, you know, sometimes I still wonder what we're all doing here."

"I can tell you what I'm doing here," said Art. "I'm getting as far away from our fat-assed brother Leroy as a man can go without falling off the edge of the earth. I got so tired of looking at Leroy, just a couple of years older than I—starting to look more like Father than Father himself. You know what I'm talking about, don't you?"

"You could say he was prematurely settled in his ways," agreed Mamie.

"That's one way to put it," said Johnny.

Art went on, "I didn't mind him being so content and all but, it's just the way he sat in Daddy's rocking chair that got to me. He would sit there rocking back and forth by the hours as happy as a pig in slop. It was as if he had not only claimed the farm but the rocker as well. And hell, we all know there were too many of us for those hard times anyway. A couple more crop failures or bank failures and another year of Leroy sitting on his hind end and we all would have starved."

"Here's to Leroy, bless his back forty, we still wish him the best. May he rock on for years to come," said Johnny, and another round of champagne was spilled for goodwill.

The women were lovely in their velvet and satin, their cut-glass jewelry, and carefully powdered cheeks. Mindy wore the only dress she owned that sparkled with color, while, in deference to the brides, Edie wore the only dress she owned that didn't sparkle with color. Beneath a black lace cloak, Rachel wore an ornate white blouse adorned by a simple gold locket. Her long black skirt nearly touched the floor. The men all wore the standard formal attire of the day, black surge waistcoats, white shirts with starched collars, and string ties. For John, the clothes were just a styled-up version of his gambler's uniform, and for the others, they were a not too radical departure from the normal apparel of funerals and other "Bible-reading" occasions. But all felt special in their fancy clothes in the elegant hotel next to the rising opera house—in the now forgotten sunset.

It was Mamie who reflected upon an earlier dinner, a Christmas dinner in 1875 when a kitchen full of Larshes feasted with all assembled. It brought a sudden, sobering quiet to the party—the thought of the distance they all had traveled in three and a half short years. Rachel from Quebec, Larshes and Lambs from the border lands of Ohio, Indiana, and Illinois. "It doesn't seem like it's been only a few short years since we were all together and our lives were so much simpler. We've all come so far. I mean you spend twenty years sitting down at the same table for supper each night with your family, and then you find yourself half a continent and a world away and you realize you likely will never sit down with all of them again. That last Christmas dinner—how we did eat and laugh and sing. It all seems so warm and safe in my memory."

In the openness of the evening, in the vulnerability and the wine of free-flowing affection they all were touched by the sad sweetness of reminiscence. Rachel thought of her father back in Canada and of her friend who rested along the waters of Clear

Creek in Georgetown. John and his brother and sisters thought of the family farm and the people they had left behind.

"Well, I've got something to say about that," said Lewis to the subdued table. "First of all, we didn't come here to this expensive hotel to sit around and mope about the past. We're here to celebrate what's happened today. I'll tell you why I'm here. I'm here to drink and laugh and eat fancy food with a bunch of fine folks and to make my Mindy feel as special as I can. Sure we all came from far away, and we miss the old ways and the old people, but it's not the first time a family has set out apart from itself to find a new home. There are plenty of Lambs and Larshes still living in the old country the same as they have for a thousand years, but some decided to try something new in America. And sure the farms are still back there in the Midwest, and it would be damn fine to all sit down and have us another great meal together, but we're here in Leadville in the mountains of the West, and I think we're a lucky bunch to have as many friends and family as we do about us here tonight. Don't you think so?"

"Good God, man," said Charlie, "I don't believe I've heard you utter so many words in a cluster in all the years I've known you. Marriage might make a politician out of a bashful farm boy."

"And you haven't heard it all yet," said Lewis as he stood up. "As long as I'm getting to be long winded—you'd think I'd become a Larsh instead of Mindy becoming a Lamb—I've got a bit more to say and I'll say it loud enough for all the fancy folks in this gaudy damn hotel to hear—I love my wife and, God bless us all, this is the happiest night of my life!"

And John jumped up and shouted, "I'll drink to that for it is mine as well! To our beautiful brides and the lives we will live. And to Leadville, God-forsaken camp that it is, the new home for which we left family and the farm. And to Leadville's future generations commenced by the marriages made today."

Revelry returned, and the room filled with the sounds of many voices speaking happiness. Then Mamie spoke up and once again quieted the festivities by saying in a voice serious, almost stern, "Then we'd better all drink up and go home right now."

"Go home?"

"Yes indeed. The sooner you two couples get to work on these new generations the more secure my job as school teacher will be. I need students."

Edie laughed and said, "Your students will have to wait—this party isn't nearly over. We haven't even had dessert."

"Speak for yourself, Sister." said John. "A man has other appetites than just for apple cobbler."

"Isn't that the truth," replied Edie, songbird of the Pioneer. Gaiety again supplanted the melancholy that underlies all joy with a yearning sadness for the impossible past.

After the table had been cleared and all were settling into the gentle mode of a good time winding down, John stood and said, "You know, with all this talk about why we're here and who's to blame or to bless for it all—there's one basic reason behind our being in Leadville."

Mamie spoke up, "And I know what it is."

"You do, don't you."

"We came out here, all of us in one way or another, because it was the most exciting thing we could think of doing."

"You're damn right, Sister! We're not in the middle of the damn West for the good sense of it—there's little sense to it all. Now, the real reason was the adventure of it, wasn't it?"

"I'm not sure I've ever admitted to such foolishness," said Rachel, "but Johnny, I think you've got a point there."

Lewis stood and said, "So, here's to the adventure of it all— bloody, foolish, or what have you—may it keep us alive and joyful!"

"To the adventure," they said as a group, as a family.

John went on, "Now that we have consumed this final course of opulence and absolutely insured that both our marriages begin with bankruptcy, Edie, would you sing us a song?"

Edie started her song in her clear and lovely voice of affection and longing, of promise and intimacy. She sang of the delicate, the fragile, the sensuous, and sublime binding that was the dream of love, and soon the crowd in the adjacent dining room grew still. The bankers and their wives, the engineers and the traveling dignitaries carefully set down their glasses, the waiters ceased the swirl of their motions about the room, the maître d' and bartenders hushed their chatter.

Edie sang with such an open heart that with her song she gave her very soul.

Her song ended, the quiet lingered for a moment, and then there was applause. Edie blushed and said, "It's not like half those so-called gentlemen over there haven't heard me sing before."

It was such an evening.

Mindy spoke, "Edie, your song makes me almost sad to feel so completely happy. It was beautiful." And then with a smile that was in its own way as deeply touching as the song, she said, "You know, this is as close, as safe and warm as people could ever need to be."

11

A Night in '79: The Life of a Gambler

Directly across from John Minor Larsh was the target of the late evening and early morning's enterprise, a genuine Denver dude, a downtown banker who had braved the fierce season to winter in Leadville and personally inspect the status of an investment. And fierce it was that night. With gusts that breached the crude fortification of the barroom, an all-night blizzard was tearing down from the cloud-smothered peaks and drifting the streets and alleyways deep in snow.

Gambling in such establishments as the Pioneer Bar was seldom purely a matter of luck, odds, and strategy. There were advantages to house gamblers for which they paid a hefty commission. There were strategically placed personnel of the establishment and communicative systems more complex than the signaling of a third base coach. And when a new deck of cards was demanded by a hapless player in an attempt to change the luck, the fresh deck was likely as clearly marked as the deck it replaced.

But regardless of the cards, the experience, or the craft of the gambler, blind luck was always a foe, and there were matters of the ebb and flow of good fortune that made the most carefully orchestrated game a challenge to wit and patience. John knew the odds and the turns of fate, but on this bitter winter night as the cards were dealt about the table and the coins cast to the center pile, he was playing with "the river's edge" and the banker didn't stand a chance.

This gentleman from the Queen City of the Plains had been losing for hours, and, though it seemed his supply of coin was no where near depleted, the beating he was taking was beginning to wear upon his upper-class manners. It was difficult for him to grasp how he could be winning his share of the hands and yet forfeiting most of his money. John Larsh was a master of the bluff.

The peripheral players had been brought along with periodic reinforcement. The freight wagon boys "hee-haw'd" and knee slapped and were having a great time of it while the miner stoically played out his cards, hand after hand, with a desperate belief that fate would eventually deal him the "mother lode." After an initial run of "luck," the banker had been tossing gold coins into the pot as steadily as he had been tossing shots of whiskey down his throat.

It was 3:00 A.M. on a winter's night, and by then most of the evening's crowd had ventured into the blowing storm to find refuge in their own dwellings. The tension of hours of shuffling, dealing, raising, calling, and—particularly—losing was heavy upon the players. John knew it was time to ease out before it erupted. With all the tricks of his trade, still elements of chance came to bear on each separate night, and this night had been exceptionally fortunate for him. Such was the flow of that evening that, even when he dealt the top of the deck and read only the markings on his own cards, fate and experience had continued to shift the game in his favor.

It was getting late, and winning for an expert gambler was not so much of a problem as winning and getting away with it. The cards were shuffled, cut, and dealt. It was time to pay back some of the night's bounty. The mule skinners were every bit as strong as they smelled, the miner was as dangerous as the depths of his disappointment, and the banker owned stock in the trigger-happy town marshal.

The banker raised the pot another twenty dollars. John looked at his hand and mentally cursed the third jack he had drawn. It was ungodly difficult to throw away good cards. The skinners and the miner had backed out at the first raise. John tossed a heavy gold coin into the pile and called. With drunken truculence bordering on threat, the man from the city laid down two pair—daring John to better him. He looked the banker in the eye and folded his superior hand.

And so went the next hour. By the time John made his escape he had sacrificed over a hundred dollars in the protection of a nice profit he had been withdrawing from the table throughout the game. He was depending upon an often observed element of human nature that a man can lose his money, his watch, and can barter the pleasures of his mistress, but if he quits on a winning streak, when he is drunk enough he'll call it a good night of gambling. The next morning he'll swear his wife "cleaned his trousers" before he'll reckon with a true accounting of his wins and losses.

When John got up from the table, the banker was elated, the miner's foolish optimism salvaged, and the mule skinners wealthy enough for a go at the "girls" on the line.

John stood at the bar having a shot of whiskey with a beer chaser. Though he wanted to get out of there as quickly as possible, a "poker face" included a well-controlled exit from the place of profit. His coat and vest pockets were laden with other men's hard earned or, in the case of the banker, complexly extracted lucre. With the ghostly chill of the blizzard invading the light and warmth of the bar, the false elation of hard liquor could quickly turn to bitter anger.

A few feet up the bar from John was a gaunt looking man with dark eyes that were at once both sad and dangerous. He wore a vest and a black coat. He leaned over his shot glass with a posture and gaze that indicated deep thought. Periodically, his contemplation of the liquid he turned pensively about the glass in his left hand was interrupted by forcefully restrained fits of coughing.

After such a bout he looked over at John and, in private tones, congratulated him on a good night of gambling. John nodded in acknowledgment. Both men were gamblers and, by the nature of their vocation, dwellers of a solitary realm. Like gunfighters, in their profession there could only be one winner, and though experience gave them empathy, no possibility existed for a bond between them.

The man suppressed another spasm. John downed the last of his beer, and as he walked away from the rail, he lightly slapped his colleague, Doc Holliday, on the back.

He stepped into a supply room through a doorway in a back corner of the barroom. Sitting down on an empty keg he quickly removed his boots. Standing, he transferred all of the money in his right coat pocket into various caches in his clothing. He also placed several twenty-dollar gold pieces into each of his boots and then sat down again and carefully forced his feet into their crowded confines. From a belt clip holster he pulled his pistol, glanced to be certain it was loaded, and stuck it into the empty right coat pocket he had cleared for it. He was ready to chance a stroll home through the late night streets of Leadville.

He had been tempted to step out the back door and leave by the alley, thus avoiding the possibility of further contact with the gentlemen he had so artfully fleeced. But there were too many who observed the turn of fate on the green felt of the gaming table, and it was no night to be risking the gifts by foolishly exposing his life and coin to the ever-present threat of murderous thieves who populated such isolated quarters of the night.

He pulled on his overcoat, though he did not button it, and walked through the barroom toward the front door. He nodded at his acquaintance at the bar who returned the gesture and then returned to staring into the pool of whiskey in the glass before him. Against the force of the weather, John opened the door and departed.

Turning right, he walked briskly past the "cribs" that by then were mostly dark. He thought of the mule-skinners and the ladies who awaited them. The vision gave him an additional shiver that cold night. You had to do what you had to do in order to make a living in Leadville.

The thoroughfare was called State Street for only a block. From that point west it was West Second. John and Rachel lived just a ways down West Second Street—not a long walk but possibly a dangerous one. He looked about to be certain he wasn't being followed and then darted the three-quarters of a block to his cabin door. He and his fortune were safe. He stamped his feet and dusted the snow from his coat before entering.

The storm seemed to have abated slightly, and he smiled, thinking of the Leadville response when someone would say, "I think the snow is going to clear up." The standard reply in this mountain town was, "You've got that right. Clear up to your ass."

Rachel heard him and lifted the bar on the front door to let him in.

12

The Fossil of Love

Some who knew him would say he was nice fellow when he wasn't drinking. Others only remembered him when he was drunk. It was the spring of 1878, and Leadville was badly in need of a new town marshal. A man named Harrison had been run out of office upon threat of his life by certain rather pervasive elements of the town's darker side. He was replaced by the city council on April 2, by George O'Connor. After three weeks on the job, while he was having a drink at Billy Nye's Saloon, a deputy of O'Connor's, a bitter man named Bloodsworth, accused him of talking behind his back. Regardless of unfortunate George's denial of the accusation, the offended deputy drew a pistol and killed the marshal on the spot. The murderer then fled the bar, ran down the street where a horse was tied, stole it, and was never seen in Leadville again.

Mayor Tabor happened to be passing through town at the time and appointed Martin Duggan marshal of Leadville—calling a special session of the city council for approval of the action he had taken. Martin Duggan was an Irishman, born in County Limerick in 1848. He immigrated to the East Coast with his parents sometime early in his childhood. Those were not easy times for the Irish in the melting pot of America, and we can reasonably assume that the young man spent a turbulent youth in the Irish ghetto of New York. Sometime during his adolescence, his family made its way to Denver.

At the age of sixteen, Duggan set out on his own. He worked as a miner, a mule skinner/wagon freighter, and as a general roughneck.

When he arrived in Leadville early in the spring of 1878, he was preceded by a reputation for violent confrontations and, specifically, for a gun fight in Georgetown where he killed another man. It didn't take him long to give credence to the rumors about his rowdy and dangerous ways. He was a man of medium height with a barrel chest and blacksmith arms strong enough to clear out an entire barroom—which he was known to do on occasion.

The research on Duggan consistently indicates his violent nature. Both in newspaper accounts—as Duggan's style was often newsworthy—and in oral history passed down through Leadville families, there is recurrent reference to his "Irish temper" when he drank.

Violence seldom seeks out a man of Duggan's temperament. It is obvious that he enjoyed it and sought it himself. Perhaps the legends are correct, and he was a "Jekyll and Hyde" drunk who was radically transformed from a gentle-natured keeper of the peace to a raging hooligan when the evil elixir of whiskey touched his smiling lips. Whatever the physiological aspects of his personality might have been, his tendency to engage others in violent encounters with fists, clubs, and guns was clearly more than a matter of coincidence.

Tabor's selection of Duggan as marshal was a classic boom town decision. What the rabble of State Street needed was respect for a bigger bully than they. The ethics and scruples of law would have to wait until there was a critical mass of people demanding a more civil concept of law and order. In the meantime, the street shootings, saloon muggings, and bloody brawls would continue. Duggan and Tabor's law was violently and selectively enforced with little consideration of any but the most primitive notions of rule by brute force. Until the citizens of Leadville became sufficiently outraged by both those who broke the law and those who enforced it and were no longer willing to tolerate such a crude and unstable code of justice, violence would continue to reign.

A covert vigilante committee was formed about that time in an effort to empower a countervailing faction whose goal was not to profit from chaos but rather to coerce it into order. In 1879, pinned to the back of one of two local criminals who were hanged from a beam in front of a building next to the unfinished court-house was a note from the Vigilantes Committee that read:

> Notice to all thieves, bunko steerers, foot pads, thieves and chronic bondmen for the same, and sympathizers for the above class of criminals: This is our commencement, and this shall be your fate. We mean business, and let this be your last warning—and a great many others known to this organization.
>
> > Vigilantes Committee
> > We are 700 strong.

Along with the warning was a list of undesirables who were encouraged to leave town. It is interesting that among the cut-throats and con men listed was the name of Horace Tabor's appointed civil authority, Marshal Martin Duggan. The demise of Duggan was to come several years later. But the downfall of his kind of law and the population it represented was to begin in November of 1880 when he shot one man too many.

What do we know of a prehistoric flower? What of its fragrance, the brilliance of its colors, the wind- and dew-touched grace of its petals?

When paleontologists study the fossilized remains of ancient life, the object they unearth is not the actual organism but rather a casting of some other material formed in the mold left by the departed plant or animal. By examining the surviving facsimile, information about life forms long extinct may be extracted. We may know the measure of a void by the rigid "plaster" of its fossil: so many millimeters of arching essence once flourishing in the momentary glow of a morning's light and so many millimeters, the girth of a once-supple stem.

So it is that the love of Lewis and Mindy Lamb may be known, not so much by its life as by its fossil. Not by its heat and caress, the secrets of its adoring eyes and private laughter but, rather, by the stone-like dimensions of the grief, the rage, the vengeance that supplanted it.

Winters aren't so fierce when you are in love, and your love is with you. Even the crude and drafty confines of a miner's cabin could take on touches of warmth and charm when inhabited by a loving wife or a loving husband.

Though Mindy and Lewis had not known each other in childhood, they had lived lives that were very similar. They grew up in farm country and with the values and experiences of land and family known since birth. They had much in common, and almost from the moment they met near Peoria two years earlier, they had known the magic of mutual affection. But it was not until they felt the security and closeness of their marriage that either openly expressed the inner thoughts and feelings they had harbored within. Mindy, the most quiet and reserved of the Larsh sisters, and Lewis, the affably taciturn miner, had revealed little more than their surface personalities to the world about them. But together in the lamp-lit, wood-stove warmth and security, the privacy of their own home, Mindy became fluid with the telling of her heart, and Lewis, it seemed, was an infinite source of wit and sensitivity. Throughout the seasons of their first year, in the openness of honesty, laughter, and love they lived the fullest days of both of their lives.

Mindy and Lewis were as reclusive as a couple as they had been as individuals. While in the summer of 1880 the scandalous Tabor love triangle—the faithful Augusta, the adulterous Horace, and the entirely too sexy Baby Doe—was a source of gossip and speculation throughout the rumor-mills of the region, in quiet patterns of work and home the bond that was the marriage of Mindy and Lewis thrived and grew strong.

No one really knows why Marshal Duggan hated Lewis Lamb. We could speculate about the mind of a bully—just think back to elementary school and the miserable bastards who terrorized the playground if you need a model for such conjecture.

It could have been jealousy. Lewis Lamb was much liked and respected; Martin Duggan was despised and feared. Lewis had a lovely young wife and a beautiful marriage; Duggan had a wife but was notorious for chasing whores.

It could have been some incident that locked the brutal sights of the ex-marshal upon Lewis. Whether based on family myth or passed-on traces of actual memory, there is some recollection that Lewis, while having a drink with John Larsh at the Pioneer, might have crossed paths with Duggan and sparked in him a primitive ire that could only be resolved in violence.

Regardless of reason—the effects of Duggan's harsh childhood, the vindictive nature of his drunkenness, or just plain meanness—all that history can clearly discern are the witnessed and recorded events of November 22, 1880.

Duggan had resigned as town marshal the previous year and was running a livery business. While delivering a sleigh to Winnie Purdy, madam of a high-class whorehouse on West Fifth, he spotted Lewis Lamb walking along the side of the street. Seizing the opportunity to inflict scorn upon a chosen adversary, Duggan swerved deliberately to the side and nearly ran over Lewis. In jumping out of the way Lewis slipped and fell in the dirty snow. Three carpenters working on a house on the corner of Fifth and Pine were witnesses to the entire episode. They reported that Duggan stopped the sleigh, laughed at Lamb, called him a "goddamned son of a bitch," and rode off.

It could have ended there with one man's pride soaking up the chill of wet snow and another man's orneriness momentarily expended. But Duggan came back for more and Lewis would have none of it.

Remember the playground bully? Remember how he would pick on those least capable of defending themselves? Lewis Lamb was a farmer and a miner and a damn fine husband, but he was no gunfighter.

By the time Mindy arrived, Duggan was sitting calmly in the sleigh, under the custody of police captain Charles Perkins. A crowd had assembled in the street in front of Winnie Purdy's establishment where Lewis lay, dead from a single shot that had entered through the roof of his mouth and exited the back of his head—his gun cocked and loaded but never fired.

Thus it was that the mortal love of Mindy and Lewis died in the filthy ruts and sun-sloshed snow of Fifth Street. And Mindy, with dress stained by the still-warm blood of her slain husband, rose from the awkward sprawl of death and with chilling stillness to her voice silenced the entire motion and utterance of the small world as she said, "Marshal Duggan, I shall wear black and mourn this killing until the very day of your death and then, Goddamn you, I will dance upon your grave."

And her rage and her pain became the fossil of their love. Mindy's grief and hatred—years of measurable dimension, the only substance from which we may infer the depth of the life it replaced.

Lewis, we hardly knew thee!

13

A Symbol of Conscience

Sometimes, when life is cheated of real substance, patterns of activity become a substitute, a ritual of motion sustaining only the façade of existence. For eight years, Mindy Lamb lived alone in the cabin that had been the home of her marriage. She would rise in winter's chilling darkness or in the glow of summer mornings, don the sable dress of her grieving, and walk along Harrison Avenue to Second Street, then west to Rachel and John's home.

Her days were spent helping with the laundry Rachel took in from boarding houses. Also, over the eight years, there were six babies born to that home, and Mindy cared for them. She knew, in their touch and the warmth of their needs, the joy of the latent love yet lingering in her heart. But also, the fullness of John and Rachel's family deepened the bitterness she felt from a life that had been denied her. She would stay long enough to help prepare supper and then walk back through town to the empty cabin. As a matter of ritual rather than desire or appetite, she would light a fire, cook, and eat a simple meal, then shut down the oil lamp and retire.

For eight years, twice daily, as she silently made her way through the streets of the town, she spoke the specter of her mourning to all who saw her. For eight long and empty years, she performed the basic motions of a life void of all but one passion—for eight years she waited for Martin Duggan to die.

Life is the antithesis of death; it is also a truth that without life there can be no conscious happiness. To dwell on someone's dying so that you can therefore be happy results in a classic contradiction. It is the same logic that occurs when one chooses greed over unselfishness.

Greed is most often the motivating force driving economic expansion. And greed seldom has a conscience. With a single vision that growth connotes prosperity, some would build the urban West until the great aqueducts are dry and the flow of western rivers a trickle. Across the country such an avaricious mentality has ruthlessly destroyed lands, environments, and even vestiges of our heritage.

In Leadville it was precious minerals: the exploitation of nature and man ruthlessly enacted for the profit of a few. In the early 1880s, it was development at any cost. What difference if the water was polluted, the workers cheated, and the investors deceived?

In a January 11, 1881, letter to the editor appearing in the *Leadville Herald Democrat*, S. J. DeLau, superintendent of the Ocean and Seneca Mining Company, addressed the problem of "wet mines" polluting the watershed. He expounds the developer's creed in his attack on those who were faint of resolve regarding the priority of mining:

> I acknowledge the importance of the citizens of Leadville being supplied with pure water, but I also recognize the fact that the prosperity of the city is dependent upon the mines from which she receives her existence, and that it would be better for the prosperity of the State of Colorado that a portion of her citizens should leave Leadville than her ore output should be reduced.
>
> The prosperity of the mines should be the first and paramount care of her citizens, and it would be as ridiculous for the city of Pittsburgh to suppress all her foundries because of smoke densifying the atmosphere as for Leadville to interfere with the development of the mines around here . . . .

Development was rampant, population was exploding, crime in the streets and in the back rooms of corporate offices was thriving, and for some it seemed to be the best of times—an era of lawlessness and unchecked greed ideally suited for the violent character of men like Martin Duggan and the entrepreneurial lust of developers like Horace Tabor. Of course, it was also a time that weighed heavily on the victims of such a chaotic and unprincipled ethos. Few were innocent of its lust, for most had come to reap the harvest of gold and silver. But few knew the fruition of material gain, and in a culture of greed, the value of human life is an expendable commodity.

It is rarely possible to honestly credit the occurrence of a single event or the actions of a single person in redirecting the course of history. I won't be so naive as to tell you that the death of Lewis Lamb and the subsequent years of Mindy's mourning effected a cessation of irresponsible behavior on the part of the low-lifes and their corporate counterparts, but it is more than mere coincidence that Lewis's death and Mindy's prolonged public display of outrage corresponded to a significant lessening of public tolerance for flagrant disregard for community values.

In the simplistic code of the West, Martin Duggan was not a murderer. He was guilty of deadly provocation, perhaps guilty of blood-thirst, guilty of ill-constrained rage. But, by the legal and practical code of the West, Lewis Lamb was gunned down in a fair fight. Witnesses even testified that Lewis was the first to draw a gun. (But then, who was going to implicate ex-Marshal Duggan after watching him blast a hole right through a man's head?) A court of law determined that the killing was an act of self defense and exonerated Duggan of any charges of wrong doing.

Martin Duggan lies forever beneath the grass of an unmarked grave. Let him rest. Duggan wasn't guilty, and Leadville wasn't innocent.

Death dwelled constantly in the silver camp. Newspaper and personal accounts of Leadville's early boom days are filled with the morbid detail of epidemics, mining accidents, disasters, and murderous violence. There is a story of four miners who were caught by an avalanche as they sat around their cabin on a claim they were mining on Carbonate Hill. When, weeks later, the site was cleared of snow, their bodies were found frozen in a ghastly suspension of their final moments. One man had a book on his lap, two others were at a table playing cards, and the fourth was finishing a letter to his fiancée who waited for him back East.

There are plenty of dynamite stories. A man skewered by a tamping rod, another cluster of three cast to the hereafter by an unexploded charge and the spark of a pick against the hard rock. There were rock slides, cave-ins, crushings—and there were shafts back-filled and abandoned to become mass graves.

In 1880 it was not uncommon for the frigid dawn of a winter's morning to reveal the rigid form of a frozen corpse with precious heat of blood spilled by the slash of a blade, the tear of a bullet, or the crack of a bludgeon. And as is invariably the case in a world built upon the cruel fantasy of instant material riches, there were many whose dreams turned to despair. Suicide was no rarity.

But when is a life more precious, more clearly mortal than when it is stricken from the earth? Lewis was ever cold, lost to the stark and bloody snows of Pine Street, and Mindy never sought another man to warm her life. Lewis Lamb had neither sons nor daughters, nor would Mindy. The resource of their values, their humor and goodness, their genes, was lost forever in "just another Leadville gunfight." Just another bloody afternoon, another excavation, another opening of the rocky earth, and closing of the rocky earth upon the pine coffin of just another dead person.

There were so many.

"Lewis Lamb?" someone would ask. "He was a fine man. You say Duggan shot him down?"

"One shot. Killed him in an instant."

"Damn. It just don't seem right, does it?"

It wasn't right. And for once, the town knew it, the law knew it, and, not only did Mindy know it was wrong, every day she reminded all who saw her as she silently spoke the message of her black dress and the solemn aura of their passing. Lewis was in the ground, and life went on. But Mindy became a living monument to the love she had for her man, the harsh and ghastly visage of death's toll, and the unforgiving fervor of vengeance.

Martin Duggan and the deadly chaos he represented were not legally guilty of a crime but, more significantly, they were operatives of a society guilty of a grievous wrong. Throughout the ordeal of the killing of her husband and the years of mourning, Mindy's public façade was such that we could be distracted into thinking of her only as a "fossil" or a "symbol." True to her character, she was not one to openly display more than the surface of her outrage and sorrow, and there is little more we can infer from either written or oral history about that period of her life. But there was an event during this period that crossed the barriers of silence and has given us some insight into the sensitive woman who dwelled beneath the black shroud of her widow's weeds.

In 1887 Mindy, Edie, and John were at the Irish funeral of Mollie May. Mollie's brothel was two doors down from Purdy's where Lewis had been slain. Mollie was one of the most renowned prostitutes in Leadville's uptown, red-light line on West Fifth. She was not only known for the professional service she rendered the gentlemen of the town, she also had a reputation for kindness. There is evidence of her charity and even a story of her adopting an unwanted child. But there was another side to her as well—perhaps a natural outgrowth of professional or personal pride. She and another Irish lass named Sally Purple owned adjacent and competing establishments. As a result of an ongoing dispute over the respective qualities of the counties of Limerick and Cork, the sites of their births back in Ireland, an all-out battle erupted between madams, employees, and whatever customers happened to be on the premises at the time. When it was over, both houses were sprayed by volleys of lead. The *Herald Democrat* reported that it was a miracle no one was killed as most of the windows were shattered.

John Larsh had borrowed a carriage to take Edie and him to the funeral and cemetery. Mollie was a part of the world in which they lived, and they felt it proper for them to show their respect. He hadn't asked Rachel to accompany them; he knew her life and the lives of their children to be separate from the elements of society with which he and Edie spent a major portion of their time.

As it came time to leave, it surprised him when Mindy showed up and said she wished to go with them.

"Are you sure?" asked John.

"Certainly."

"I mean, Mollie wasn't exactly the most respectable of citizens to have made their homes in this town."

"I know exactly who Mollie May was. I knew her well."

"You knew Mollie May, the Fifth Street hooker?" asked Edie in amazement.

"Yes, I did."

Mindy's black dress and public deportment, even after seven years, still had a sobering effect as she passed through the streets of the community, but within the family, her "mission of mourning" was accepted and they went on with normal processes of love and humor and communication. They respected her resolve, but instinctively they all knew, including Mindy, that healing and survival were more the product of the simple rituals of daily living and human interaction than of the most just and exacting act of revenge.

"Mollie May was a friend of mine. I spoke to her several times a week on my way to or from this house."

"Mollie and Mindy—I would have never guessed," said Edie.

"How did you ever get to know Mollie May?" asked Johnny. "I hardly knew her myself and you know the crowd I associate with."

"It was just a few days after Lewis's killing. This dull dress I wear today was shiny and new. You know, except for you people, most everyone seemed afraid to even approach me—most of them still are. I was walking along Harrison Avenue when a pretty lady wearing a flashy dress stopped me. I was in such a fog of sadness in those days that her voice startled me. She said she didn't mean to scare me. I assured her I wasn't afraid. Then she said, and I can remember it clearly, 'You don't know me, but I wanted to tell you that what happened to a decent man like your husband was a dirty rotten shame and I'm really sorry for you.' We've been speaking friends ever since, and I'm really going to miss her. Isn't it a strange town where a murder can be the law of the town, and a whore the goodness of it?"

As they started out the door, with a quick smile that bridged the sorrows of her recent years, Mindy said, "At least there's no doubt I'm dressed for the occasion."

Mollie was honored by one of the town's most sizable funerals. A local poet wrote some lines in remembrance of her and recited them on that day.

Think of her mournfully;
Sadly—not scornfully—
What she has been is nothing to you.
No one should weep for her,
Now there is sleep for her—
Under the evergreens, daisies and dew.

Talk if you will of her,
But speak not ill of her—
The sins of the living are not of the dead.
Remember her charity,
Forget all disparity;
Let judge they whom she sheltered and fed.

Keep her impurity
In dark obscurity,
Only remember the good she has done.
She, to the dregs has quaffed
All of life's bitter draught—
Who knows what crown her kindness has won?

Though she has been defiled;
The tears of a little child
May wash from the record much of her sin;
Whilst others weep and wait
Outside of Heaven's gate,
Angels may come to her and lead her in.

When at the judgment throne,
The Master claims his own,
Dividing the bad from the good and the true.
There pure and spotless,
Her rank shall be not less
Than will be given, perhaps unto you.

Then do not sneer at her
Or scornfully jeer at her—
Death came to her and will come to you.
Will there be scoffing or weeping
When like her you are sleeping
Under the evergreens, daisies and dew?

14

Strike One

The laboring class of Leadville in 1880 was diverse. In the mix of immigrants, transplanted coal and lead miners, desperadoes, El Dorado dreamers, cowboys, and college graduates, there developed a level of pride, an element of self-esteem that prevented them from being just another contingent of the legion of the down-trodden and oppressed. The westward movement of the nineteenth century brought with it the belief that private land ownership could override the demands of the public weal. Observers who traveled west during this period noted in the mining camps of Colorado a new phenomenon, a "sense of pride in the workers." One observer called it "a blatant insolence in their self-assertiveness."

I say more power to the insolence of our Leadville progenitors. It seemed, contrary to the tradition of Western civilization, that these citizens actually considered themselves to be equal to any others in the society, regardless of finance or position.

There is no record of serious labor unrest prior to 1880. It is almost as if the miners were saying, "Okay. I'll work a ten-hour shift for your miserable wages. I'm proud of what I do, and between the pittance you pay me and a little pocket or lunch pail bonus, I'll get by. Just don't mess with me. I have my pride."

But mess with the miners they did.

It started with our old friend H. A. W. Tabor. He and two partners, United States Senator Jerome Chaffee and financier David Moffat, had controlling interest in the Little Pittsburg Mine in Big

Evans Gulch. At the time this mine was the best-known operation in Leadville and had been touted to the extent that eastern investors were clamoring to buy stock and share in the amazing profits it was generating. Tabor knew the Little Pittsburg was playing out (as did the miners who shoveled the ore). Its seemingly inexhaustible bounty was diminishing in the closing months of 1879, though no indication of impending failure was given investors. He and his partners maintained the semblance of unfaltering confidence while negotiating their own separate exit from ownership. Tabor, with the timing of a Swiss watch, accepted a buy-out for a flat one million dollars. Chaffee and Moffat, though publicly stating that they lost fortunes in the Little Pittsburg, managed to quietly leave the scene with very deep pockets, abandoning the sinking Leadville economy to handle the crash that occurred after the directors failed to pay a monthly dividend in March of 1880. The value of Little Pittsburg stock fell from sixty-five dollars a share to about six dollars.

Not only were individual investors ruined as a result of this blatant stock manipulation and mismanagement, but the collapse of the Little Pittsburg also severely shook the investment community's confidence in the entire Leadville Mining District. The riches of Leadville were known throughout the world, and the failure of the Little Pittsburg was a matter of international concern.

Disquieting words of panic were whispered along the subterranean grapevines of the mines. The railroad was on its way and with it an anticipated lowering of the cost of living. Word had it the mine owners would expect to trim expenses by matching the drop in the cost of goods with a drop in the daily wage of the miners.

Membership in the recently formed Miners' Cooperative Union increased dramatically as a strike seemed imminent. The seeds of empowerment were sown, and they were nourished by the energy of discontent. Industrial "Goliaths" were being challenged by working-class "Davids." The advocates of the Declaration of Independence were broadening the girth of organized labor.

Activity focused on Tabor's Chrysolite Mine up on Fryer's Hill, an extremely successful operation that was nevertheless experiencing pressure from the business community due to the failure of the Little Pittsburg. In a series of actions, management seemed to be intentionally trying to provoke a dispute. An attempt to charge a compulsory medical insurance payment of one dollar a month to each miner was met with predictable reluctance. In the past, the company had regularly refused to pay benefits to injured workers, and now they wanted to impose a fee for doing nothing. It's the kind of issue that creates political extremists. Next, management instituted a policy of insult and petty harassment that prohibited smoking and talking on the job. Somebody up there in the higher strata of authority was really pressing for a strike.

On May 26, 1880, half a year before disaster struck the Larshes and Lambs with the bullet that left Lewis dead on the frozen November ground, catastrophe of a different sort struck Leadville. Shift bosses tried to up the quota of production expected of each miner during a day. That did it. The strike was on. As miners from one shift left the mine, they told the next crew that they were going on strike, and nobody went to work. As word spread, miners throughout the area walked off their jobs.

There are several theories as to why the management of this profitable enterprise would intentionally want to incur the debilitating effects of a strike. It's all hindsight and speculation, and one must be cautious not to slip into regions of economic paranoia when examining the mechanization of greed. Some have said that the strike was viewed by the owners as winnable and used as a means of culling out the malcontents and labor agitators who could have eventually become more powerful. Back in the coal country of Pennsylvania, Irish miners had formed an American version of the Irish secret society known as the Molly Maguires and supposedly committed violent acts in the name of the labor movement. It was likely that some of the miners in Leadville in 1880 had been associated with such activities, and perhaps it seemed a good time to root them out before they became more organized. There is no evidence that major, organized Molly Maguire-like plots were afoot in the district in those days, but it is true that the best way to cripple a labor movement was to suggest outside subversive elements and to thwart a strike before it got fully organized.

At the time, some observers suspected that the strike was the result of a plot by the local management of the Chrysolite to undermine the value of stock in the mine so they could buy it up themselves. This theory is certainly consistent with the idea that the masses are merely pawns in the chess game of the big guys.

Regardless of motivation or justification, the strike began the morning of May 26, 1880, and within a short time most of the miners in the region had refused to go to work. There were parades with bands, meetings, threats, counter-threats, and a dabbling in negotiation. Then the Colorado National Guard showed up, and the labor movement was squelched for another ten years. All of these developments occurred within three weeks; the miners then returned to the shafts to make the same two-and-a-half to three dollars a day they had earned before the strike.

The quick and thorough defeat of this first major labor insurrection was accomplished by a coalition of self-serving citizens unofficially led by H. A. W. Tabor and officially under the charge of a local newspaper editor and zealot, Carlyle Channing Davis. A "Committee of Safety" was formed with Davis, its elected leader, and the strike was doomed. The committee formed its own militia, and it seemed the forces of commerce and the forces of labor were about to do bloody battle—or at least that is what Governor Pitkin was meant to believe. He was sufficiently impressed by the barrage of communication from members of the committee and by the questionable opinion expressed by his lieutenant governor, Mr. Tabor, to feel the need to send in the National Guard to deter the democratic actions of Leadville citizens. Martial law was proclaimed, and within a few days, on June 18, the strike was officially over.

The events were not this simple, but the result was: The mine owners won, the miners lost. If it had been a game, the box score would have read:

MINE OWNERS: 1
MINERS: 0

15

Badger Fight: The Atmosphere

The badger fights are Leadville's best-kept secret. They appear in no newspaper accounts, and many residents to this day don't know anything about them. The first one had to have been planned by young miners—bright, hard-working activists who had ventured to Leadville in the late seventies. They were not the immigrants who were satisfied with three dollars a day. These young adventurers had come to Leadville from the East, against the grain. Many were college boys; all were disenchanted. It was one thing to be offered a job after fleeing a potato famine, a job where the tools were a pick, a shovel, and a carbide lamp; it was yet another thing when you were a farm boy from Indiana where there was plenty of food, and you were enchanted with the western myth of finding gold nuggets on your own claim high in the Rockies. As these young men were handed the same pick and same shovel, the mine bosses were told to keep a close eye on them—there was a good chance some of those malcontents were labor agitators. They had heard of Andrew Carnegie and had come to Leadville where, with hard work and a good head on your shoulders, you, too, could be rich and famous. They had part of the formula right, but they were soon to learn that a non-thinking head on a good pair of shoulders made you a more desirable miner—same pick, same carbide lamp, same hole in the ground.

The socio-economic dynamics of mining towns, especially in Leadville, created an ethnic and cultural simmering pot. Leadville sits at an altitude of 10,190 feet. The mines were scattered through-

out Stray Horse Gulch all the way up to the Ibex. There the altitudes are over 11,000 feet. Water won't boil at 212°F—it takes
more heat than at lower altitudes. The air is clearer; there just isn't
much of it. To stretch a metaphor, the mine owners wanted the pot
boiling, and they knew how to turn up the heat.

Laissez-faire was the economic system in place; Manifest Destiny
was the dream that drove both miners and mine owners. All operated under the delusion that infinite resources were available. Tabor
had made millions by 1880; Lewis Lamb, the O'Mahoneys, and the
Kitts had made three dollars a day and had been told not to smoke
or complain. Western adventure had given way to corporate realism.

Men who had access to money formed corporations; they
owned the mines. These mine owners did not live on Chicken Hill
or West Second Street; they lived in Washington, D.C., St. Louis,
New York, Chicago, Denver, and other points east of the Mosquito
Range. They were aware that some of the young pioneer prospectors who were forced to work as miners and some of the older veterans of labor movements back east could pose potential problems.
The seeds of confrontation had taken root down in the shafts.

As 1880 rolled around, the stage, both literally and figuratively,
was set for a powerful encounter. The magnificent opera house
was completed and had been filled with the music of New York
stage plays, the oratory of a major funeral ("Texas Jack" Omohun-
dro from Buffalo Bill's show), and other local spectaculars. Tabor
moved to Denver; 30,000 people came to Leadville. The Pioneer
Bar was in full swing, as were the doors of eighty-one other saloons.
Strikes, bad press, scams, real economic disparity, and adultery at
the highest level—Leadville had it all.

By July of 1880, the strike was over, though the discontent and
inequity were no where near resolved. The first train was due to
arrive, and the first badger fight was due to take place. The planning for both events had a common impetus. Often the intersection of unlikely elements resulting in an event, while seemingly a
matter of chance, is actually the product of a complex set of both
large and small circumstances. A particular set of circumstances
leading up to the big fight of July 24, 1880, can be documented.

The people of Leadville were well aware of the formidable walls creating a xenophobic distortion for the second largest city in Colorado. Fremont and Mosquito passes were difficult in the summer and nearly impossible in the winter. You couldn't go west over Mount Massive, could you? The only reasonable way in and out of town was down the Arkansas Valley to Weston Pass and then over to Fairplay, or down to Buena Vista, Trout Creek Pass, and on into South Park. These difficult passages were the routes on which the stage coach depended—along with four horses, a damn good driver, and a firm grip on your rosary beads. Leadville was indeed in need of a train.

The first train, which arrived on July 22, 1880, established a precedent by rolling into Leadville nearly three hours late. The Denver & Rio Grande train carried a famous passenger on that first run, General Ulysses S. Grant. No one will ever know exactly how many people were in Leadville in July of 1880. Some say 20,000, which is probably a conservative estimate; others say 30,000, likely on the liberal side. Whatever the number, most of them were there that night of the train's arrival to witness a 100-gun salute, five fully uniformed bands, Civil War veterans, five infantry companies, all the ladies of the evening, the patrons of all the saloons, the miners, the kids, the Lambs, the Larshes, the Cavanaughs, at least one Tabor, and, no doubt, all of the jackasses.

Needless to say, with a three-hour delay in the arrival of the train, there had been ample time for everyone to have a few drinks, and hundreds were totally intoxicated. As Grant stepped from the train to the waiting buggy, he was slapped vigorously on the back by H. A. W. Tabor who shouted, "How're ya doing, General? Welcome to Leadville!" Recovering from this enthusiastic welcome, Grant headed into a ninety-six-hour drinking contest with the mountaineers of Leadville. Grant was good, but in Leadville at 10,000 feet, he was out of his league.

Few of the thousands who were there that summer evening were sober enough to notice that the carriage in which Grant and Tabor were riding was being drawn by four magnificent black horses whose backs glistened with ounces of gold dust. It would have taken a crystal ball to recognize this ominous symbol of changing money standards and the demise of the supremacy of silver.

The plotters of the first Leadville badger fight made sure that their "pigeon," one of the dignitaries traveling in the former president's entourage, had arrived on the train and was up to his elbows in food and spirit at the banquet room of the Clarendon Hotel. The miners began preparing for a bit of pioneer justice. We give this gentleman, the first in a long line of out-of-town victims, the fictitious name of Howard Smith, but we know he was a certifiable representative of the bankers who had depleted the minerals, the money, and the credibility of Leadville over the previous year.

Members of the elite political planning committee arranging to have Grant arrive on the first train into Leadville were also schemers of the first order. Tabor, although not the architect, was in the middle and was being used by Moffat and others. It was not only Mrs. Elizabeth "Baby Doe" McCourt that Tabor coveted; he also had his eye on political office in Washington, D.C. His ambition made him vulnerable to those who knew how to manipulate political scenarios. Silver King or Don Juan, how sophisticated could he be considering his Leadville origins of groveling in the gravel up California Gulch?

An indication of his total lack of awareness of the times in which he lived was his disregard for the mores of the Victorian Age that valued appearance over integrity. Tabor's sudden rise to wealth and notoriety, accompanied by his national political aspirations, clouded his ability to see the hypocrisy of the real world. The mining camp ethos accepted and honored Tabor as an honest, hard working, and generous man. He knew how to make deals and money. He owned the world's greatest silver mines along with a couple of whorehouses. He knew miners, gamblers, marshals, bankers, governors, and sleaze balls. All of this was not only tolerated but even applauded in Leadville. However, the day he dumped his loyal wife, Augusta, for a petite, blue-eyed, blonde divorcée named Baby Doe, he was disgraced; his political ball game was over.

Eugene Field, in a succinct description of Tabor in 1880, wrote, "Stoop-shouldered; ambling gait; awkward with hands; black hair, inclined to baldness; large head; rugged features; big black mustache which spreads at ends; dresses in black; magnificent cuff buttons of diamonds and onyx; no public speaker; generous and charitable; carried his hands in his pockets; worth 8 million dollars."

The same newsman/Hoosier poet also described both Tabor and his investment partner, United States Senator Jerome B. Chaffee, in a two-verse poem written about the same time:

> *Chaffee had a little lamb*
> *Who wore a fierce mustache,*
> *And people wondered how that lamb*
> *On Chaffee made a mash.*
>
> *What makes Chaffee love the lamb?*
> *Incessantly they cried.*
> *The lamb has got a golden fleece,*
> *The knowing ones replied.*

That spring, the lines had been drawn. Tabor lined up with the owners, the bankers, and the crowd from Denver. The miners lined up with themselves. The townspeople on the sidelines engaged in lengthy conversations about both parties posturing for a strike. A measure of the hostility existing during the strike was the reaction that occurred when three of the *Herald Democrat*'s printers clandestinely published "The Crisis Paper" in support of the miners. The printers, Howard Lee, Robert Higgens, and John Sorenson, each received a handwritten notice as follows:

> Sir,
> You are hereby ordered to leave Leadville before sun up tomorrow morning, to return no more. Disregard this notification at your peril.
> By order
> Committee of 100.

So much for freedom of the press! It is likely the threat was written by the paper's editor, C. C. Davis. Howard Lee's defiance of the letter has been an inspiration for those who cherish the Bill of

Rights. Lee sat on his front porch with a sign leaning against the railing that read: "I was here in this camp before any of the Law and Order Gang and plan to stay." Resting close by was a long rifle, and in his lap was a pistol. He was determined to stay and stay he did.

On the top of Imogene Pass, a jeep road crosses the San Juan Mountains. There is a plaque honoring the militia that held back the miners who were striking for similar causes in those southern Rockies mining camps. When I travel that wonderful country, I can't help wanting to erect a plaque to Howard ("Hop") Lee, perhaps on top of Mosquito Pass. The plaque would read, "To Hop Lee, a newspaperman who held off his own editor and a gang of illiterates who either could not—or had not read the 'First Amendment.'" I would sign the plaque, "The Son of a Printer from Leadville."

Just exactly who originated and orchestrated the first Leadville badger fight can never be determined, but we know they had to have help from someone who was "learned in the law." When the miners needed legal advice during the strikes that preceded the badger fight, they knew where to go; and after they lost—they also knew a big-time lawyer who could teach them a few tricks. Tom Patterson believed in their cause and needed votes. A liberal lawyer with outstanding credentials, he was an astute Democratic politician and a man of courage. (He was also the great-grandfather of Sybil Downing, the chairwoman of the Colorado State Board of Education in the early 1990s and the primary source of information.)

Thomas McDonald Patterson was born in Ireland in 1840. His parents brought him to the U.S.A. when he was six years old. The family settled in Indiana; young Tom first became a printer and then went on to Wabash College where he earned his law degree. After serving in the Union army during the Civil War, he moved his young wife and family to Colorado Territory in 1874 and was instrumental in obtaining statehood for Colorado.

In 1879 Patterson and his partner, Charlie Thomas, opened a law office on Chestnut Street in Leadville. Tom was always a believer in silver and the Democratic Party. He became the first elected United States Congressman from Colorado. He championed the causes of the little people. He abhorred martial law, believed in labor unions, wanted the railroads to be nationalized, and supported the idea of women's suffrage. It is almost certain that he was involved in planning the first badger fight.

Though the failed strike was finished, the lines of division were very clear. The miners went back to work, the gamblers continued to gamble, the girls on the lines continued their various positions. All of Leadville had looked forward to Grant's arrival, including John Minor Larsh, who had agreed to be the odds maker and money changer during the upcoming "sporting" event. The plotters knew the fight between Bad Pete, the town's bulldog, and a ferocious Rocky Mountain badger would be irresistible to the greed and drunkenness of the town's most honored guests. Up and down the streets and in the bars and gaming houses, word was out that the fight was to be held on July 24 at 11:00 P.M. in the gambling area of the Pioneer Bar.

16

Badger Fight:
Don't Muck with Leadville

Bad Pete, the 1880 version of a series of town pit bulls of the same name and general deportment, slept in a corner of the Silver Dollar Bar on Harrison Avenue between Third and Fourth streets. He usually awoke around 9:00 A.M., whereupon he would move outside to Harrison Avenue to sleep on the sidewalk across from the newly built Tabor Opera House. Around 3:00 P.M., after following the sun from one angle to another, Bad Pete would begin his afternoon rounds. The bartender at the Silver Dollar would place a pan of warm beer on the floor. Bad Pete would quickly quaff the brew and then slowly work his way down Harrison Avenue, stopping at the bar that sixty years later would be converted into Ed's Printing Shop, then on down to State Street and the Pioneer. Finally, Bad Pete would stop in at the Pastime before heading back to the Silver Dollar where he spent the remainder of the night.

Bad Pete's bar-hopping was interrupted before it ever began on July 24, 1880. He was in training. Two rugged-looking miners were manning a wooden beer barrel that had a door cut into one end. A chair was propped against the door, to which an eight-foot piece of rope was attached. A serious noise emanated from within the barrel. Bad Pete crouched about ten feet away. Upon hearing the noise, he could hardly be contained. The strong chain holding him was straining at every link. Every eye in the tavern was focused on the barrel. Bad Pete growled and lunged. The men with the barrel were quite aware of the ominous sounds that were demanding all of the bulldog's ferocious attention. They positioned themselves so that, just in case the door of the barrel were suddenly to pop open, it would be the dog rather than themselves that would be in direct line with the charging contents.

After a short time, the training program ended. Bad Pete was ready. The "badger barrel" was pulled back out of sight, and the men stepped up to the bar where they had a drink and speculated on whether justice rather than beer might be served that evening.

That same afternoon, Mindy and Rachel were sitting at the table at 230 West Second. They were counseling Edith, who was ironing the dress she intended to wear to the evening's event. John Minor entered the room and instantly was sorry he hadn't sneaked in the back door. The three women all started talking to him at the same time.

John knew he was trapped and said, "All right, if you ladies will let a man speak, I'll tell you what I can. A week or so ago while our fair town was being protected by Governor Pitkin's army, a group of the Irish lads who were temporarily out of work got a lesson in Leadville politics from Danny Donovan."

"Who?" asked Mindy and Rachel in unison.

"Danny Donovan, an Irish poet and one of the strike leaders."

Rachel couldn't help but interrupt, " I hope there's an explanation for why Edie's going out buggy riding with those Denver phonies who have been trailing Grant around by the coattails. And what all this has to do with you being arrested at what Edie says is going to be some kind of a fight between a dog and a wild animal!"

"If you'll listen I'll tell you some of it. A few bankers in Denver and the East can buy stock in mines at a low price and then sell it later for a great profit. This is all fine and good unless it's stock in a mine like the Little Pittsburg. Last year it was the most productive mine in the district. The trick is knowing when to sell the stock. Tabor and his partners, David Moffat and Jerome Chaffee, knew the mine was playing out and dumped their shares before word got back east to the other investors. The fact that the ore in the Little Pittsburg hadn't been worth a plug nickel for months didn't stop Tabor from making a million on the deal before everything crashed. You know that the panic and confusion that followed the failure of the Pittsburg were a big part of what eventually got everyone riled up to strike."

"It doesn't seem quite fair," said Rachel.

"It's not fair. And its not right for all the money to be hauled out of Leadville and spent in Denver either. And it's not right for people with money to be manipulating miners and the common people like they do."

"So, what does this have to do with buggy rides and badger fights?" asked Mindy.

"It's all about getting even, Rachel. It might just be a token gesture, but it's time for a little poetic justice. Danny and the boys have it all planned. Now, I've got to get going and Edie does, too. She's got to take a ride up to the pine forest near Iowa Gulch in just half an hour with one of Tabor's cronies, Mr. Smith. Trust me, you and Mindy and Lewis show up at the court house tonight around 11:30 and it will all make sense. Get in early, take a seat, and then you'll see a few ragged-assed miners do some manipulation themselves."

John took a cloth money bag, a notebook, a sharpened pencil, and his Derringer pistol and walked out the cabin door and up Second toward Harrison Avenue and the Pioneer Bar.

It was almost dusk. Patrick Griffin, who seldom needed an excuse to drink, loved boilermakers (a shot of whiskey with a beer chaser). He was downing another in a series of rounds that had begun hours earlier and, in preparation for the night's developments, he slipped a plug of tobacco into his pocket even though he well knew that the combination of booze and any kind of tobacco invariably made him violently ill.

Bad Pete was sleeping near the piano. The barrel was in the storage room that opened out onto Tiger Alley.

Strange bedfellows were shaping an exciting scenario on this warm July evening. There, on State Street, as the sun created a magnificent sunset over Mount Massive, the curtain was opening on what has to be one of the great undiscovered secrets in the American West, the drama of the Leadville Badger Fight.

By 11:00 P.M. the line in front of the Pioneer had turned into a mob. The swinging doors were not swinging because with the crowd of miners on either side there was no place for them to swing. Springhetti, the head bartender, wouldn't let anyone stand on the bar, but on this special occasion a few were allowed to sit on it. Bar stools were being used as corner posts with an inch-thick rope defining a square—creating a rather precarious barricade between the crowd and stage center. The normal sounds of the Pioneer, the mixed sounds of questionable leisure, had given way to the sound of nervous apprehension.

Around 11:30 a group of Denver's finest gentlemen made its way into the bar through a back door. H. A. W. Tabor, in the lead, was followed by a group of men, some of whom would have been recognized in Washington, and all of whom would have been recognized on Seventeenth Street in Denver. Perhaps out of some respect for the White House, Grant had been dissuaded from joining them.

With the arrival of the honored guests—including two men, William Arnold and Howard Smith—Mike Marratta, the owner of the saloon, stepped over the ropes into the center of the ring. Springhetti rang the fire bell, and the Pioneer became quiet.

"Gentlemen," began Mike, "what we are doing here tonight is illegal, but Leadville is full of 'illegal.' Johnny Larsh, who's had a bit of experience with wagering, is taking the bets. William Arnold, one of our esteemed visitors from Denver has agreed to assist Mr. Larsh—his banking credentials surely make him an honest enough man to entrust with the cash. The current odds are eight to five in favor of the badger. You put up eight and get back thirteen if the badger wins. You put up five and get back thirteen if Bad Pete is victorious. Joe O'Leary over here will be the judge of which critter is the winner. Gentlemen, you've got ten minutes to place your bets and fill your glasses!"

The stage was set. Bets were collected and vouchers returned. John Larsh closed the book and the bag just as the Yelenck brothers worked their way toward the ring. The miners quickly gave them ample room as ferocious noises were coming from the barrel being hoisted through their midst. Bad Pete, who seconds before had appeared to be in a comatose state, was suddenly growling and lunging in such a furious way that many who had bet on the badger wished they could reconsider their bets.

The barrel was placed in one corner of the ring. The Yelencks, who were strong Austrian athletes, were busily directing the barrel into a frontal attack position. When the wooden barrel was on the barroom floor, the audience realized that something was about to happen. The bulldog was ready for action; Patrick Griffin, swaying and trying to hold the rope, was straining to maintain his balance.

Marratta got everyone's attention and announced that the event was about to commence. He said, "Now there are certain necessary safety precautions that we have to insist on. No one enters the ring except those who are the active participants. We are honored to have four gentlemen who have, more or less, volunteered to assist us. We know from past experience that having a bit of protection for these corner men is very helpful. Larsh, you and Griffin as well as Mr. Arnold and Mr. Smith, put these eight-inch stove pipes on your legs."

All four men, after first removing their shoes, stepped into the stove pipes and with considerable assistance, managed to get their shoes back on their feet.

Marratta continued, "Now, the timing of this fight is extremely important. To be fair the release of the combatants has got to be exact, and for that reason I'm going to ask that two of our friends from Denver do the honors. Mr. Arnold, if you would be so kind as to take the rope that will release the dog, and Mr. Smith, a distinguished banker and politician, would you do the honor of handling the release of the badger? We want this to be done right, and who could be more honest and fair than a banker and a politician?"

The miners cheered.

Arnold and Smith stepped forward, obviously pleased that the peasants of this crude camp held them in such regard. Each took a rope and crouched, ready to pull and also ready to get out of the way of the beasts. The barrel rumbled and Bad Pete tugged to get at his prey.

"Ready, gentlemen?"

"Yes," they both shouted over the rising sounds of the crowd.

Marratta raised a pistol. "At the sound of the shot, sirs. Get ready . . . set . . ."

The gas lights dimmed for a second and, suddenly, two of Leadville's biggest and finest Irish cops appeared at ringside—in uniform and with guns drawn.

With a shout one of them commanded, "Hold it right there, you merciless bastards. You're under arrest."

Arnold and Smith immediately dropped the ropes and tried to step out of the way. Stepping out of the way with your legs encased in stove pipes takes some doing under any conditions—especially given four bar stools with tangled ropes, at least four hundred miners all moving in different directions, dance hall girls leaning over the upstairs rails, a snarling bulldog being held by a drunken Irishman who was also wearing stovepipes, two giant young men wearing police uniforms and brandishing fire arms, and a barrel full of a mountain badger. This would have been a challenge for anyone.

"Now where do you think you're going?" asked Kelly, the bigger of the two policemen.

"Let go of me," demanded Smith. "I've done nothing wrong."

Tabor, who had been in the background, came forward and said, "Hold on there, Kelly. These gentlemen are guests in our town and are friends of mine."

In a booming voice that brought down the house, Kelly replied, "Friends of yours, aye. That bit of incriminating evidence alone could get them both hanged!" Then over the hoots and hollers and laughter of the mob he shouted, "Handcuff 'em, Tommy. And I guess we'd better take Griffin and Larsh in as well."

Smith was in shock. Arnold was livid. In an angry and condescending voice he threatened, "You two are making a big mistake! This gentleman is Howard Smith and, I'll have you know, I'm a good friend of Governor Pitkin. I demand to know the nature of the charges against us. You'll have my lawyer to deal with."

"Welcome to Leadville, U.S.A. Your lawyer, you say. For two weeks we had your damn militia to deal with and they taught us something of law and order. Well, your soldier boys are gone now, and we'll show you what justice is really about. The marshal sent Tommy and me down here to the Pioneer tonight because word was out about this badger fight of yours. Whether you're aware of it or not, badger fights are in violation of the 'Act for Humane Treatment of Dumb Animals.' And there the two of you were— holding the ropes, and standing there in stovepipes with Griffin just looking guilty, and Larsh over there holding the money. Let's go, gentlemen, night court is in session."

"Night court?" asked Arnold in disbelief.

"Hell yes, night court. It's been doing a land office business ever since you and your buddies showed up on the train."

"This is ridiculous," said Smith. "Horace, do something."

Horace Tabor might not have been formally educated or accepted into high society, but he was clever enough to know when his hometown was up to something. He looked at Officer Kelly and said, "Hell no, they're liable to hang me right along with you, Howard."

"Gentlemen, I can give you two choices. Either you can go along with me to Judge Donovan's court, or I'll just take the cuffs off and you can tell your story to that group of shanty Irish over there who lost their jobs last month because of some bankers who didn't think them worthy of another twenty-five cents a day. I might remind you that last November some of the same bunch here in this saloon strung up and hanged two men just spitting distance from the courthouse."

The distance from the Pioneer Bar in the middle of the block on State Street to the Lake County Courthouse on Harrison Avenue between Fifth and Sixth streets was less than four blocks. It would have taken Bad Pete about four hours to make the trip, but then Bad Pete made a lot of stops. The miners, not waiting to hear Smith's or Arnold's decision regarding their civil rights or welfare, headed for the courthouse en masse, getting there in record time. Without even slowing down at the Bucket of Blood, the Miner's Club, or the Silver Dollar, 223 of them crowded into the seats and another hundred or so stood in the area behind the last row. Seated directly in the center facing the witness stand were two women who had first met in Deadwood, South Dakota. Mindy, who was seated next to her husband, Lewis Lamb, was searching the crowd for the pretty face of her younger sister Edie. Rachel who, although anxious, seemed resigned to accepting something over which she had no control was wondering where her gambler husband might be at that moment.

The judge rapped his gavel only once. The sound reverberated throughout the newly opened courtroom. When the judge looked up, the audience was aware of a pontifical presence. Judge Donovan, a 280-pound Irish-Welshman, spoke in tones of authoritarian habit. In a commanding baritone voice he said, "I am pleased you good citizens have chosen this evening to perform your civic duties by observing justice in the determination of those who have transgressed the laws of this land and this community. Regarding the clamor occurring as you entered this courtroom, such disturbance will not be tolerated again, or I will clear this room without further warning. Bailiff, what in the hell is that racket in the hall?"

The bailiff, quickly standing at attention, shouted from the rear of the room, "Your Honor, Officers Kelly and O'Toole seem to have four transgressors in tow." Even the judge smiled faintly at the quickness of imitation. The bailiff opened the door. The first to enter was John Minor Larsh, head bowed and very solemn, wearing stove pipe leggings. He was followed by Arnold, then Smith, and finally Griffin who under ideal conditions didn't have the best of balance and in the present circumstances found navigation extremely difficult. With each stagger he collided with Smith, who was offended not only by Griffin's demeanor but by his aroma as well, not to mention the clanging of metal leggings.

The two out-of-town prisoners were incensed. "We demand to know why we are being treated in this fashion!" bellowed Smith.

The judge brought down his gavel once again—a little harder than the first time. As he looked around the room, all the demimonde ladies standing in the rear of the room, out of habit, shuddered at the glare of the law. In a low and constrained voice he said, "Suppose we try to find out why you are being so treated, sir. Mr.

O'Toole, what cause do you have to arrest and handcuff these men?"

"Your Honor, the marshal assigned Kelly and me to check out the rumor that there was to be a badger fight down at the Pioneer tonight. He instructed us to interrupt any wrong doing and to arrest those that were putting on the bloody fight."

"And what happened?"

"When we got there, the fight was just about to begin. Marratta was explaining the rules and . . ."

"Just a moment, officer. If Marratta was explaining the rules for the fight, then why isn't he standing here in handcuffs?" quizzed the judge.

Kelly decided to enter the discussion, "Sir, just as we were about to arrest everyone involved, the lights went dim. When they came back up again, Marratta was gone, but we did catch Griffin and this fellow Arnold holding back the dog and Smith there hanging on the rope to the barrel that held the badger. And Larsh was holding the stakes. We grabbed them, I don't know what happened to Marratta."

The judge faced the accused, he said, "Gentlemen, before I hear your side of this barbaric affair, let me inform you of the seriousness of the charges. May I also ask why the four of you are wearing stove pipes?"

"Judge," said Smith, "Let me say a few words. There has been a serious misunderstanding, and I demand you recognize who you are dealing with here. I am Howard J. Smith, vice president of one of the largest banks in Denver and currently in Leadville in the company of General Ulysses S. Grant, former president of the United States of America, and as the personal guest of Horace Tabor, lieutenant governor of the State of Colorado. And I'll have you know my personal attorney is Herbert R. Johnson of Denver, Colorado, and I insist that Mr. Arnold and myself be released immediately and until such a time as proper legal council may be consulted and this farcical proceeding dealt with properly."

Judge Donovan was not only a large man, he was also a mighty man, and when he stood up from behind the bench in his long black robe, his mass and demeanor made him appear to be a sandy-haired giant. He was not smiling. "You insist! You demand!

You call this court of law a farce. If you continue to insult this proceeding I'll put you into a cell on the charge of contempt of court, and then, after you've apologized for your behavior, I'll bring you back to this court for your trial. Do you understand, gentlemen?"

Smith, beginning to sense the hopelessness of his position, just looked down.

"Regarding your defense. If you choose to postpone this trial, I cannot guarantee your safety. This courthouse is full of angry men who are bent on witnessing some form of justice this night— whether by the authority of this court or by the mandate of the streets of Leadville."

With that the room burst into a roar of shouts, applause, and foot stamping. The judge glared out at the hollering and whistling mob, and before he could rap his gavel there was dead silence. "Don't interrupt these proceedings again!" he warned. Then he turned his attention back to the four men in front of him and said, "You are entitled to a trial by jury tonight. I strongly recommend you risk the judgment of this court rather than the whim of the streets. If you choose to do so I will appoint a man of considerable reputation to represent you and, if you please, Mr. Smith, a fine lawyer as well. You are fortunate that a man of such standing happens to be in the courtroom tonight. Mr. McKay, will you confer with the defendants?"

"I will, Your Honor," replied Mr. McKay, a respectable looking man wearing a lawyer's suit. A murmur moved across the courthouse audience, for here was a man who had risked a great deal by representing a poor miner against the establishment of political and economic power.

"Good. We'll take a ten minute recess so the defendants can consider their choices."

Just then, Griffin, having taken a large chew of tobacco moments earlier, staggered to his left, stared at Smith with bleary eyes and a complexion of a pale and ghastly hue, and vomited. Though he gave it a superb effort, Mr. Smith was unable to leap from the path of the violent discharge and took the bulk of the blast just below his watch chain. The semi-liquid bilge cascaded down the vest, with some of the waste dripping through the stove pipes onto his leather shoes.

As the gavel hit the bench everyone in the room was laughing except for the judge who exhibited great composure, Griffin who was still too ill to perceive mirth, and, of course, Smith who literally had been splattered by the insult of it all.

McKay spoke with his prospective clients. First he told Griffin not to chew any more tobacco; then he advised Larsh that gambling had its limits and told the two of them to admit guilt at their first opportunity. McKay said everybody in town knew of Smith's role in the scam at the Little Pittsburg Mine and of his position against the recent miners' strike. Arnold wasn't so well known but was traveling with the wrong crowd from the common man's point of view. "You don't have much of a chance at getting an impartial jury, but its got to be better than some lynch-happy mob."

"People keep talking about lynchings," mumbled Arnold.

"Do you want to go on with this? And, if so, do you want me to represent you?"

Both nodded in agreement. "I just want to get out of this damn town," said Arnold.

"I'd settle for a clean pair of trousers," said Smith. "Is this guy Donovan likely to show us any sympathy? I mean we're educated men, surely he . . ."

"Mr. Smith, the last defendant who asked Judge Donovan for sympathy was told if he wanted to find sympathy he could look it up in the dictionary between 'shit' and 'syphilis.'"

"My God," said Arnold.

"All rise for the honorable Judge Daniel Donovan!"

"Be seated," said the judge. "Mr. McKay, will you be representing the defendants?"

"Yes, Your Honor."

"Very well, we shall proceed. You have each been charged with the illegal promotion and conduct of a fight between a bulldog and a mountain badger. In addition, you are charged with operating this illegal and sadistic event for the purposes of personal gain through gambling. Mr. Griffin, how do you plead?"

"I did it. It's true, I'm guilty, sir. Yes, I did—now what was it I . . ."

"Mr. Larsh. How do you plead?"

"Guilty, Your Honor."

"Mr. Arnold?"

"I'm not guilty, Your Honor."

"Mr. Smith?"

"Not guilty. I wish to strongly protest this entire process."

"All in due time," replied the judge. "Griffin, you and Larsh will be sentenced at the end of the trial of Mr. Arnold and Mr. Smith."

"Mr. Wyman, our prosecuting attorney will conduct the state's case. Let's begin. It is already 12:30 in the morning and I want this finished by 3:00. In Leadville we pride ourselves on respect for the right to a speedy trial."

"Mr. McKay, the defense attorney, and Mr. Wyman, our prosecuting attorney, will select twelve members from this group of citizens assembled here. The process will be as follows: each attorney will select eight possible jury members; then each of you can reject two. It is now 12:30 A.M. You have twenty minutes to select the jury."

All sixteen potential jurors were asked if they knew Mr. Smith or Mr. Arnold personally; all sixteen answered that they did not. All were asked if they knew of Mr. Smith or Mr. Arnold; all but four said they did not. The four were then asked what they knew about the defendants; they all answered that they knew that Smith and Arnold were bankers and shareholders in Tabor's mines. For the first and last time that evening McKay and Wyman agreed; neither wanted a juror who knew that the defendants were in bed with Horace Tabor, albeit at different times than the most famous ladies in Colorado.

The jurors were sworn in. The prosecuting attorney, Thomas Wyman, addressed the jurors. Smith and Arnold were observing and listening with rapt attention. Wyman was in many ways even more impressive than Judge Donovan; a very large man in immaculate dress with a kind face, a born orator in the tradition of Daniel Webster, he was well versed in the nuances of body language, especially his own. He carried with him a gold-trimmed Bible as he leaned against the banister, beyond which sat twelve jurors, many of whom looked to be exactly what they were—raggedy-assed Leadville miners.

"Gentlemen of the jury, I am appalled at the behavior of some of our most distinguished visitors. During a short visit to Leadville those whom we have read about and honored have displayed a total lack of respect for the decorum of your city, and I might add, a total lack of respect for you. Debauchery, in one word, describes the actions of these well-dressed Denverites. They ascribe to you, who work for a living down in a hole in the ground, designs to become their equal; and they, no doubt, wonder how men who wear overalls dare associate with those who wear suits.

"We, as a community that desires to be civilized, to be fair, to be decent, deserve more respect. We cannot arrest people just because they do not respect us, but let me tell you a reason for which we can arrest people. I witnessed a fight between a bull dog and a badger once; I won't ever do it again. I have also seen the bank building in Denver where these two men work. They would not dare do in their bank what they did today here in Leadville.

"When a bull dog bites another animal, he latches on until he breaks the bones; if he has found the other animal's neck, he breaks the other animal's neck. But a badger is different. The badger has four powerful legs with long, sharp, steel-like claws that, before the bull dog can kill his opponent, can rip and cut so that after a minute or two the dog has his entrails hanging with his excrement being thrown about. The dog, at this point, does not quit and run. He is confined to a space in which to die at the pleasure of depraved human beings seeking sport. There is never a winner. The difference is one animal dies before the other. Certainly the men who stage such an outrage cannot be winners. What does a man win by orchestrating cruelty over God's dumb creatures? Men who do such things reduce us all to something less than noble.

"The state of Colorado has passed laws saying that those who promote or are responsible for such acts have committed a felony. I intend to prove that these two men have violated the Humane Statutes of Colorado, and you, after hearing the evidence, will have the responsibility to find them guilty. I can assure you, at that point in the proceedings, that the honorable Judge Donovan will assess a sentence that will meet the severity of this crime."

At this juncture in the criminal proceedings, Griffin, who was attempting to overcome nausea, developed one of his infrequent alcoholic fits. He grasped the legs of the nearest person, who happened to be Mr. Smith. Griffin writhed and convulsed, dragging Smith to the floor. Donovan stood up and announced that Mr. Griffin was having a seizure that would soon subside. He instructed Larsh to place a wooden ruler in Griffin's mouth so as to protect the victim from biting his tongue. Larsh experienced difficulties in placing the ruler in Griffin's mouth as Griffin's head was between Smith's legs. The mission was finally accomplished, but not before many miners had to leave the courtroom to prevent laughing. The fear of being thrown out of the room by the domineering judge also created a problem for Rachel, who had the choice of not laughing or running to the restroom to avoid wetting her bloomers.

Order in the court was soon restored. Smith, somewhat the worse for wear, exchanged seats with Mr. Arnold, while the judge asked the defense attorney to make his opening remarks.

"Gentlemen," began McKay, "This is a highly unusual trial. Because of that fact you, the jury, must be very careful in judging the facts. Two of the four charged here with a violation of the Humane Treatment of Animals Statute have pleaded guilty. Both are from Leadville: one is a well-known gambler, the other is a well-known drunk. They know that they will receive a relatively light sentence because what they were doing tonight at the Pioneer they do every night, only in some modified form. But these two gentlemen from Denver have pleaded not guilty because they fear the wrath of the Leadville miners; not because of what they did tonight but because of what the miners believe they did last month.

"If you find them guilty, you must do so on the trivial part they played in the badger fight tonight; not on what part they may or may not have played in the labor strife that this mining town experienced in the past."

At that remark, Mr. Arnold leaped to his feet and shouted, "Judge, I would like to plead guilty!"

Judge Donovan said firmly, "You will be given the right to testify as a witness in your own defense. I will not allow any more outbursts from you or others. The jury will decide your fate. Please call the witnesses for the prosecution."

"Your Honor . . ." Mr. Smith began.

This time Judge Donovan rapped the gavel and said loudly, "Mr. Smith, you are a slow learner. I am tempted to judge you both not guilty, and turn you over to the Baldessari brothers, but that would be a cruel and unusual punishment! Now shut up and sit down." The judge cast a menacing glance at the crowd of miners as a notice not to applaud. Then he said quietly, "Mr. Wyman, call your first witness."

Wyman called his first witness, an actress performing at the Tabor Opera House who had been portrayed by the local paper as "a Broadway star, one of America's greats!" He asked the actress, who was more appropriately dressed for the theater in New York than the drama which had started in the Pioneer that evening, "Were you asked by Mr. Marratta to attend a function at the Pioneer this evening?"

"Yes, I was," said the actress.

"Tell us about the invitation, please," asked Wyman.

"Well, Mr. Arnold here along with Mr. Smith were having a late dinner two nights ago with Mr. Moffat and Mr. Tabor at the Clarendon Restaurant. Mr. Marratta was introduced to all of us by Mr. Tabor. Mr. Marratta asked us all if we were interested in seeing a dog fight another animal. I thought then, as I do now, that Mr. Marratta, who seemed a rather crude man, was trying to embarrass me. However, both Mr. Arnold and Mr. Smith agreed to accompany Mr. Tabor to the fight. I asked them if it weren't illegal. They said, 'Of course, it is illegal.' I declined."

"Did they, in fact, go to the Pioneer this evening?"

"Yes, I was on my way to the opera, and we, my escort and I, dropped them off at the Pioneer around 9:30." The actress was excused and Wyman asked John Larsh to take the stand.

After the oath, Wyman asked Larsh, "What do you do for a living?"

Larsh replied, " I work at the Pioneer as a card dealer, both faro and stud."

"What were you doing tonight at the Pioneer?" asked Wyman.

"I was asked by Mr. Marratta to hold the money that was being bet on the badger fight," said Larsh.

"Was anyone else in this room directly involved in staging that badger fight, Mr. Larsh?"

"Yes, sir, that person was holding Bad Pete, the dog, and that person was holding the badger," Larsh exclaimed, pointing at Smith and Arnold.

"Have you any personal grudges against either of these two?" asked Wyman.

"As a matter of fact, I do, sir," said Larsh. This revelation was shocking to everyone in the courtroom as they all had expected a negative answer.

Wyman had no choice but to ask, "What reasons do you have to feel antagonism toward these gentlemen?"

"Well, sir," said Larsh, "that one, Mr. Smith, picked up my sister Edith this afternoon, took her to Iowa Gulch, tore her dress in an attempt to rape her, and didn't have the courtesy to bring her home."

Smith jumped to his feet and shouted, "These are all goddamn lies."

McKay, Smith, Wyman, and then Judge Donovan were all on their feet shouting. It wasn't until Judge Donovan gaveled for silence, that his deep voice prevailed. "Mr. McKay, you will have adequate time to cross examine this witness and call any witness on your own. You will also have time to counsel your client, Mr. Smith, on the protocol of this court and on the penalty for contempt. Mr. Smith, the prosecuting attorney is a man of firm religious beliefs. I might add, the members of the jury are mostly Irish Catholic or Austrian Catholic. I suspect you should apologize for using the Lord's name in vain."

After a stumbling apology from Smith, the judge declared a

fifteen-minute recess. Bang! The gavel was louder than ever.

It was now after 1:30 A.M. on Thursday morning. Many of the people had been at the court house since 9:00 P.M. on Wednesday night. None of them was anxious to leave, although most of them were wearing overalls and were expected to work ten to twelve hours that very day.

McKay, when asked by the judge to call his witnesses, described to the jury what he intended to do and why. "The defense will call only one witness who will offer testimony about the character of these two victimized men. Then I shall call a witness who has already pleaded guilty and ask you to weigh the veracity of his testimony. I will ask that witness's sister to come forth with real evidence that she was, in any way, violated. Finally, I will call Mr. Arnold and Mr. Smith to explain this bizarre episode."

McKay then called his first witness, H. A. W. Tabor, who talked of Smith's and Arnold's reputations as businessmen, politicians, and family men, of their impeccable integrity, honesty, and good will. The jury listened carefully and incredulously; here was their former friend, former postmaster, former lieutenant governor, and former mayor who had encouraged the militia to force them back to work only a month ago. Here was a man who was leaving his wife, whom they all admired, for a divorcée. Here was a man who was moving to Denver, taking the money from the mines of Leadville to build opera houses and mansions in that city. His recommendations as to someone else's character were only valid in comparison to his shortcomings.

McKay then called John Minor Larsh to the stand. "You testified that you were guilty of participating in an illegal badger fight. Is that correct?"

"Yes, sir," said Larsh.

"Do you know that such a felony could result in going to the state penitentiary for six months?" asked McKay.

"I do now," said Larsh.

"Would you, knowing what you now know, still plead guilty?" asked McKay.

"Yes, sir," replied Larsh.

"Why?" questioned McKay.

"Because," responded Larsh, "I gamble every night. What I did last night was collect bets on a dog fight. I did not know how serious that was until I got here. I was doing what the owner of the Pioneer, Mr. Marratta, asked me to do. I was collecting money from many of Leadville's distinguished citizens. So I am, as the judge pointed out, 'guilty,' but not any more than a whole lot of other people."

"Thank you," McKay said. "I now call Edith Larsh." Edith walked demurely to the witness stand. She was dressed in a simple, blue cotton dress. It would be she, rather than the New York actress, who would have created murmurs in any society gathering. "Miss Larsh, what is your occupation?"

"I am an entertainer," she said very quietly.

"What does that mean, an entertainer?" asked McKay.

"I sing and dance at the Pioneer," Edith replied.

"Do you also entertain men in the rooms above the bar room at the Pioneer?"

"I do . . . at my discretion," she answered.

"Your brother testified that yesterday afternoon Mr. Smith escorted you in a buggy up the road toward Iowa Gulch. Is that correct?"

"Yes, sir, that is correct," she answered.

"He also said that Mr. Smith tore your dress and attempted to become very familiar with you. Is that correct?"

"Yes, sir, that is also correct."

"Young lady, you are under oath to tell the truth. Don't you think it strange that this gentleman would do such a thing when he could purchase your sexual favors in the rooms of a saloon rather than risk possible detection in the woods near Iowa Gulch?"

"Sir, Mr. Smith, late on Monday night, asked me to his hotel room, not to the rooms in the Pioneer, because he did not wish to be seen going up the stairs with me. He asked me to come to the Clarendon. I told him that I would not. He begged me, gave me $20.00 and this key to his room, number 233. He then asked me to accompany him on a buggy ride up to Iowa Gulch for yesterday afternoon. I took the precaution of asking two young men to watch the glen where we would be sitting around four o'clock. They saved me from the embarrassment, but not before Mr. Smith had torn my dress. The two young men are seated here in the courtroom and will be happy to verify my entire story."

Judge Donovan spoke in a very firm voice. "Counselor, this trial is a trial about man's inhumanity to animals! I don't think you want your client tried on attempted rape, but if you continue this line of questioning, it may come down to Miss Larsh's word against your client's word. It would appear that she has some witnesses of her own. What do you want to do, Mr. McKay?"

"Judge, I would like a ten-minute recess to confer with my clients."

The judge rapped his gavel and announced to all, "If you leave this courtroom you will not be allowed back. This recess will last only ten minutes, and this trial may not last a whole lot longer, God willing."

The recess was exactly ten minutes. The judge asked Mr. McKay to step forward and then said, "What do you want to do, Mr. McKay?"

"Your Honor, the defendants would like to testify individually before the jury without benefit of counsel. After you hear their statements, they would like you to judge, *a priori* to the jury's verdict, the feasibility of *a nolo contendere* plea and place themselves at the mercy of the court."

"Do you have any objection to this rather unusual procedure, Mr. Prosecuting Attorney?"

Mr. Wyman, in his righteous way, responded, "I have no objection, Your Honor."

Mr. Arnold took the witness stand. "Gentlemen of the jury, Your Honor, this has been the most enlightening and terrifying night of my life. Mr. McKay has told me of the attitudes that exist here in Leadville, attitudes held by the majority of the men who work at the mines. He also has told me how stupid I have been to be part of what I innocently thought was a sporting event. In my innocence I was flattered to be asked to help with the dog. I know now that that was wrong, and I am willing to pay for my part in that crime. Mr. McKay has informed us that if the jury decides our fate, it will be difficult for you to separate what happened tonight from what happened last month up at the Chrysolite and Little Pittsburg mines. So I ask you, Your Honor, to be the judge, to mete out whatever punishment you deem fair. I do need to say that I am not from Denver. I am from New York City. I have never owned stock in any mine, and I do not aspire to be governor of Colorado!"

Mr. Smith was livid. He shouted, "Arnold, you son of a bitch!" He then dropped his head on his soiled vest and began to sob.

The judge quietly said, "Please go on, Mr. Arnold."

Mr. Arnold continued, "I have a wife and three children and a reputation as an honest businessman. Imprisonment or jail here in Leadville will destroy a lot of that! I want to finish with what may appear to be a foolish statement. In the three days that I have been here, I have met the friendliest, nicest people in all my experience. Thank you, Your Honor."

"Mr. Smith, you may now take the witness stand."

Smith had entered the courtroom immaculately dressed; his arrogant manner testified to his belief that he was truly of a superior class. He was now reduced to a sobbing, incoherent, unhygienic, pathetic figure. He started to describe his family and his relationship to Grant and Tabor, but, unlike Arnold, he didn't have his act together. He started to get down on his knees between the loud sobbing sounds.

The judge rapped the gavel and said, "I have heard enough! Mr. Smith, I am going to sentence you rather than ask the jury to decide on your guilt or innocence. This is Leadville and I find you guilty."

The audience all stood and applauded. Judge Donovan motioned them to be seated. "As part of your sentence I want you to see the beautiful wild animal that because of your actions we have had to destroy. Bring in the dead badger!"

From the rear of the room, the two Slovenian blacksmiths carried the wooden barrel toward the judge's bench. The barrel was silent, but at the sight of it Bad Pete, who had been curled up next to Griffin, lunged forward, proving that he was sufficiently trained to do battle twice within a twenty-four hour period. The barrel was placed in front of the judge, who said, "After you have seen the badger, I will give you your sentence. Pull the rope and look at the misfortunate beast!"

Standing behind Smith was Bad Pete, grinding fangs exposed, ready for battle. Smith looked forlorn and pathetic.

"Pull the damn rope!" shouted Donovan.

Smith finally pulled the rope. The door on the slanted barrel opened, and a flowered chamber pot emerged onto the court house floor.

It took a full two minutes before the judge could gavel the audience, standing in their overalls and roaring with laughter, to silence. It took a little longer before Mr. Smith realized that he had been had.

"There are two more parts to your sentence, Jackass," Donovan announced. "The first is some kind advice. The early train back to Denver leaves at 6:10 A.M. You just have time to make it. One last thing, our printer friend, who was advised to leave town last month because he dared to print a miner's view of the strike, printed up this card as a gift to you, just to remind you of this evening. I want you to read it loud and clear."

The courtroom once again became very quiet. Smith, looking as if he had been hung out to dry on the gallows frame up on Printer Boy Hill, read the card loud and clear:

ADVICE:
Don't wrestle in the mud with pigs;
Don't get into a pissing contest with a skunk;
Don't play leapfrog with a unicorn;
Don't get in the middle of a badger fight;
And finally, don't muck with Leadville.

Bang! The gavel hit the bench. Donovan declared, "This trial is over!" Legend, folklore, and oral history would have us believe that not one miner or miner's lady left the court house without a deep sense of well being. Not one would have traded places with Mr. Smith. They all knew who they were, and they liked what they knew. It is one thing to work for $3.00 a day and lose a strike to the powers that be—that is the realism that sets in on top of the dreams. It is still another thing when you discover the power of a critical mass which seems to include magic. In Leadville, whenever the diverse ethnic groups coalesced, you had a critical mass whose power could and did perform miracles. The important aspects of the Leadville badger fight were not the how or the what, but the reasons why.

Legend would have us believe that Donovan, John Larsh, the two Yelenck brothers, Griffin, twelve Irish jurors, a comely prostitute named Edie, a New Yorker named Arnold, and a lawyer named McKay drank boiler makers at the Pioneer until it was time for old "Number Four" to depart at 6:10 A.M. from the Denver and Rio Grande Depot up on Poplar Street. Around six they walked up to the depot to make damn sure a Mr. Smith had gotten to the station on time.

The train pulled in as the sun rose over the Mosquito Range. The rays were sparkling off the glacier up on Mount Massive. Tom Wyman quoted Hebrews 12:23, "The Spirits of just men made perfect."

My father believed that education should not be limited to school. He constantly encouraged us to seek learning experiences from a wide range of sources. It was with this in mind that he convinced my friend John Swenson and me to accompany him to the Lake County Courthouse late one evening in July of 1937. We didn't know it at the time, but what we attended that night was probably the last badger fight in a non-scheduled series beginning in 1880 and spanning the turn of the century, Prohibition, and most of the Great Depression.

As we sat waiting for the "trial" to begin, he told me about the involvement of my grandfather and my great-aunt in the first badger fight. I was fourteen at the time, and what I remember most about the incredible evening was the performance of three well-known Leadville characters. Tom Ryan owned Ryan's Pool Hall, where the badger fight was held, and inherited the role of the prosecuting attorney. Tom O'Mahoney, a shoe salesman, was cast in the role of the judge; Tom had learned his role through his father, who had been the Lake County sheriff, starting in 1896. I later found out that Tom O'Mahoney was Lee Schraeder's uncle.

But the most memorable actor was Jack Laing. He was impressive in his role as defense attorney—a big man with a white face, white hair, and pink eyes. When he spoke at the trial, he made a believer out of you, as he did in real life. His physical presence was commanding enough but, as chief lawyer for the Climax Molybdenum Company, he had the legal expertise to give the proceedings a powerful credibility.

For obvious reasons, the badger fights of Leadville were never recorded nor even openly discussed. I knew the best place to start tracing the oral history of the badger fights was with Jack Laing. He knew and loved Leadville for over eighty years, and he had a fantastic memory for people and events. It was Jack who established that the timing of the first fight coincided with the arrival of the railroad and the Ulysses S. Grant entourage. He said labor strikes, the one in 1880 and more so the big one in 1896, took away any pretense of miners and mine owners working together. He also told me that when Ryan opened his pool hall on Seventh and Harrison streets, the badger fights were moved there from the Pioneer Bar. He named the prime players who participated in them during the 1920s and 1930s, not forgetting himself or Bad Pete, the bulldog. He described the process in detail from the moment the "badger" was brought into the room (carried in a wooden barrel by two miners) to the statement of the judge upon finding the defendant guilty. He described Ryan, the prosecuting attorney, and O'Mahoney, the judge, in terms usually reserved for stage stars.

Though it is difficult to tell exactly how often badger fights were held, it seems they were a fairly regular event up until World War I, when there was a moratorium for a period of four or five years. They returned with renewed vigor during the 1920s when the additional element of illegal drink could be tacked on to the charges brought against the defendants in the trial. Prohibition created a unique case for Leadville to tap. Even teetotalers during that period saw the futility of legislating morality.

Leadville had little difficulty in accommodating the risk-taking majority. Bootlegging was big business in the mountain town. Leadville booze was well known throughout the state of Colorado. On any given night during those Prohibition years between 1919 and 1933, you could buy liquor by the drink across the counter and by the jug out the back door of any bar on State Street or Harrison Avenue. Producers with stills hidden in the hills and down in the mine shafts distributed their bottled goods by various means of conveyance to Larimer Street and other centers of night life in Denver and other cities. It was a money-making enterprise. But, nevertheless, it was illegal, and you could go to jail if caught and proven guilty.

The laws and penalties for violating Prohibition were perfectly suited for setting up badger fight victims. Not only were the unfortunate individuals apprehended holding the rope in one hand, they invariably were nabbed with a drink in the other. It was during this prime era of informal justice that Jack Laing, a talented young Leadville lawyer, began his role as defense attorney.

According to Jack Laing, Gerald McMillin, Lee Schraeder, Bill Rose, and others, the stage I witnessed in 1937 was set almost exactly as it had been in all the previous trials. Though the scene of the "crime" had been moved to Ryan's Pool Hall, and the current version of Bad Pete, the bull dog, was at least the fifth incarnation of the original canine conspirator, little else had changed. The principals in the play were as much a part of the town as were the mines, the bars, the hard times, and the social and economic inequity—all type-cast and steeped in the tradition of social justice a lá Western mining camp jurisprudence.

Authenticating the history of the first badger fight has been a challenge. I was fortunate. My family is a family of storytellers. My dad, a newspaper man, knew many people who knew Leadville extremely well, such as Ezra Dickerman, Grandpa "Doc" Rose, Walter Peck, Harry Schraeder, the O'Mahoneys, and Dad's good friend, Jack Laing (whose father was a conductor on the train to Johnny Hill in the nineteenth century). Gerald McMillin, who sometimes played the defense attorney, was my brother-in-law's brother. (His father was in the grocery business in Leadville in the nineteenth century.) The list of sources is lengthy; the stories have been told and retold.

The history of the first badger fight has now been written, albeit by grace of oral history and the storyteller's art rather than by the academic historian's science.

17

Center Stage

"Who the hell is that guy hanging up there?" asked Horace Tabor as his Tabor Opera House was in its final decorating phases in the fall of 1879. "Why that's the immortal bard William Shakespeare," replied the interior design consultant who had been imported from Denver.

"What did he ever do for Leadville?" Tabor demanded. "Take him down and put me up."

Today it is one of the features I first recall about the Opera House. Tabor's portrait is hanging just left of the stage. It is one of the many connecting points that fill this place with ghosts.

For Leadville people, there are many personal stories associated with this venerable old hulk of a building: stories of the theater, stories of the town, stories that have been passed down through families for generations.

You can read about the Tabor Opera House and you can tour it. Give three dollars to the lady behind the counter out in the narrow, unpainted entrance and you will be allowed to walk up the stairs and through the exact same doors Augusta and Horace Tabor entered on opening night, November 20, 1879. After you step into the theater and encounter its dimension and haunting vacancy, you may sit down in any of the eight hundred wooden or velvet seats and listen to some of the history of events, performances, and remembrances of over a century of songs and plays, orations and circuses. This historical review comes from a ten-minute tape that is played over and over. The voice that echoes through the cavernous antiquity is that of Mrs. Evelyn Furman, the current proprietor of the Opera House. Very likely it was also Evelyn who sold you the ticket to get in, and she who will sell you the book she has written about her historical edifice as you leave. If your interest is piqued by the novelties that clutter the room behind the counter, she will gladly escort you into her shop where a random collection of antiques, curios, and artifacts is on display and for sale. But, don't plan your outing to the Opera House on a Saturday. Mrs. Furman is a Seventh Day Baptist and retires every Saturday to spiritual endeavors.

Mrs. Furman inherited the property from her mother in the sixties and since then has committed herself to personally applying first aid to the place—patching the roof, filling in holes in the walls, and generally attempting to slow the atrophy inherent in any structure abandoned by the purpose of its creation. The Tabor Opera House is an old dream waiting for restoration—it is a shell, a museum displaying what was once a vivacious venue of theatrical art and showmanship. Only the ghosts remain to dance and sing and recite the heroic poems and comic monologues of other eras. If you sit there long enough, during the interlude between broadcasts of the tape, when only the footsteps and scattered conversations of a few other visitors disturb the quiet, you can hear the ghosts—you can feel their presence.

The Tabor Opera House is not like any other opera house, but then Mrs. Furman is not like any other lady nor is Leadville like any other place. And for those of us for whom this old building has personal significance, it is not only the haunting presence of long-gone thespians, crooners, and soft-shoe hoofers that fill the place. We are also joined by a reflected manifestation of our own lives.

When I have been in town during the summer (and it wasn't a Saturday), I have often paid my three dollars just to sit again in this old theater and let my mind seek out what hovers in the shadows of the great stage and the hall about me. There is something in the reverberating sounds of these scattered visitors that add a dimension of realism to my mind's ability to revel in the past. Having heard it numerous times, I try not to listen very carefully to Mrs. Furman's tape. I also avoid looking at the people wandering about in a self-guided tour—you can see them in Dallas, Central City, or Aspen.

There in the velvet unholstered, orchestra section you can free your imagination. You slouch down, close your eyes and play the game of seeing. Certain words drift in from the tape evoking connected thoughts and events. I hear names: Jack Dempsey, Oscar Wilde, John Philip Sousa, Cornelia Otis Skinner . . . old Horace Tabor's mustache is somewhere up there on the wall . . . the ghosts and memories come alive.

Tabor's Opera House was a high priority in the town of Leadville back in 1879. Tabor was mayor, he was rich, he owned the property, and he needed the influx of some class to enhance his dream of being the "Silver King." Construction was started in August of that year and whole thing completed in one hundred days—a marvel of productivity, especially considering the quality of material and design: built of brick and mortar and finished inside with imported hardwood, imported velvet seats, and a giant stage with a ceiling over three stories high. Every seat, brick, board and piece of cloth was hauled by wagon over Weston Pass. No shortcuts or compromises were considered—this theater was intended to make a statement: By God, Leadville is a first-class city with first-class culture and it is here to stay. With curtains, back-drops, dressing rooms, gas lights, orchestra pit, and eight hundred seats, it was ready for the grand opening on November 20, 1879.

We could not determine the exact number of opera houses that opened between 1637 and 1879, it surely was in the hundreds. We do know that none of these opera houses opened on the same day two men were hanged by vigilantes from an exposed beam of a building being constructed across the street.

On the morning of the twentieth, Mr. Frodsham and Mr. Steward, an alleged thief and an alleged rapist, were still hanging around where the local committee had left them along with a note advising certain undesirables to leave town. Among those being advised to depart was our favorite marshal, Martin Duggan. The *Leadville Herald Democrat* reported the coincidence of the hanging with the opening of the Opera House by saying, "Theater goers were in no mood for frivolity, accounting for poor attendance."

The Tabor Opera House has another claim to fame. In its relatively short but colorful history there has been a wide variety of performances attended by millionaires, presidents, and a full house of ragged-ass miners. Among these performances and events have been funerals, prize fights, New York stage plays, high school graduations, recitals by musicians; recitations by famous poets, writers, governors, and lecturers, and entertainment by beautiful actresses (one of whom was showered by twenty dollar gold pieces)—but never an opera!

While sitting there in the orchestra seats, the names I heard penetrated my thoughts, resulting from connections both local and distant I realized Leadville and the Tabor Opera House can connect you to other historical eras and locales—to other mining towns in whatever era.

18

Art, Ice, and Sisyphus Hill

When you pray for ice, you pray for mud.
—AN OLD LEADVILLE PROVERB

In 1896 a collective, creative, artistic impulse emerged from the same human beings who had developed the Leadville mining district with all its attendant destruction. Grandiose vision combined with a hearty sense of humor to create something unique from nature's simplest material, water, and Leadville's most abundant natural resource, cold air. Leadville would build a magnificent palace of ice, the likes of which had never been seen before.

It was a palace that was home to no royalty, nor meant to be; a palace that began its own destruction before it was finished; a palace graced with statues that would gleam in their glorious moment and then disappear into rivulets, some of the water making its way down the north slope toward the Evergreen Cemetery to water the graves and some finding its way to the southern slope of Sixth Street Hill to water the early summer dandelions destined to become vintage Slovenian wine. It was absurd, it was art, and it was definitely Leadville.

Some would view the outrageous notion of building the most extravagant ice-block edifice in the world on Capitol Hill as motivated solely by economic factors. But to look at the winter festival of 1896, the Leadville Crystal Carnival, in strictly economic terms doesn't begin to do justice to the spirit and vision and downright craziness of the community. There were any number of much more practical ways of boosting the economy, if that had been the sole motivation. And conditions for the population in the area were not as desperate as one might suppose following the loss of the silver standard and ensuing Panic of 1893. Horace Tabor went under, as did others, but the mining went on, and the quantities of silver and gold did not decline. Eighteen ninety-five was second only to 1880 in the amount of silver extracted from the Lake County hills. The mines produced nearly 9.5 million ounces, a total production of over nine million dollars. People have never needed much of an excuse to celebrate, and the people of Leadville were alive and working and no more broke than they had been for the previous eighteen years.

The Leadville Crystal Carnival began in the summer of 1895 when a committee was assembled to discuss the organization of a winter carnival to attract tourists to Leadville. A real estate agent, E. W. Senior, made the point that crowds of people from around the nation could hardly be expected to travel the difficult miles to Leadville simply for a couple of runs down a toboggan slide. What was needed was an attraction that was as spectacular as it was unique. He had read about ice structures that had been built in other Nordic climes, St. Paul in Minnesota, St. Petersburg and Moscow in Russia. An ice palace would be spectacular enough, but to make it sufficiently unique it would have to be the grandest ice palace ever built.

Great ideas require great leaders if they are to be realized. Unfortunately, Mr. Senior, though no one could fault his powers of vision, apparently lacked appropriate "character" to spearhead such an ambitious endeavor. He was a suspected Mormon: he didn't drink and he was from Salt Lake City, Utah. To the mine operators, proprietors of the bistro establishments, and the people who spent their days and nights frequenting these environs of industry and depravity, this stigma was serious enough to justify withholding enthusiastic endorsement of his vision. It wasn't his religion that troubled the masses so much—it was America and it was Leadville and a person had the right to any belief he or she fancied—but who could trust a man who didn't drink? By September he had raised only $4,000 of the estimated $10,000 needed to commence the project. There is no evidence that the man's honor was in question. But, regardless of the extent to which he intended his efforts to benefit the community, as a non-drinker he would always be considered an outsider and, thus, treated with suspicion. Perhaps in Salt Lake City a different ethic prevailed.

On October 25, the winter carnival committee accepted Mr. Senior's much encouraged resignation and relieved him of his responsibilities. In his place, it appointed the dynamic and popular manager of the Lilian, Benton, Agwalt, and Antioch mining companies, Tingley S. Wood. One can assume that Mr. Wood was not only an extremely competent administrator, a respected public figure, and a natural leader, but he must also have been "honest" enough to take an occasional drink.

He agreed to accept the appointment on condition that before beginning construction of the palace there would have to be at least $20,000 up front. Some sources say that Wood even agreed to match that amount from his own funds. The "Unsinkable Molly Brown's" husband, James Joseph Brown, was said to have immediately started the newly invigorated fund-raising campaign with a contribution of $500.

Exactly one month later, on November 25, 1895, the cornerstone of the Leadville Ice Palace was laid on a five-acre plot of land on Capitol Hill between Seventh and Eighth streets.

Just as fishermen sometimes promote the myth that the object of their sport is to acquire food while it is really to escape matters domestic and responsible, the purpose of the Ice Palace was supposed to be the creation jobs and the return of great monetary rewards to investors. In truth, it is likely that such economic enticements served as but a surface motive. At the heart of the Ice Palace was the spirit of Leadville, the celebration of life, and the utter disregard of anything as mundane as reality.

You don't read much about it, but surely someone pointed out to the frenzied advocates of this massive work of ice that the damn thing was bound to melt. But then the mines were bound to play out, too, and that hadn't diminished the desire for opera houses, grand hotels, and electric lights. It was Leadville, not Peoria.

Charles E. Joy, the most famous living "ice architect" in America, designer of the ice palaces of Montreal and St. Paul, was contracted to come to Leadville and create the grandest project of his career.

The initial source of the ice was local lakes as well as the ice flats over Tennessee Pass where Camp Hale was built many years later. Under the direction of W. H. Cole of the Leadville Ice Company, slabs of ice were hauled to the construction site by eighteen, four-horse teams pulling sleds. There the ice was cut to uniform size, five feet by two feet by two feet. At first the ice was cut by stone cutters, but they were too slow. Contradicting the stated goal of the project to create local jobs, lumberjacks were imported from Canada to chop the large slabs of ice into blocks. When the regional resource of ice was depleted, it was cut from Palmer Lake, located a great distance away between Denver and Colorado Springs, and shipped to Leadville on rail cars.

Areas of the palace walls were to be used for colorful displays of products and advertisements frozen right into the ice. A diversity of participants agreed to have their wares exhibited. There were ice-suspended presentations by railroads, packing houses, hotels, newspapers, and dry goods companies. (Interestingly enough, the Cornforth Fish and Oyster Company was represented—quite a way for a saltwater mollusks to travel.) The Adolph Coors Company of Golden, Colorado, sent six bottles of beer to be frozen in the wall along with an extra case of twenty-four as insurance in the case of breakage. Shortly after delivery, H. B. Hardt, the gentleman in charge of displays, determined that the case was missing. After a bit of a search he found it, discarded and, to his surprise, with most of the bottles unopened. Considering the intemperance normally exhibited by most of the workers as well as the supervisors of the project, he was amazed that all had not been consumed. It was then, I suppose by tipping one himself, he discovered Adolph had sent them thirty bottles of colored salt water for fear that the real stuff would freeze.

The entire production was threatened in early December when Chinook winds—gusting, down-slope blasts of compressed and heated air—attacked the winterscape with temperatures upwards of sixty degrees. Tingley Wood came up with $5,000 worth of muslin cloth to insulate the assembled blocks during the ten-day siege of balmy breezes. The *Leadville Democrat* commented on Leadville's fickle turns of climate: "When a fellow wants a linen duster and a palm leaf fan to visit the Ice Palace . . . and a fur-lined ulster and toboggan suit to attend a Fourth of July picnic, the less I hear about the weather the better."

Regardless of the weather, the expense, and probably the voices of reason, on New Year's Day, 1896, right on schedule and enhanced by the vigor of a brilliant, eight-below-zero day, the gala celebration began—the Leadville Crystal Carnival commenced, and the magnificent Ice Palace was opened for the world to visit.

One day that month, John Minor Larsh walked north on Harrison Avenue with a four-year-old boy riding on his shoulders, on their way through the extravaganza of the carnival to see the wonderful Ice Palace up on Capitol Hill. The little boy was Eddie, his son, who grew up to be my father and to tell me about the experience.

When Dad spoke about the winter festival of 1896, part of his knowledge was based on the stories of his parents and older brothers and sisters, and a portion was from things he had read. But the whole story was colored and given life by the sights and sounds and emotions experienced by a four-year-old kid. It was a day of bitter-cold sunshine. In the illusion of mildness created by clear skies and brilliant light, they ignored the sub-zero temperature and were warmed by the excitement of wandering through an everyday world that had been transformed into a carnival.

My grandfather and, from his shoulders, my father saw the bands and heard them playing in a continuous parade up and down the middle of the street. In one formation after another they marched, the rigid men in brightly colored uniforms trimmed with shining brass buttons and epaulets of dangling golden cord. They saw the rhythmic puffs of breath-steam escaping the bells of blaring horns. They heard the driving power of drums. There were carriages and horse-drawn sleighs filled with revelers and driven by strange looking men wearing knickerbockers and crimson capes. And between the music and sleigh bells and the mobs, in silent and serious syncopation, stepped a precision snowshoe brigade in perfect "dress-right-dress"—regardless of the horse manure. Along the familiar sidewalk were scores of laughing strangers, tourists, and a seasoning of friends shouting greetings. The scent of meats simmering on red-coaled braziers and the delicious aromas of breads and pretzels and cookies emanated from carts and storefronts.

As father and son approached Seventh and Harrison, they could hear the screaming of passengers both thrilled and terrified as toboggans were pushed off an elevated station high above the street to swoop in an exhilarating rush along a glazed run at speeds faster than the gallop of a horse or the plodding pace of a passenger train, faster than any form of transportation known to those times. Eddie was a bit young for such a ride, but Rachel and the rest of the family were already up ahead of them, and John was certain there would be a share of Larshes plummeting down the icy track. Just being there was excitement enough for Eddie.

Then they walked on up the steep hill to Eighth Street and west to the Ice Palace. Almost any article or pamphlet written about the Ice Palace goes into great detail about the proportions of this great edifice. In modern America's official unit of measurement, the football field, it was more than one field long and over one and a half fields deep. It was built as a full-scale replica of a late medieval castle, with high walls and great towers on each corner. The octagonal towers flanking the main gate were as high as nine-story buildings. Inside were luxuriant ballrooms and a skating rink where scores glided to the waltz tempos of an orchestra.

Julius Van Linden, a "special correspondent" for the *Chicago Record,* in the full purple of Victorian prose, described the Ice Palace as follows:

Leadville's ice palace, blazing in myriad colors under the brilliant influence of incandescent light, is a material thing and an attraction worthy of the Cloud City. . . . The poet alone can paint the glories of this marvelous creation of frozen beauty. It was planned on a scale of magnificence never before attempted. Moscow, Montreal and St. Paul have had their palaces of ice, but these were mere dwarfs to the crystal castle on the summit of Capitol Hill. It is not merely a noble picture to the eye, all cold, cheerless and desolate inside. Within the ice walls are interior frame walls, affording comfortably heated halls. Within the giant castellated walls are ballrooms, in which are to be seen the most beautiful effects that artistic skill and cunning can produce. Between these beautiful apartments extends the great expanse of the ice rink, covering 16,000 square feet of skating surface, illuminated with the bewildering splendor of electric lights . . .

Four-year-old Eddie Larsh likely had few words to express his amazement at the massive structure that loomed before him—not so much due to the limitations of his young vocabulary as to the lack of anything in his brief life to which he could compare such a wonder. His father was probably nearly as dumb struck himself. It was art and spectacle on the grandest scale he had ever seen.

Johnny fetched seventy-five cents from his pocket, and they headed for the entrance. Before it stood the nineteen-foot-tall ice sculpture, "Lady Leadville," glistening as, with an extended arm, she gestured toward the eastern hills and the excavations there that had provided the wealth she celebrated. In her left hand she clasped a ledger bearing the figure $207,000,000—the total worth of precious metals shoveled from the depths of shafts up Stray Horse Gulch and Johnny Hill. As they passed, little Eddie just pointed back at her in awe.

"Let's go find your mama and your brothers and your sisters— they're waiting for us inside . . . and let's see about renting you a pair of ice skates."

The bands played on through January and February. By the trainload, crowds from the lowlands thronged to the spectacle. The locals strove to do their part in keeping the party alive, but before the first of March it was obvious the thing was melting. Actually, the crowds had been impressive but not nearly so large as had been projected by the dreamers and developers. And, while before the opening it had been feared Leadville would be hard put to accommodate the arriving masses with food and lodging, in fact many of the visitors were amazingly thrifty in their planning and made little use of local resources. By taking advantage of special round-trip fares offered by the railroads, they could ride the night train and arrive in Leadville in the morning, spend the day at the Ice Palace (admission was fifty cents for adults), eat the sack lunches they had packed for the trip, take a few runs down the toboggan slide, and catch the evening train back to Colorado Springs or Denver. They could accomplish the entire odyssey without contributing more than a dollar or two to the economy of the host city.

Whether or not anyone really believed it, the optimistic prospectus offered when shares were being peddled in saloons, lodge halls, churches, and shops throughout the town promised a healthy profit of five dollars for every dollar of up-front money raised. Though no accurate tally was ever made following the cessation of events that spring, a conservative estimate places the loss at about ten dollars for every dollar invested. The Leadville Crystal Carnival of 1896—a masterwork of impermanence—was a financial disaster.

But it was fun for a while. Anyone from the down-slope world who attended was sure to have spoken about it for years thereafter, surely taxing the patience of grandchildren and anyone else within hearing. And the locals and their children and their grandchildren have kept its moment alive.

At the crest of a steep hill overlooking the town of Castleton, England, in black-gray stone beneath the weight of a heavy gray sky, stands a 900-year-old fortress—a castle as enduring as the dense rock of its construction. On a hill above Leadville, there is a section of real estate that some people claim has not completely dried up in the ninety-six years since the Ice Palace melted.

Some were foolish enough to think that with insulation of hay bales and gunny sacks the Ice Palace might survive the summer and with a little upkeep be reopened for years to come. Others, a little more realistic, believed the wooden superstructure and the steel-work of the wide ceilings could be kept in place, and in succeeding years all that would have to be done would be to replace the ice blocks. But no such renovation has occurred.

By the first week in March, the party was over, the spirit dispersed, and the joy expended. Tourists were heading for other diversions, and local stars of the grand skating rink were tiring of their own figure eights and daring leaps. No one could recall an earlier or a warmer spring than that of 1896. After three months of existence, what had been the grandeur of a splendid palace had been reduced to a puddle of slush and mud. The Leadville Crystal Carnival was officially closed on March 28.

"See, I told you so. The damn thing melted," some hind-sighted, "armchair" visionaries said. Sure it melted. Ice usually does that when winter is over—even at ten thousand feet.

"Big waste of money, it was. Everybody lost their asses on that foolishness. No doubt about that." It would be hard to argue the fiscal aspects of the undertaking.

"So, why bother—why spend $140,000 to build something that's going to end up being a five-acre mud puddle?"

Now that's easy to answer. Why bother to build anything, whether it's a three-month palace or a six-hundred-year empire? It will all end up as mud puddle or something worse.

Eldon Dedini, the famous cartoonist and artist of Carmel, California, told me about something that happened when he and his two elderly aunts were touring Italy. They were wandering around the Roman Forum one day, the very place where Edward Gibbon sat over two hundred years ago and was so inspired that he spent the rest of his life writing *The Decline and Fall of the Roman Empire.* The two women came hurrying over to Eldon in a state of obvious distress and disbelief. After calming them down, he asked what it was that had gotten them so upset. "Well," exclaimed the older of the two, "right over there beyond that ancient wall there are three Italians pissing on the ruins." Why build an empire if it's just going to end up being used as a urinal?

If the ancient Greeks were right about eternity, Sisyphus is still rolling his rock up a hill on some Hell's Island in Hades. It's hard to tell just how long it takes him to struggle from the base up to within a few feet of the crest where invariably he slips and has to go back down to start over again. By the measure of our own experience, his cycle of futility could be equated with either a single day, a lifetime, the duration of an empire, or the entire epoch of humankind.

So, who needs a celebration? Who needs to create or just build something for the hell of it? Who needs an empire or an ice palace or a rush down a toboggan run? Who needs to drive a wedge beneath the backside of the boulder it is our task to move, take a break, and try to enjoy the richness of life that can accompany the toil?

That summer the dandelions were as pretty as roses, and the wine was delicious.

19

Strike Two . . . and You're Out

In the summer of 1896, the Silver Panic of 1893 continued to depress the economy of those who were in the business of stock manipulation; the miners were still making $2.50 to $3.00 a day; and the mine owners were more intractable to the demands of labor than ever. A strike was inevitable—there were too many forces at work to avoid an impasse and an eventual confrontation.

It started back in 1880, when the first strike managed only to maintain the status quo. Most of the miners had walked out. But after all their efforts at organization and unification of the local proletariat, they eventually walked back in at the same wage to work the same ten-to-twelve-hour shift as before the grand adventure. Some of the mines called an eight-hour shift a day's labor, but they were the exception and had done so before the strike.

If indeed the paranoid perspective of history is correct and the strike of 1880 was part of a plot by mine management to suppress the labor movement before it grew too strong, then the same Machiavellian logic might have been at work a decade and a half later when the second major dispute began to materialize. But there were other forces involved as well, and the resolve, organization, and resources of the miners were different. Times were not as simple as they had been. The strike of 1880 can be simplistically called a conflict between the greed of the owners and the naive expectations of fairness by the miners. To this standard equation of capitalist versus proletariat, in the case of the second strike, we must add the effects of the crash following the Panic of 1893 and the world's lessening demand for Leadville's standard precious metal, silver.

The Silver Panic had its precedent back in 1880 when Tabor, Chaffee, and Moffat manipulated the limited glory of the Little Pittsburg Mine to their advantage and to the tune of about 2.5 million bucks among the three of them. Eighteen-eighty was the year when silver mining was at its zenith in Leadville. In real value, over 11 million dollars worth of carbonate ore was extracted while many more millions of dollars were mined from the investment districts of Denver and New York. Chris Bradley, Clear Creek County's archivist, calls this practice "corporate mining" and has said that most of Colorado's great mineral fortunes of the nineteenth century were the result of such speculation. The problem with paper profits is that somewhere at the base of all the shuffling and lies there had to be a fellow with a pick and a shovel producing some genuine ore, and at the other end of the process there must be a real demand for it. When either component was weakened, all the beautifully engraved stock certificates Wall Street could print weren't worth any more than Confederate dollars.

In 1880 the direct connection between supply and demand was broken when the Little Pittsburg Mine ran out of high-grade ore. As a result, those whose livelihoods were based upon speculation were stuck holding the certificates. In 1893 the opposite end of the supply and demand continuum proved catastrophic to the banking community. As a prime early example of the presence of a global economy, consider what happened to the silver market due to a decision made on the opposite side of the planet from Stray Horse Gulch. In 1893 the British colonial government of India decided to stop purchasing silver to mint their coins and created a huge reduction in the demand for the mineral. This had a radical impact on the value of this increasingly less-precious metal and was a factor in the repeal of the Sherman Silver Purchase Act that had guaranteed a market for silver ore.

Some had seen it coming, others didn't know any better, and a few notable silver barons apparently had chosen to ignore it. In any case, as the culminating event in a series of devastating financial developments, the Silver Panic of 1893 finished off Horace Tabor and a number of his colleagues.

While some of the big names in Leadville were toppled by the panic, others of less renown picked up the pieces and kept the district going. John Campion and J. J. Brown, to name two, were instrumental in the resurgence of the economy in developing mines to tap gold deposits on Johnny Hill.

In the meantime, steady as ever, the miners had agreed to accept a conditional reduction in pay down to $2.50 a day. The stipulation was that when the price of silver returned to 83½¢ an ounce, a condition that was unlikely to occur during the working lives of most of the miners who were affected by the agreement, the old rate of $3.00 a day would be reinstated. A labor union document from this period estimated that the minimal living expenses for a mining family were about $65.00 a month, while the average income for a man working twenty-four to twenty-eight shifts a month was about $75.00. It didn't take much of a financial setback to burden a family with debt from which it could not recover. The Leadville miner was still staving off starvation by a little high-grading and a lot of labor.

Once again conditions were ripe for revolt in the mining camp. A strong labor organization, the Cloud City Miners Union, was formed; the mine owners established an intractable position, refusing to even recognize the existence of the union as a negotiating body; and on June 19, 1896, Leadville's second mining strike began.

There were major differences between the strike of 1880 and that of 1896. The earlier strike was short lived, lasting only twenty-three days. The second dragged on for a grueling eight months. During the first strike, at least a façade of communication existed between the miners and the mine owners. In 1896 the mine owners, rigidly adhering to a secret agreement, refused to even enter into a semblance of negotiation. The most dramatic difference between the two disputes was that the first was for the most part non-violent; the second erupted into what some eye-witnesses described as an all-out bloody battle.

On September 20, there were explosions and fires at the

Coronado Mine, considerable gunfire and resultant casualties, and by the time the episode was over the miners had lost another strike. Whatever public support they might have enjoyed was destroyed by acts of violence and, particularly by the unintentional killing of Jerry O'Keefe, foreman of Hose Company No. 2.

O'Keefe was an east-side Irish Catholic. He didn't like working for $2.50 a day in the cold, damp mines any better than any other miner. He jumped at the opportunity to work for the city of Leadville as a member of the fire department. He was, as were most Leadville boys, a strong, hard worker endowed with a work ethic: do a little more than you are asked and be loyal to your boss. Everyone seemed to like Jerry. Most of his friends were Shanty Irish and many of them were miners, but some of them were his buddies at the fire department.

Jerry O'Keefe went to work with a heavy heart on the morning of September 20, 1896. His neighbors and closest friends (the miners) had given him a hard time the night before. Some had accused him of selling out to the bureaucrats down at City Hall. They asked him how he could line up against his own friends who were only asking for a twenty-five cents a day pay increase. Some questioned his working for a fire department that was willing to do whatever A. V. Hunter, a powerful businessman, politician, and founder of the Miners Exchange Bank, told them to do when even Mayor Nicholson was on the side of the miners.

Jerry O'Keefe had only one answer, "I fight fires with a fire hose; that is what I am paid to do."

O'Keefe was a victim. When the fire broke out at the Coronado Mine (started by the miners), the guards hired by the mine owners manned their posts. O'Keefe, the foreman of the firefighters, moved into the "no man's land" with fire hose in hand. Some of the miners started shooting wildly in the air. The guards, who were badly trained, had been told to return any shots, and shoot they did. O'Keefe was mortally wounded in the cross-fire. The state of Colorado, the mine owners, and the managers all blamed the miners for O'Keefe's death. Edward Blair, in his book *Leadville: Colorado's Magic City*, writes:

The city council and community, by unanimous, though not official, consent, determined to give Jerry O'Keefe a hero's burial. His death in St. Vincent's Hospital, his family and friends around him gathered, was faithfully reported in the local newspapers. The Excelsior Lodge of the United Workmen, in which O'Keefe was a member, handled the details of the funeral. The city council agreed unanimously to pay all costs and asked that as many of the militia companies as could be spared participate in the funeral ceremony.

The O'Keefe family agreed to the arrangements for financial reasons and also because the city council, who had employed O'Keefe, agreed to invite the Colorado State Militia to participate in the funeral to avoid an escalation of the tragedy. The militia had been called up very early in the morning on September 21, the day after O'Keefe had been killed.

But in Leadville in 1896, before you had an Irish Catholic funeral, you had an Irish Catholic wake. The young Irish compatriots of O'Keefe got permission from the family to have a wake for Jerry, and therein lies another well-kept secret of the town; the event wasn't recorded in any of the city newspapers or journals.

Mayor Nicholson, on the afternoon of the twenty-first, held a community meeting in the Tabor Opera House. As a result, a large body of community leaders asked the governor to declare martial law. A small group of Irish miners asked the managers if they could hold a wake for Jerry O'Keefe in the Tabor Opera House. The answer was a definite "no."

The miners arranged to have the Pioneer Bar closed at 8:00 P.M. on the evening of September 22, 1896, for its first and last wake, in honor of Jerry O'Keefe. It was by oral invitation only. There was to be no gambling and no selling of booze at this wake—for an Irish boy caught up in the cross-fire of bullets and contradictory beliefs. Many women, miners, and male friends of O'Keefe all came to the Pioneer that night. John Minor Larsh was there as a friend of Jerry's.

Before the dawn of September 23, 1896, the bar was opened to all the guests. Jerry O'Keefe was propped up behind the bar. The Irish miners became a choir that serenaded O'Keefe with the

Emerald Isle's best. A jig was danced on the walnut bar top to the strains of the Irish Washer Woman. The piano player played the beginning chords of a familiar song, silencing the crowd immediately. A clear alto voice changed the mood of all; there wasn't a dry eye in the crowd nor any that was not focused on beautiful Edith, standing alone on the balcony as she sang the ancient Gaelic song: "Oh, Danny Boy, the pipes, the pipes are calling . . ."

The story of Jerry O'Keefe is more than a Leadville Irish wake tale; more than a story of a conflict between laborers in the mines and the owners in the banks and the state house. It was the statement of a beginning . . .

All changes emanate from a vigorous re-evaluation, a reorganization of the paradigms. The little people of Leadville's east side were not conscious of cosmic laws when they organized a wake for O'Keefe in a new and creative way, but they nevertheless expressed the ultimate moral power that has been in evidence since the beginning of recorded history.

Kenneth Boulding may have said it best: "In this way, we may come to understand that there exists an independence of spiritual and mental growth which, though conditioned by circumstances, is never determined by circumstances." The miners articulated that philosophy in an unusual Leadville fashion at the Pioneer Bar that night. They were affirming a consciousness of the qualitative uniqueness of human life as a universal principle.

For all of the differences between the strike of 1880 and the strike of 1896, there is one critical point of similarity: The mine owners won; the miners lost. The box score would have read:

MINE OWNERS: 2
MINERS: 0

Leadville Baseball, 1947, front row: (left to right) Bill Brady, Ed Larsh, J. J. Coble, Al Berger, Leo Ryan, Bun Ryan. Back row: Bill Bodycomb, Glenn Lane, Kenny MacElroy, Kenny Reynolds, Jack Tanner, Pete Donoher, Earl Coulter, Bud Guy, Don Moffett.

Part 2

Being There: Looking Back

Leadville Baseball, 1948

20

The Silence of East Tennessee Gulch

Their real task was to find the song theme of the river,
Not study rivulet to rock the pattern of wear.
The course the river took and why not considered.
They wanted to find out the song of the river,
Lie on its banks and listen to its tones,
Discover which tones were music,
And which were just the tumble of rocks.
—FRED GEIS FROM "THE TONES OF THE EAST TENNESSEE"

Long before people, the connections began: the shifting mass of
rising mountains, the trickling persistence of waters, the universal
power of gravity; the rains and the snows, the dew drops condensed
by the chill of night, the secret sources beneath the rocks erupting
in the pristine clarity of springs. Thus commenced the gathering of
waters to flow down the sloping crevices and canyons of the land-
locked regions to touch the distant seas. Water is the transient yet
eternal force of the planet. Where water is, there is life.

Leadville, to be seen as an art form, cannot exist without life
blood—the headwaters of the Continental Divide. In pulse of
freeze and thaw, gather and flow, the seasons are the beat of
nature's heart.

Tennessee Creek is neither wide nor long. It begins on the
crown of the Continental Divide and ends just short miles downstream where, in confluence with the Arkansas River at Leadville

Junction, it contributes its substance to the continuity of all waters. Leadville Junction is where the Colorado Midland Railroad crossed the Denver & Rio Grande—a place where water, railroads, and mysteries mingle and then go forth.

The source of the Arkansas is equally humble on the slopes of Mount Democrat above Fremont Pass. Meandering through meadow lands and cascading down deep-grooved ledges, it falls to the rocky slopes on which the town of Leadville is superimposed. The life-line waters of Leadville are ancient, persistent, and strong, for they reach the Mississippi and the Gulf of Mexico and the oceans beyond.

What do the truths of the wind and the elements, the creatures of the wild, speak of the collective consciousness of Leadville? What of the infallible logic of gravity applied to the procession of geology, the harsh discretion of predators expressed by the survival of species? What of the wisdom of field mice in fetal-ball slumber beneath the frigid snows? What of the will of mosses on the sunny face of reality?

And of humankind, with the loudest voice, that connived in greed to buy the world with gold and silver coin? The quiet voices owned the world with love and laughter. I can tell you of the mind and the heart that is the essence of Leadville, this life that lives by the blood-line of waters, the pulse of seasons, the mind of nature. I can tell you there are mysteries up the gulch of East Tennessee Creek— matters defiant of understanding, gifts left by the invisible winds.

Each year, about two weekends before Christmas, we enacted a ritual in my family. My dad and his brother-in-law Clyde would throw an ax and a saw into the trunk of the family car and head toward East Tennessee Gulch where, on the north side of the hill above the frozen stream, grew a large forest of Colorado blue spruce trees.

The ritual went something like this: Uncle Clyde and Dad rejected tree after tree as being too small, too wide, too narrow, graceless, wanting a proper top, too bushy, too sparse, or too perfect to take from the mountain; and after trekking through seeming miles of knee-deep snow, they would settle on the first tree they had spotted an hour earlier. They would cut it down and carry it to the car far down the mountain along the side of the road. Binding it to the roof with ropes, they would head triumphantly toward home, some ten miles away, knowing they had accomplished their important mission.

It seemed that, invariably, the carefully selected tree was too big for the corner of the living room and would have to undergo considerable alteration so as not to crowd the family out of the small house. I can still hear my dad and Uncle Clyde saying as they shook their heads, "I could have sworn that tree was just the right size." (Trees are always smaller in the great forests than they are between the walls of a living room.)

Often, having suffered the surgery of domestication, what had once been resplendent with blue-hued boughs, was transformed into a human attempt at improvement on perfection. At this point in the ritual, my mother would traditionally proclaim the tree to be the worst we had ever dragged into the house and disavow herself of any responsibility for its adornment. We would plead with her, for there could be no Christmas in our house if the Christmas tree were not blessed by her touch. Begrudgingly she would always acquiesce and say she might help out a little with the higher branches (". . . but it needs a branch right here").

By Sunday evening, with tinsel glistening and lights aglow, fragile ornaments hung in artful balance, and a snow-rug of cotton at the tree's foot, my mother, with tears in her eyes, would announce to all that this was undoubtedly the loveliest tree we had ever had.

All who live and love near nature know that there are places where the energy is different. Areas that give off a different vibration. Places where the silence is louder. In such magical zones exists a presence, an ambiance of indistinct mystery. East Tennessee Creek has that kind of special and disquieting energy.

When I was five years old, my father decided it was time I joined Uncle Clyde and him in the annual event and, along with the ax and the saw, they loaded me into the family car and headed for the spruce forests of East Tennessee Gulch.

In December snow is plentiful in the mountains near Leadville. As my dad drove up into the trees of East Tennessee Gulch, it was soon too deep to go on, even with chains on the rear tires. But, even before we stopped, I could feel the magic of the area, and I wanted out of there. When Dad stopped the car on the snow-packed road, both of them realized that the snow was almost as deep as I was tall. They'd have to leave me there while they went after a tree.

In one of those rare instances of lucid recollection of an event occurring in early childhood, to this day, I can still feel the uneasiness I felt as my father assured me that he and my uncle were just going to be gone for a short time and soon they would return with a wonderful Christmas tree. They amplified my fears by saying, "Now Eddieboy, there isn't anything to be afraid of; you are going to be just fine. You wait here in the car and we won't be gone long." The two of them departed with crunching sounds as they broke through the crisp snow and soon disappeared up the hill. There are places where the energy is different.

I lived in a house full of voices and the cluttered harmonies of dish sounds and sweeping sounds and the booming sounds of full laughter and spirited debate. I was unaccustomed to such stillness. The footstep sounds were gone and the mountain-wind sounds ceased. It was so strangely quiet and desperately lonely in the chilling car with the windows fogging over from my rapid breath.

I don't know the source of my fear. Perhaps it was in a small boy's creative imagination; perhaps it was just the first time I had known the full voice of mountain silence. I don't know why, but I can still feel the terror that overcame my most ardent effort at being Daddy's brave little boy.

I started screaming for my mother. Loudly. So loudly that my scream pierced the silence and climbed the snowy slope to where my rescuers were doubtlessly engaged in aesthetic and philosophical dialogue about "too bushy, too short, too perfect." They came rushing down the hill like deer before an avalanche, leaping and stumbling and tumbling into the haze of my tear-blinded vision.

My father was first, Uncle Clyde just behind him. The door was flung open, and my father hugged me in his arms to quiet me and said, "Don't worry, Eddieboy, we'll take you back home to Mama. It's all right, it's all right. We'll wait until you get a little deeper yourself before we bring you back again." I sat between them as we drove back down the road. They joked with me, and I didn't feel too bad about what had happened, though my thoughts were of my mom.

Beneath the ice trickled the waters of Tennessee Creek.

When we pulled into the alley and stopped behind our house, my mother was waiting in the yard. I can remember her there in the snow. She was wearing an apron—no coat.

"What's wrong with Eddieboy?" she cried. "I could hear him calling for me. Is he all right?"

Over ten miles of rocks and ravines, rises of land mass and turns of the wind, in her heart she had heard my cry. The bloodwaters, the connecting waters flowed, pulsed by the driving seasons; the spirit-reach of a mother's love transcended the petty limits of the physical world.

I think of that day every time I drive over Tennessee Pass. The road up the gulch is still there. Whenever I am not too rushed by the demands of the day, I slow down and let the emotion of that marvelous day be timeless; a sense of awe and warmth settles over me. I am tempted to turn and drive up the gulch but never do. I fear that the years and the effects of scientific scrutiny may have changed reality.

I prefer to believe the same magical waters still flow.

21

Our Hearts Were Young and Gay

When I look down at the empty ball field from the porch of the house that was once my family's home, I can relive scenes vividly in all their sensuous and emotional detail. I can hear the honking horns, the crack of the bat, the rowdy good spirit of the grandstand crowd. There were so many great Sunday afternoons. I'll tell you about one.

It was the Fourth of July, 1934. Mom, Dad, my brother Donald, and I were sitting up on the porch watching Leadville play Salida. Skully was playing shortstop; Tony Yelenck was catching; Jimmy Connors was out in center field. The Bearcats got Salida out in the top of the ninth and came to bat down by six runs. It was looking pretty bad in Leadville (Mudville?) that day, but the team hadn't given up and neither had the crowd. A walk, a hit batter, a couple of singles, a new pitcher, a fly ball: one out. Another hit, a grounder to short: two outs. By the time Tony Yelenck came up to bat, we had runners on first and third, two outs, and were two runs behind. Then on a full three-and-two count, he pulled a line drive just inside third base, and it kept on going. The ball rolled over into the ditch down by Joe Sadar's house, and by the time the left fielder found it and climbed back up to field level, it was all over.

My mother was going crazy. Beating Salida on the Fourth of July by scoring seven runs in the bottom of the ninth was really too much for her. She went into labor. My dad called Dr. McDonald and gave Donald and me thirty-five cents and told us to go the carnival just up Fifth Street from the ball park.

We walked around the midway for a long time, debating the best way to spend our windfall. We kept circling back to the Ferris wheel and finally decided it would provide a thrill worthy of our investment. I gave the lady thirty cents for two tickets, and we stepped onto the platform. The operator, a burly sort with tattoos, a gravelly voice, and an attitude to match—a real malcontent—pulled the brake lever and growled at us to sit down. He locked the bar into place, and up we flew. At the very apex of the arcing flight, the great wheel came to an abrupt halt as another set of thrill-seekers climbed on board. Below us rocked the festive town; and, out and about us, the blue sky and mountain-peaked horizon circumscribing all the world we knew, rose and fell with the giddy swaying seat.

I leaned out over the side and spat, hitting the operator squarely on the top of his head. In a grand swoop we fell back and back, brothers of Icarus, to the mundane realms of the earth below. With an angry jerk on the brake lever our celestial journey was terminated at the end of but one revolution. "Get your asses away from here before I tan your hides," the irate operator shouted as he furiously rubbed his head with his free hand. We jumped from the seat and took off running. Donald was mad at me all the way home, even after I offered to give him the nickel I had left from the thirty-five cents Dad had given us. Come to think of it, to this day Donald might still harbor a bit of resentment over the incident.

As we climbed the stairs up to the porch, Dad met us with the news that we had a baby brother named Jack. It is only by the limited measure of physical reality that time is on an irreversible continuum. I can still clearly hear the honking horns, the crack of the bat, and feel the surprise at the news of a new brother.

By the time I was in my late teens, I was playing on the town team. Contrary to most of the dynamics of the community, it didn't take me long to realize that competing on the playing field transcended ethnic prejudices. It was only later I recalled that short-stop Skully (Frank Skala), first baseman Satchel Ass (Al Broadnick), and catcher Tony (Tony Yelenck) were Bohunks.

Later, in 1947, Jackie Robinson, who probably influenced civil rights in this country at least as much as Supreme Court Judge Thurgood Marshall, proved the premise that ability surpasses circumstance. He was one of the best second basemen ever to play the position. It also happened that he was the first African-American to play in the major leagues.

I recall the summer of 1941 and the seeming harmony of a parochial world. Times will never be so simple as they were one Sunday afternoon in July when we, the Leadville Bearcats, were in Aspen to play a game. Just as there were idiosyncrasies to the home field in Leadville, every other town we played in had its own ground rules due to a less than standardized notion of what constituted a baseball field. We were in the Colorado Rockies where a scarcity of level acreage dictated the conditions of play more than Abner Doubleday and his successors' visions of regulation. It often took five or ten minutes to elucidate the peculiarities of the park, interpretation of which the visiting team knew would always assure the home team an advantage.

We played in Oak Creek, where the field was level out to second base but then climbed straight up a hill so steep that not even the great Dimaggio could have played there with any sense of grace. Dimaggio was having a pretty good summer himself in another league as we all followed his fifty-six-game major league hitting streak on the sports page of the *Denver Post.*

It was pure Americana back then—the spirit of small towns combined with the sport of baseball. Over in Cripple Creek, they had a first-base umpire who robbed us on so many calls that Broadnick, after grounding to second for the third and final out of the game, upon hearing the ump's resounding, "Yer out!" shouted, "And so are you," and knocked him on his ass. The ensuing battle would have put a John Wayne brawl to shame, subsiding only when it spilled across the street to the bar at the Empire Hotel, where the idea of a cold beer on a hot day was sufficient to pacify the warring factions and quell the rhubarb.

But it wasn't a fight that ended the game in Aspen that July in 1941. It was a line drive.

Our pitcher's name was George Hiduck—we just called him Ducks. He was a good man and had held our opponents scoreless through two-and-a-third innings when he pitched a fast ball a little high, and this big farm kid from Carbondale lined it right off his forehead. We had to stop the game right then, load Ducks into a '34 Chevy, and run him down to the nearest hospital forty miles away in Glenwood Springs. It wasn't only that our pitcher had been knocked silly—he was fine the next day—but we had been ahead. I'd hit a "ground rule" double off the side of a barn in left field and had driven in a run.

It was just good baseball back then. Cripple Creek, Aspen, Oak Creek, Leadville—ball players were the same wherever we went. We won a few and lost a few and learned a lot. It didn't matter what your last name was or how you spoke English. The name of the game was baseball. What mattered was whether you gave those mountain Sunday afternoons your best shot.

By the end of summer I learned that there were great similarities among ballplayers, whether they came from Leadville, Aspen, or Cripple Creek—I didn't know much about New York or Yankee Stadium.

In 1941 Raymond Chandler wrote *The Big Sleep*, Dimaggio went zero-for-four against a pitcher no one had ever heard of; Ted Williams hit over .400 (no one has since); the Blitzkrieg was on in Europe; and I was working at the Climax Molybdenum Mine near Leadville. The summer faded into fall, and I decided to take Coach Paul ("Frosty") Wright's offer of an athletic scholarship to go to college at Western State. A classic example of alternative education: the alternative was to remain at Climax up on the Continental Divide near Fremont Pass, breaking my young back in the rumbling, dust-choked environs of Bartlett Mountain.

Western State College at Gunnison, Colorado, had four hundred students and a small cadre of caring faculty. Within the male population of students were two distinct factions. There were the men who took classes from Dr. Schuman, Miss Kansgen, and other academic-type professors who expected you to know the difference between "their" and "there" and the significance of dangling modifiers. The other group consisted of young men who were athletes—high risk, educationally deficient bodies, recruited from small towns by the lure of gridiron glory and "free" tuition. We were the sons of miners, farmers, smelter workers, and at least one printer.

My scholarship allowed me to work for my room, board, and tuition. In the present atmosphere of sports fanaticism, young stars are enticed by college scouts with offers of fancy sports cars. By contrast, I was given the keys to a garbage truck and the privilege of driving it around the campus for a couple of hours every morning before eight o'clock classes. I frequently smelled like garbage.

That fall of 1941, many of the young "Mountaineers" wore big heavy sweaters that bore the school colors and numerals designating the year they would graduate. Mine had a "45" on it.

I remember Ray Holman sitting on the large red couch in Ouray Hall and insisting that Gunnison was the greatest place in the world and that we'd all better appreciate it "now!"

In the fall of '41, before the world was forever changed, the air smelled different—something in the dim light of late afternoon was different then; it was a magical blending of the autumn chill, the aroma of smoking leaves, and the optimism of youth. It felt good to wear those crimson-and-slate sweaters with the numerals on them. Later, after the bombs and the blazing sea and the sunken tombs of Pearl Harbor, Frosty, our caring, loving coach, told us that war was not a game. He said crimson was the color of blood, and numerals the count of casualties.

I guess if I had to choose, I would say that the fall of 1941 was the happiest time of my life. I had escaped the mining holes of Leadville. I had matriculated at an institution of higher education—Western State College in Gunnison, Colorado—though it is true I didn't know how to spell "matriculation" much less know the meaning of the word.

That fall I successfully played some football, pledged into a local fraternity, and was a starting guard on the freshman basketball team. Coach Wright and Doc Taylor were looking out for me. I had made four or five close personal, life-long friends, especially

Paul Becker from Hotchkiss and Rodger Rigdon from Cripple Creek. I wasn't burning up either the athletic or academic league, but I knew with a little luck I could. Truly, in those brief days, our hearts were young and gay.

I can still remember ten of the boys who were waiting for the cafeteria to open on one December morning. We were standing around talking and looking off at "W" Mountain. The air was clear and cold—maybe five or ten below zero. The guys were all athletes, all in the Kappa Delta Mu Fraternity. Many were wearing their letter sweaters, all were young, and all were innocent. Rodger Rigdon and Paul Becker were there along with Lennie Stewart, a Cherokee Indian from Littleton, Ray Holman and Herb Kaczmarek from Milwaukee, Jack Neelan and Chuck Hitchcock from Pueblo, Bob Moss from Alamosa, and Ed Larsh from Leadville.

Doug Hoffman came running over from Ouray Hall. He told us an announcer had just come on the radio and said that a place called Pearl Harbor had been bombed by the Japanese and that the United States was at war. It was Sunday, December 7, 1941.

Before December 25 of that year, all ten of us had volunteered. Rodger and I took the oath at the Custom House on Nineteenth and Stout in Denver and then went home for Christmas vacation.

My mom called Thelma and Gene out in Oakland, California, and told them I had enlisted in the United States Army Air Corps and for them to get a train ticket because we were all going to have Christmas dinner at home together. She reminded Thelma to bring warm clothes for their baby, Jeri.

On December 31, I paid my second visit that year to the old Tabor Opera House. This time it was not for a graduation but for a party in what was once Horace Tabor's private suite. We danced to Duke Schultz's magic accordion, only stopping twice the whole evening, once at eleven for a moment of silence for departed Elks and then around midnight for "Auld Lang Syne." As Thelma and Gene and I all hugged and toasted the new year, 1942, we all knew things were never going to be the same again.

It is difficult to write about a time of innocence. It all becomes a mixture of memory and myth that might never have existed, and yet is as real as the pain of its loss. I suppose every generation passes through the lie of immortality and into the reality and disillusionment of frail flesh's decline. Ignorance or innocence, it doesn't matter what you call it. When it's gone, when you've passed from the economy of cupie dolls and jack knives to that of bank accounts and mortgage payments, to squirming burdens and the responsibility of diapers and college educations—you know an era has passed in your life.

For my generation, and, to a certain extent, for everybody who happened to be around at the time, our bitter enlightenment was somewhat more abrupt than the normal transition into the cynical realms of adulthood. The official date for the end of our innocence is December 7, 1941. This day changed the future for millions—most of them innocent victims. A few were born and grew up in Leadville. I was one of them.

It takes time to organize a massive war effort, and some of us were in the fray much sooner than others. Before Rodger and I were called, several of our buddies had already been killed. It was spring, and our sweaters had long been put away. We waited for our call to wear the uniforms of war. Word came that Ray Holman had been shot down over Germany—a numeral. And we heard Lennie Stewart had stalled out on take-off from an aircraft carrier and was lost to the slate-gray sea.

Innocence. Crimson and slate.

In April Rodger and I got our notice to report to Fort Logan in a week. We left Western State, and he went home to Colorado Springs and I to Leadville.

After several days at home, Mom and Dad drove me down to Colorado Springs where Rodger and I were to catch a bus to Denver at one the next afternoon. We stayed at the Rigdons' house that night. Rodger and I went out on the town for our last night of civilian life. We talked a couple of girls from Colorado College into going dancing with us by telling them we were juniors from Dartmouth just out for a bit of a tour of the West. They seemed impressed but almost caught us when they asked where this famous Dartmouth College was located. It was uncanny, Rodger and I almost on cue answered in the same feigned voice of amazement, "You mean you Colorado girls don't know where Dartmouth is?"

The next day, after we said good-by to Mr. and Mrs. Rigdon, Mom and Dad took Rodger and me downtown to the Greyhound Bus Terminal. We shook hands, we hugged, we cried, we said good-by, and they left. Rodger and I walked into the terminal and found out the bus was going to be an hour late so we decided to walk around the town while we waited. We wandered through the Woolworth's Five and Ten and, looking down the aisle, we saw Mom and Dad. It was strange. We had already spoken our farewell, and in this meeting of our eyes, the hesitation of the instant, there was absolutely nothing to be said. I looked into my father's face and into my mother's eyes, and my parents were gone.

I thought about that second farewell for the next three years. It came back to me later, after the war, when I read Ernie Pyle's book, *Brave Men*. There is a scene in the book where the mother is dying, and the young son, not knowing what to say, hopes his mother is proud of him. Before he can say anything the mother asks him, "Son, are you proud of me?" It occurred to me that in that silent moment at Woolworth's, my parents and I had had a similar moment of poignancy.

I remember an afternoon in 1940 after basketball practice, standing with Louis Horan at the corner of Seventh and Leiter. I don't remember what we were talking about, but I can still feel the air and still see Mount Massive filling the western sky, not as it does today but just as it did that precise day. Young Doc McDonald walked by on his way home. Don Moffett came by riding his Monkey Wards bicycle. It was a moment in which nothing memorable or significant happened—just one of the myriad moments that make up most of our lives. Yet it is locked into my memory as if it were some kind of mental time capsule.

Young Doc graduated from Leadville High School in 1939. Louis graduated in the spring of 1940. I was in the class of 1941. Don Moffett graduated in 1942, and my brother Don in 1943. Louis, along with his merchant marine ship, went down somewhere in the Pacific. Doc, trying to limp his B-29 into Iwo Jima, hit the same briny sea.

Don survived, and we played ball together for three years, start-ing in 1948, but it wasn't until 1992, in the Silver Dollar Bar, that Don, in his great easy way told me that he was one of the boys who landed on Iwo Jima on the D-Day when 5,000 other young marines never made it beyond where the Pacific meets the sands.

Don described jumping from the landing barge with an extra belt of ammunition wrapped around his neck and, being only 140 pounds soaking wet, sinking like a rock. His nearly drowning may have saved his life, as the lethal spray of the Japanese machine guns passed above his submerged Leadville Irish head.

Throughout the long war, in scattered conflict about the globe, those of us who had been college kids back at Western State in the fall of '41 kept the memory of that special time alive in our minds. The thought of crisp, clear autumn mornings, college girls, dances, coaches, classes, games, "W" Mountain, roommates—hearing the haunting voice of a nostalgia that could only speak through the pre-sent when it was forever in the past, I realized, in the lucid contrast of circumstances radically altered, that it was a time that no longer existed nor could it ever exist again. Perhaps it was the juxtaposi-tion of one short era of a life with the shock of the next that made it all seem so perfect. But, more than most of the remembrances that touched those warring days, I craved the scent of that autumn air, the simplicity of a crimson-and-slate letter sweater.

I was on Iwo Jima when the *Enola Gay* dropped "the Bomb" on Hiroshima. I talked to the crew after their return, and all they could say was that the war was going to be over soon. The nuclear age had begun. I had been serving my time with the Fourth Emer-gency Rescue Squadron of the Twentieth Air Force. Our mission was to fly around the Pacific in a B-17, spotting fallen flyers in sink-ing B-29 bombers and coordinating the rescue of survivors.

In succeeding weeks the action had all but ceased following the Japanese surrender on August 15. I went to my colonel and told him I had a brother who was with the Sixth Marine Division on Guam and requested permission to catch a plane and go see him for a few days. We were just sitting around waiting for notice to fly back home to the strains of "Sentimental Journey" and the "Stars and Stripes

Forever." It would be just a matter of time before we would be looking down again at the Golden Gate Bridge and San Francisco Harbor the same as we had when heading in a different direction three years earlier. The colonel, a man whom I had learned to respect, said he didn't want to be the first commanding officer in the Pacific Theater to be involved in case of someone going AWOL from an island four hundred miles out in the middle of nowhere. He told me he didn't want to hear any more about it but would expect to see me at breakfast in exactly one week. I felt like saluting, which was something I hadn't done for a couple of years. But I didn't.

I left my Quonset-hut quarters, walked over to the airstrip, boarded a plane, and flew to Guam. The Marines were easy to find. They were still sleeping on the dirt floors of pup tents, and when I got there a group was standing at attention while some sergeant checked how neatly they had made their beds that morning. I asked around, and they directed me to where I would find my brother. I counted the specified number of precisely regimented rows of white tents and walked into the area.

I asked a corporal standing there about Donald Larsh. He pointed and said, "That's him sitting in front of his tent."

I saw him.

Something terrible had happened. The last time I was with my brother, he had been a junior at Leadville High School—a curly haired, blond, happy, seventeen-year-old kid.

In the spring of 1942, Donald had convinced Mom and Dad to write a letter giving the Marine Corps permission to accept him upon graduation even though he wasn't yet eighteen. The Marines wanted a few good men but were willing to take a few good boys as well. In Donald's case they got both. Six weeks after graduation, Donald finished basic training at Camp Pendleton and was on his way to Guadalcanal, where he joined the First Brigade of the Sixth Marine Division, which was staging an invasion of the Mariannas and then Okinawa—and if there were any Marines left—on to some islands called Japan.

It's been almost fifty years, and he still doesn't speak about it. His unit received a presidential citation, and he was awarded three battle stars, a marksmanship badge, a good conduct medal, and an honorable discharge. He saw his buddies killed as they stormed the sandy beaches. He saw other young men wearing different uniforms fall before his rifle and his bayonet. He was a well-trained, fighting Marine, and did his job properly.

There is good reason why the young heroes who survive a war—old before their time—don't talk about combat in detail. They don't know what to say.

How do you describe your feelings when you are seventeen and huddled down in a landing barge after having spent the night faking bravery, not sleeping, making sure you have the bare essentials: your hand grenades, your rifle, your bayonet, and clean underwear (just in case you make it to the sand)? How to describe a night with buddies who are having the same thoughts as you but don't talk about them any more than you do? The landing barge is only going to go in one direction. You know the odds, and you also know the odds are better if you don't foul up. So you just do it. I don't believe any marine has ever made more than two such landings and stayed mentally and emotionally intact—the human mind just isn't that insensitive. You make your first landing because of your training, and it is a piece of cake until you realize you're in the middle of hell. The second, seasoned by experience, is horrible, damn near impossible. The third, fourth, fifth—it isn't you; it's somebody else using your body to dash through the exploding waters. You can train young men to kill, but you can't train the mind, the heart, or the soul not to be affected.

When Don saw me that day in August of 1945, he jumped up and grabbed me and threw me around and probably would have cried if he hadn't been a marine.

It was good that he knew me. I wouldn't have recognized him.

His hair was gone, his teeth missing. He looked very tired and much older than his nineteen years. He was extremely nervous. He still is. The malady that had so cruelly transformed the youth and vitality of my brother into the war-ravaged form I encountered that morning was not of germ or virus or wound of flesh. It was the physical manifestation of a wound of the spirit.

The war was over, and a world was ready to return to normal. A victorious army came home from Europe and North Africa and the Pacific. Sailors came home from the seas and airmen from the skies, and it was time for life to go on in peace and plenty.

In my moments of political anger, I sometimes think of the letter my dad wrote giving his permission for Donald to join the marines before he was of legal age. It was back before yellow ribbons became the public relations symbol of the U.S. Department of Defense (then more honestly known as the War Department). The country needed to be defended, Donald wanted to go, and our parents consented.

A question arises concerning the country's values and whom we honor as heroes. Maybe the heroes in the age of innocence were those who excelled in the context of games played by children, but in the real adult world of political sleaze and economic corruption where we become the victims of the high-tech media, we honor those who conform to the cosmetic spin. I don't know.

I do know that on a sunny morning in the late summer of 1945 on the island of Guam, I could have written the last line of Harris's classic baseball story called *Bang the Drum Slowly,* "From now on I rag no one." On that day, I suddenly felt much older as Donald and I looked over the pup tents at the coral beaches and out at the Pacific beyond.

I also knew something about the innocent heroes and victims.

Donald proved that, even though the experience had cost him dearly, had taken his youth and scarred his body, it didn't destroy his heart. He went ahead to get his degree at Western State, where he was a "four-way event" leader on the first NCAA Championship ski team. He became a good educator, a good husband, a good father.

Life went on.

22

1946, When Jack Was 13

Baseball has its rituals, but they have nothing to do with religious beliefs or moral structure or political power. Baseball is more akin to another human activity: art.

I went back to college after the war, and the following spring I convinced some of the Western State College baseball players to come to Leadville that summer and play against the Leadville Bearcats. The game was scheduled for the Fourth of July, 1946, in the ball park that I could see so well from our front porch.

It seems as if the whole town turned out that Independence Day. Cars were double parked up and down Sixth Street, the grandstands were full, and the Leadville team was raring to show us college boys how the sport of baseball was played. The Bearcats were a good team; I knew almost everyone of them. But our Western State squad was hardly a bunch of boys. We were all in our twenties; most of us had been through a war; and all of us were serious about the sport. Our catcher was Cy Rambo, who could fire the ball to second like a rocket; and Bill Andreas, the second baseman from Cripple Creek, may have been the best athlete ever to go to Western State.

In the first inning, with one out, Leadville had men on first and third and tried a double steal. As the runner on first broke for second, Rambo fired the ball to Andreas who immediately returned it to the plate where the runner from third was out by a mile. Meanwhile, the fellow who had been stealing second came on around and tried for third. Rambo burned the ball to me, I tagged the guy out, and the inning was over. After eight more innings of play, the final score was Western State: 7, Leadville: 0.

I said goodbye to my buddies, and they headed on out of town. Then I went over behind the grandstands to find my youngest brother, Jack, who was gathering up some equipment for me. The crowd had dispersed, and the place was almost empty. I stepped around the end of the stands and was greeted by a hostile gang of rather large young men—Austrians, Hungarians, Slovenians—a fearsome cross-section of Leadville's Bohunks. With a sinking sensation, it occurred to me that even though I was within a few hundred yards from my own safe home, I was deep in their neighborhood and it was obvious something was troubling them.

The spokesman for the group was a big smelter worker named John Bogunovitch. He had the courtesy to explain the nature of their dispute with me and, furthermore, took the time to give me the Bohunk version of the Marquis of Queensbury Rules.

"Larsh," he said, "you smart ass, you come over here from some farmer college with a bunch of ringers and try to show us how smart you are by making fools out of everybody. Well, now you don't feel so damn smart, do you?"

He had a point there.

"We're going to fight you fair and square—one at time and, guess what, I get to go first," he said, then tackled me. We were rolling around in the gravel, and either he had my head or I had his head, but whatever, it was going to be one hell of a long afternoon for this third baseman. Jack saw what was happening and went running to get Donald.

What occurred next is all mixed up in the horror of war and the rowdy, brawling innocence of baseball and the immortal stuff of families. Now that I think about it, John must have had me in a headlock because I still remember his letting go. We were there on the ground, looking up at Donald above us with the baseball bat that Jack had handed him. "Hold it!" he shouted with a voice right out of the South Pacific and, believe me, everything ceased. But it wasn't his voice that scattered the mob that day—though it's true when he explained to the circle of my adversaries that the rules had just changed, there wasn't a one who didn't hear and believe him. Nor was it my thirty-six-inch Louisville Slugger that struck such terror into their hearts. It was the metamorphosis they saw in the blond-haired, shy kid whom they remembered from high school just a few years back that sent them steadily shuffling down the streets and alleyways of the west side. His eyes were the eyes of Tarawa and Guam and Okinawa, the eyes of bloody beachheads. He didn't look tired and old as he had when I saw him on Guam. He looked fit, ready, and deadly as hell and, for the second time that afternoon, the locals realized the ball game was over in the early innings.

It was an heroic moment, and I was grateful for the rescue, but I think I might have been more frightened by what I saw in the eyes of my little brother than in the eyes of those who opposed us. It wasn't just a baseball game and a bunch of hot heads and sour grapes. Nothing could ever be that simple again.

Donald and I started up Sixth Street Hill with Jack trailing along behind us, carrying my glove and the bat that just moments earlier might just as well have been an M-1 carbine with fixed bayonet. All around us, the mountains were taking on the red glow of one of those great Mount Massive summer sunsets, the kind that only seem to emit their special light when you're close to home.

Our folks were sitting up there on the porch, and we knew Mom was happy. Her three boys were coming home up the hill to dinner. The pot roast was on. Jack's dog Lucky came bounding down the hill toward us.

El Dorado.

23

Rails and Rhythm

Imagine—you are eight years old. You have to get up at 4:00 A.M. this August morning in 1918. The whole family is going to ride the last passenger train from Leadville to Basalt, through the two-and-a-half-mile Carlton Tunnel.

Doc, your dad and the town dentist, has a sense of history. A friend has alerted him to this event, and he doesn't want his family to miss it. He gathers you three kids, your mother, and your grandparents in the kitchen and tells you what to expect. We are going to take the Overland down to the depot on Spruce and Fifth, he tells you. Then we will take the Stub down to Leadville Junction. We change trains there and catch Train number 3 pulled by Engine number 51, the famous engine that made the first run from Leadville to Basalt in 1887. The same engineer who was at the throttle that day is going to be the "hog" on our trip. His name is W. P. Bates, and he has promised me he'll let you kids ride in the engine cab after we leave Hellgate. The train leaves Leadville Junction at 5:25 A.M. and we will arrive in Basalt before 9:00 A.M.

Remember, the Colorado Midland Railroad has failed because of the war, he tells you, but that railroad represents what makes this country great. Pay close attention this morning; one day you will be very proud to have been on the last Midland passenger train. The Midland Railroad is the greatest railroad in the U.S.A.

Bill Rose, or Doc Rose as he still likes to be called (with his father and grandfather, he represents ninety straight years of dental practice in Leadville), did remember that morning, and he told us about it sixty-four years later.

You can get an idea of his trip by taking a Jeep over Hagerman Pass, or better yet—you can walk from Leadville to Basalt. In either case you go up past Turquoise Lake, around Windy Point where a Midland engine once went over the precipice, then up to the Carlton Tunnel, past Ivanhoe Lake on the northern slope of Mount Massive, and on down toward Hellgate. From there it is all downhill through one of the most beautiful valleys in the country: green hills, red rocks, and the cold, clear water of the Frying Pan River.

You can see the Schuck cabin on your left, and then on a bit is Doc Rose's house on your right. Soon you will see the Seven Castles, a colorful rock formation. As you pull into Basalt, you see the old Midland Depot. It is now a bank. If you are a bit sentimental, you might shed a tear.

Trains are still the backbone of America's freight-hauling system, but few serve people anymore. Hundreds of railroads across the continent have gone the way of the Midland—fading in the memories of old-timers and into the history books and into the hearts of the rail buffs who walk the remaining roadbeds. Amtrak provides the only passenger service, and it misses most of the country—including a small town called Leadville.

The railroads, for better or for worse, opened the continent. The West would still be "that vast frontier that will take a thousand years to develop," as Thomas Jefferson said in 1804. Technology and economic growth proved him wrong by nine hundred years.

Colorado and Leadville were major stages in the drama of westward movement. Leadville, because of its mountain-top existence, was a costly addition to the network of railways that eventually unified the whole country. When the railroad finally arrived in Leadville in 1880, it opened convenient access to thousands of people and made the movement of goods and ore more economical and efficient. Competition for freighting minerals inspired the romantic folly of the Midland Railroad as it fought its way up Ute Pass near Colorado Springs, across South Park, up the Arkansas to Leadville, and then, amazingly, right over Hagerman

Pass to the Frying Pan River and down to Aspen—one of the great American engineering feats of all time.

The Colorado & Southern was equally ambitious. It followed Clear Creek up from Denver to Georgetown and there executed the famous Georgetown Loop up to Silver Plume. It also had an inner loop connecting South Park by way of Boreas Pass, where during one run the crew had to use the elephants from the circus they were hauling to push the train over the top of the four-per-cent grade. From there the C&S crossed over to Breckenridge, Kokomo, Robinson, Fremont Pass, and Leadville.

The C&S came to Leadville after the Denver & Rio Grande. It created a right of way down from Fremont Pass to enter on the north side of town. After years of steaming up the mountains from the plains, the railroad finally brought the track across Graham Park on the northeast side of town, an idea the competing D&RG did not exactly approve of. On the morning the C&S engine arrived with men and materials for the last section of rail coming into town, the crew was met by a large party of men, mules, and equipment from the D&RG intent on plowing under the new tracks at a junction for an intended spur line. But the newcomers had been forewarned. Fifty men jumped off the C&S train and, using rails as battering rams, staked a claim to the right of way. The C&S then brought in seven armed men to guard the track. It was a close call, but the dispute was finally resolved without violence.

No connecting trains are left in Leadville, where once the tracks served every mine on Carbonate Hill. No passenger service joins Leadville to the world. You can go down to Malta and wave to the engineers as the freights go by with their load of automobiles for the West Coast, but the rest of the tracks have all been pulled for salvage.

When the first train arrived in Leadville in July 1880 with U. S. Grant on board, it was met by literally dozens of brass bands as well as a one-hundred-voice choir. By now you know we are shameless sentimentalists who seek unity and meaning in connections that may not be obvious, who constantly try to "see" rather than to just look. We have "seen"—or rather, heard—something while thinking about railroads and history and remembering our last train ride, barreling through the landscape, listening to the 2/2 beat of the wheels on the rails. It is the connection between trains and music.

The steam engines and the rails connecting America at one time were the ultimate in technology, but this industrial wonder was built on the sweat, blood, and lives of slaves and poor workers. Having no part of the wealth and grandiosity that the railroads represented, they responded with all they had: their bodies and their voices. They danced, sang, imitated, clapped, and interpreted what they saw and what they heard. Gandy dancers working on the rails regularly sang the blues to the strike of spike hammers. African culture was the source of the blues, but the rivers and the railroads helped give it locomotion and made it jazz.

How many people have stopped for a moment at the sound of a distant train at night, reflecting, perhaps unconsciously, on the chilling, existential loneliness of the sound? Quilling, the art of train-whistle blowing, gave and still gives voice to the dismal dark. How many souls have sung in two-part harmony with that mournful sound? And how many songs have been written from that nearly universal experience?

It was in the saloons where songs like "Those Gambler's Blues" made their appearance and left an impression lasting until today.

> *It was down in old Joe's bar-room*
> *On a corner by the square,*
> *The drinks were served as usual,*
> *And a goodly crowd was there.*
>
> *On my left stood Joe McKenny,*
> *His eyes bloodshot and red,*
> *He gazed at the crowd around him*
> *And these are the words he said:*
>
> *"As I passed by the old infirmary,*
> *I saw my sweetheart there,*
> *All stretched out on a table,*
> *So pale, so cold, so fair.*

"Sixteen coal-black horses,
All hitched to a rubber-tired hack,
Carried seven girls to the graveyard,
And only six of 'em comin' back.

"O, when I die, just bury me
In a box-back coat and hat,
Put a twenty dollar gold piece on my watch chain
To let the Lord know I'm standin' pat.

"Six crap shooters as pall bearers,
Let a chorus girl sing me a song
With a jazz band on my hearse
To raise hell as we go along.

"And now you've heard my story,
I'll take another shot of booze;
If anybody happens to ask you,
Then I've got those gambler's blues."

The lyrics of such songs are often the result of borrowing lines from other songs or poems and making them fit. The first verse of "Those Gambler's Blues" was adapted from the poem, "The Face on the Barroom Floor," a nineteenth-century folk poem. The third verse is the same as one in "St. James Infirmary Blues," a later improvisation. And the fourth is from a version of "Frankie and Johnny," which goes back to when women first found out about men. In every case, the lyrics speak a similar theme of a sublime despair, and whether sung by a black man in New Orleans or a sultry white woman in Leadville, they all tell the truth of the blues. They all have a steady rhythm, and they all are moving on—just like the railroad that brought them all the way from Rampart Street to State Street.

From the beginning music was a rich part of Leadville, whether performed on the stage or in the orchestra pit at the Opera House, in the bars of State Street, or in the parlors of houses all over town. Scores of wagons coming into Leadville before the turn of the century had, strapped against the sideboards, upright pianos that eventually found their way into family homes.

The town was full of piano players—and an unbelievable number of marching bands. Every major organization in town had a band, and some organizations were formed just as an excuse to have one. During the first miner's strike in 1880, within a few hours of the walk-out there was a massive gathering of miners and a parade down California Gulch and right up the middle of Harrison Avenue, all accompanied by the driving rhythms of a hastily assembled marching band. Later, in an effort to show solidarity (along the route to ignominious defeat), there was another march to the accompaniment of the cacophonous sounds of five different bands. In the 1880s, someone wrote that it seemed nothing could be accomplished in Leadville without at least one, and often several, marching bands blasting away. Leadville might have been short on summer days and certain other luxuries, but from its earliest times, there was no dearth of pianos, trumpets, or trombones, or of people willing to wail away on them.

In the early days, John Philip Sousa and band played the Tabor Opera House. His opening number was "The Stars and Stripes Forever," followed by the "The William Tell Overture." That night, all eight hundred seats were filled, not just with the typical, habitual, theater-goers, but with a sizable number of miners and smelter workers and their wives. Under the spell of Sousa's music, all the people there felt a surge of patriotic unity. It wasn't until they left the driving tempos, the trilling piccolos, and the powerful brass, and headed back to their separate ethnic ghettos that the reality of heritage and cultural bias was reclaimed.

The Irish on the east side, the Swedes up on Chicken Hill, the Austrians on the west side—they all played the music of their respective "old countries" and, once the radio entered the scene, the music of the new country. The Irish played it loudly. The Swedes were a bit more restrained and Lutheran in their touch. The Austrians mixed it up—the fast tempo of the polkas and the oom-pah-pah of the Tyrolean regions were all there, but so were the classic strains of Mozart.

Once, on a train trip, looking about me at the diversity of my fellow passengers, I had an image, almost a vision, of all humanity as a band or orchestra, every race, every class, every individual even, playing a separate instrument—but all in the same band. If we could only play together! I saw the train trip as a song, as a metaphor for a possible harmony of peoples.

When the piece starts, all the players are in line: marching, singing, drumming together. Speaking their many voices, piccolo shrill and bass bassoon mellow—with percussion-driving, wood-wind-winging, violin-reaching mellifluous, Lord-praising, flag-waving, soul-saving gifts for the world. Whether crescendo bombast, woodwind sigh, a bluesy seventh, or battalion halt—it's the whole band that plays the show. And, when the maestro drops his baton, the show is over.

When the locomotive stops, all the cars of the long train with all of the passengers arrive at the same time. The woman with her kid who sang "One Hundred Bottles of Beer on the Wall" for the past fifty miles, the delegation from the convent, the soldier looking like a child beneath his freshly shaved scalp, even the man who owns the railroad—it's end of the line for all. "Everybody off!"

For a final moment on the platform, regaining the stability of static earth, we're all still in the same band, and the song we all played just ended for all of us at the same time.

There's something wonderfully egalitarian about that last beat.

24

From Sea to Shining Sea

The view of the mining district from our front porch was directly over the ball park. Looking past the town, if you have a discerning eye, you can note the difference between Carbonate Hill and California Gulch. There are very few mine dumps in California Gulch. Most of the minerals taken there were mined on the surface by sluice box and placer techniques. However, this area is not without blemish. In the 1940s and 1950s, the Resurrection Mining Company dumped its tailings in the lower part of the gulch, filling the watercourse with a fine white material so chemically sterile that even dandelions won't grow in it. Only in relatively recent times has concern about the pollution of the head waters of the great river systems of America gotten serious. The toxic threat of Leadville's mine-tainted waters is connected by the arterial system of the continent to the Arkansas River, the Mississippi River, the Gulf of Mexico, and the Atlantic Ocean beyond.

However, there are places potentially more dangerous than the watershed of Carbonate Hill and California Gulch: the zinc mines near Gilman on top of Battle Mountain and the Climax Molybdenum Mine up on Fremont Pass.

The town of Gilman, located on a ridge dropping down from the top of Battle Mountain between Minturn and Redcliff, is Colorado's best-preserved ghost town. Just a few strenuous, mountaineering miles to the north is the town of Vail. It can be extremely difficult for tourists to get reservations in this expensive mountain resort, but reservations in Gilman are impossible. It was abandoned when the Gilman Mine closed in the 1960s and has been sitting up there in a strange, suspended state ever since. Large gates prevent access to souvenir-seeking vandals. Seen from the highway, this deserted town projects the atmosphere of a science fiction movie set. When you look at its rows of empty white houses and the brick school building and see the swings on the playground eerily blowing in the wind, you could believe the whole population was spirited away by encounters of the "Third Kind." To add to this sense of the uncanny, consider that the whole community rests on a grassy slope just steps from the Eagle River—the last step of which encompasses a drop of 1,500 feet straight down the face of a sheer rock canyon. The children who grew up in Gilman were not allowed to ride tricycles!

It was here the Eagle Mine allowed the poison of its metallic waters to spill from its operation and plunge down the mountain into the upper waters of the Eagle River and on into the Colorado River system of which it is a tributary.

The whole town was for sale, but lawyers suggested that along with homes, schools, and avenues, purchasers might well be acquiring responsibility for its environmental impact. So Gilman sits on the precipice, guarded by steel fences and the EPA.

Terry Fitzsimmons reminded me of the not so distant past in reference to the Eagle Mine at Gilman:

The impacts of the Eagle Mine, its mine drainage and tailing ponds are real and are being addressed. That is as it should be. Ed, you and I remember going over Battle Mountain and down to Glenwood Springs when we were greeted by the sight of numerous "privies" built out over the banks of the crystal clear upper waters of the Eagle River. During the winter mounds of human waste accumulated beneath each outhouse. Each spring the snow melt runoff filled the river and washed the feces downstream into the Colorado River system. Who forgets the smoke-filled community of Minturn and the snow banks turned dirty black from the cinders and soot as steam locomotives double and triple teamed long freight trains over Tennessee Pass? The "privies" and locomotives were inherent to the Eagle River Valley from the 1890s until the early 1960s. Perhaps it wasn't quite as pristine as we would like to think.

The Climax Mine is a very different story. It is a victim, an industrial-age giant caught in a western mining scenario, written as usual by the global economy.

The mine itself is on the crest of the Continental Divide. Directly in front of the main gate that leads from Colorado 91 into the complex itself is a sign declaring the apex of the United States of America. You spill a cup of coffee six inches on one side of the sign and the atomic particles of the liquid will flow into the Mississippi watershed, six inches to the other side and the liquid makes its way down 11,000 vertical feet to the wide Pacific by way of the canyons of the Colorado River.

Dirt from the mines went to the crusher and then on to the mills and through the chemicals, the residue of which has stained the Mother Earth. We aren't talking about littering with two cups of coffee—Climax never did anything small.

From the mid-1920s until the 1980s, the Climax Molybdenum Company up on Fremont Pass was the predominant economic force in Leadville. For over half of this century, it has been the fate of the community to thrive or struggle as the world's supply and demand of this element fluctuated.

In the early days, molybdenum was mistaken for galena, the ore from which lead is extracted. It wasn't until a scientist in England examined the dark ore that it was determined to be molybdenum, a material suitable for producing an extremely hard steel alloy. Full-scale production up on Bartlett Mountain began in 1918. After years of complex litigation over various claims to the property, a crusher, a mill, and some miners' quarters were completed and a sixty-five-year venture commenced. During this span, the demand for molybdenum varied and the boom and bust, roller-coaster economy so common to Leadville was again the case. After World War I, a national labor shortage opened up more cultural doors at the Leadville smelters and up at the Climax Mine. It was then that a large Mexican-American population established itself on the south side of Leadville—having made its way up the corridors connecting Mexico with Texas: New Mexico, the San Luis Valley, Trinidad, Colorado, and Meyer Guggenheim's smelters. This Hispanic influx provided another element to the work force of Leadville's mining economy—joining the Irish, the Austrians, and the Swedes in riding the roller-coaster.

In the post-war economy, there was no market for molybdenum. Climax shut down after just over a year of operation, beginning a pattern of on-again off-again production lasting until the 1930s. While the rest of the country was flying into the twenties, masses of local miners were being forced to flee the hills. Leadville's population dropped from 30,000 in 1880, to 12,000 in 1900, to 4,500 in 1920.

From 1918 until late into the 1930s, the primary market for molybdenum was not the United States but Europe. The Weimar Republic, soon to become the Third Reich, was a legitimate market for this alloy that hardened steel. This fact signifies nothing other than that the business market around the world may have been headed for globalization long before the Japanese made a science of it. It is only in the afterglow that political embarrassment occurs.

During the twenties, Baby Doe hung on to the Matchless, water flooded the shut-down silver mines, and the price of metals dropped drastically. The Roaring Twenties had begun as a dry decade throughout the United States and, making the best of a difficult situation, Leadville converted Prohibition into its "best shot," called bootlegging.

The badger fights were revived, with the Irish still trying to get even with Denver. There was another Leadville mining strike, and again the effort failed. Miners returned to work for fifty cents an hour less than they had been making before they went out. The Pioneer was purchased by Mike Magone, and the Bartalluccis owned most of the girls on the line. Leadville was down again but not out. Prohibition helped. During the twenties and into the depression years, the price of metals remained so low that only gold was worth the effort of mining.

In 1933 Franklin D. Roosevelt came into office and, with realistic social programs, saved capitalism. Climax was up again and so was Leadville.

Climax was called "The Glory Hole" and for many years ran three shifts a day: day, swing, and graveyard. Safety and working environment were of little concern anywhere in the U.S.A. until more recent times, and consequently, the health of the miners suffered.

Danny Donovan, one of my closest boyhood friends, came to Leadville (interestingly enough, from Galena, Illinois) as a child. He graduated from Leadville High School in 1939 and went to work at Climax in the mine. He volunteered to be a hang-up man—the most dangerous job in the mine—because it paid an extra twenty-five cents an hour. His friends talked him out of it. The life expectancy of a hang-up man was less than promising. Heeding the advice of his buddies, he quit a dangerous job and took on what, in those days, was also a deadly one, though not recognized as such—working on the crusher, the massive machine that turned rocks into powder. For two years he breathed tiny particles of hard rock. He went to war, survived the Battle of the Bulge with Patton's Third Army but then returned to his home country to die in a lonely apartment on Logan Street in Denver before he reached the age of thirty. Cause of death: pneumonia, bad lungs, "rocks in the box," silicosis, Climax, Leadville.

Leadville was not Climax, but Climax from the mid-1920s until the 1980s was a major part of Leadville. It was also a connecting force that influenced the Larsh tribe. My dad, trying to supplement a meager salary at the *Herald Democrat*, took a weekend job as a watchman at the upper compound of Climax. It was up there that my sister Thelma took some of her first steps in a walker— making her way up and down the long halls of the empty bunk house a few feet above timberline.

My Uncle John, Dad's brother, went to work in the mines up on Johnny Hill when he was fourteen years old. Except for a period when he lived in St. Louis, Uncle John stayed with mining the rest of his life. When they got back to Leadville from St. Louis, they moved into a little house on West Seventh Street. John and my mom's brother Clyde claimed a few acres up on the south shoulder of Mount Arkansas and spent the summer of 1935 looking for gold. They pinned their hope for riches on the family story about my grandfather's brother, Charles Larsh, stumbling over a piece of quartz that was entwined with wire gold while walking from Alma to Leadville in 1880. Most of the families of Leadville have similar stories. Every gold-mining town in America has similar families, and the El Dorado search will probably continue as long as there are people to pass on stories. Uncle John and Uncle Clyde had a great summer up on that ridge, but the elusive mother lode is still undiscovered. It proved to be Uncle John's last shot at working in clear air. He returned to Leadville and spent the last ten years of his life working on the crusher at Climax.

Thelma has a story about Aunt Margie, John's wife, that is part of family folklore. Soon after they moved into the house on West Seventh Street, Thelma suffered one of the major embarrassments of her high school years. She and a group of her girlfriends were walking past Aunt Margie's house on their way to school one morning; at the same time Aunt Margie was using a garden hose to give an enema to an ailing burro named Mildred. This incident, perpetrated by a relative and in front of sensitive young ladies, created a lasting impression.

Leonard E. "Gene" McMillin was one of my dear friends. He also happened to be my brother-in-law. He and Thelma were married on the front porch of our house in 1937. Gene's granddad was a wagon master after the Civil War, helping fellow immigrants move west. He finally settled in Texas. Gene's dad came to Leadville around 1890 and opened McMillin's Grocery on the corner of Fifth and Poplar. Mr. McMillin was an avid reader and passed his enjoyment of the written word on to his two sons. He would read to his family from the classics, ending the evening with a few verses of Robert Burns. Never did he forget Burns's birthday or the haggis (a favorite dish of Burns and all true Scots consisting of ground vital organs, oatmeal, and spices, boiled in the stomach of a sheep.)

Gene's dad was a very close friend of Frank Zaitz, Sr. They were both successful businessmen, and neither was ever seen in public in anything but a business suit with starched white shirt and neck-tie. Both were imposing men—well over six feet tall and on the heavy side of 250 pounds.

Gene liked to try to describe the smells of his father's grocery store: barrels of pickles, freshly baked bread, sawdust on the butcher shop floor. He would point out that Thomas Wolfe did it better in *You Can't Go Home Again*, but for Leadville, McMillin's Grocery was in a class by itself.

At the time of Thelma and Gene's marriage, Gene was working at Climax. Rather than earning a daily wage, he and three other men worked as contract miners, being paid by the amount of muck they loaded and removed from the lower colon of Bartlett Mountain. They drilled and blasted, cleared "hang-ups" from slopes, slushed out the ore, and loaded it in two-ton mining cars. Gene was not born to be a miner. He just happened to be a miner because he was born in Leadville. What else if you graduated from Leadville High School in 1932? The depression was in full swing. He wasn't a big man like my Uncle John. He was about five-nine and weighed only 135 pounds. Gene was more suited to be an intellectual—well read, quiet, and gentle.

One day in 1940 (by then he had transferred out of the mine and was working in the crusher) he walked out of the swirling granite dust into the fresh air of Fremont Pass, got into his '37 Chevy coupe, and joined the line of cars heading back down the thirteen miles home to Leadville. He stopped long enough to pick up Thelma and their little boy, Jeri, said farewell to all of us, and headed west for California. He never looked back.

Unlike Gilman, there is nothing left of the town of Climax to remind us that once it was home to hundreds of people. Climax is no longer a town, but it was—a cluster of houses, a gathering of people with all the elements of a community, and an autonomous commercial enterprise that even "minted" its own currency. Laytons operated the Climax Company Store where miners and their wives purchased the basic necessities for living with credit tokens, plastic coins bearing the name of the employer (Climax Molybdenum).

The miners called it "chit," and the pun was probably intended. Some of them spent most of the working years of their lives trying to break even on the debits they had accumulated.

During 1961 and 1962 Climax (the company) moved the entire community of Climax (the town) down the Arkansas Valley and planted it on the northwest side of Leadville. The population of the Leadville "metropolitan area" doubled. (The town's population remained the same because it didn't bother to annex the land that was to be the new subdivision—the loss in tax revenue has been significant. But then, Leadville had never been famous for its forethought.)

Fremont Pass doesn't look like it did when John C. Fremont came by in 1843. By the 1970s, the miners had blasted and slushed so much muck from the bowels of the mountain that it became easier to cave it in and turn the project into an open-pit operation.

To fully appreciate the extent of this visually disturbing crest of America, we'll take a drive up Fremont Pass from the Leadville side. Imagine a two-lane mountain highway rising in wide, sweeping curves up through the high meadows of the serpentine waters of the Arkansas River. All about you is the rich green of alpine flora and above you, in succeeding splendor, shoulder to shoulder stand the great peaks of the crest of a huge continent. You round another curve, and you can feel the strain on the car's engine as the grade steepens. Then, as you look up the road that climbs before you, there is the stark and horrid specter of a ruin, a crater where once a mountain stood. It is the denuded heart of a giant. On across the pass, another specter can be seen where there was a once green valley; it is now full of fine, white silt—the tailing ponds of Climax.

In some sections of the valley, the residue is five hundred feet deep and half a mile wide. During the second half of the twentieth century, Climax has poured millions of tons of tailings down a beautiful Colorado mountain valley and, in the process, has buried two authentic mining towns, Kokomo and Robinson.

The mining camp called Robinson was eighteen miles from Leadville, just over the Continental Divide from Climax on the back side of Copper Mountain and about twelve miles east of the

Mount of the Holy Cross. Robinson was an important early settlement and had a history similar to California Gulch. Placer and sluice boxes in nearby McNulty Gulch produced half a million dollars in gold in 1860. After the surface gold played out, the Ten Mile Mining District was deserted until 1880, when gold and silver deposits were discovered underground. As a result, a mining company was founded with ten million dollars of capital provided by sale of stock to the New York banking community. Mines—the Oriental, the White Quail, the Rattler, the Wheel of Fortune, and others—were built, and a town of two churches, a bank, a newspaper, a telegraph office, a few stores, and 1,500 people was established.

The Robinson folk were competing with Kokomo, another mining town that had sprung up two miles across Ten Mile Creek. Both towns wanted to be another Leadville. Neither could have known back in 1880 that the real competition was going to be a man-made volcano called Climax. The flow from the "Glory Hole" was not to be hot lava but sterile silt, the tailings of a massive molybdenum mine. Climax Molybdenum Company bought the entire valley and the towns of Robinson and Kokomo. They are still down there somewhere.

These towns were bulldozed and buried years ago. When I see them, it is through my mind's eye looking down from the peak of the Mount of the Holy Cross at a time that has long passed. What is visible today is the white and lifeless inorganic residue of the short-sightedness of expedience. It is only fair to add that none of us could see the future through the dust of industrial success.

One day in the summer of 1939, my dad (my first mentor) and the rest of the family piled into the '34 Chevy and drove to Robinson. Along the way up to Climax, Dad explained a bit of the history of Kokomo and Robinson. As we crested Fremont Pass on the narrow dirt road we could see Ten Mile Creek meandering down through the green meadow land with splashes of Colorado wild flowers glowing in patches of brilliant color amid the lush green grasses. Kokomo was a weathered wooden town of maybe a thousand people. Across the valley was a cluster of about twenty buildings in disrepair. "The town of Robinson!" my dad announced.

"Only two people live there now. Two old men, a couple of old miners. Let's go see if we can find them—I know them both."

As we drove around the abandoned stamp mill we saw Jake sitting on a piece of what was once a sidewalk. We stopped, and Dad struck up a conversation, reminding Jake of their first meeting in 1919 at the upper camp at Climax. Dad asked Jake how Willy was doing. Jake's answer is the part I remember most clearly.

Jake said, "Come on, Ditto," (Ditto was one of my dad's nicknames), "you know Willy and I haven't spoken a word to each other for almost four years now."

"I know about that," said Dad. "But I didn't ask about your conversations—I just want to know how he's doing."

"Okay, I guess. I see him everyday over there where the C&S Depot used to be. He ain't there today though—he meets somebody over in Kokomo on Saturdays for some damn reason I don't know or care about."

We left Jake still sitting on the abandoned sidewalk. On the way home I asked Dad what Willy was like. Dad said, "He's a lot like Jake—they're brothers. The two of them sort of look out for each other there in Robinson. They don't talk any more—they've probably said everything there is to say, but they still care."

Gilman is a ghost town. Climax, as a town, is a transplanted suburb. Robinson and Kokomo are memories. Climax Molybdenum Company (AMAX) is operating with a skeleton crew of less than two hundred as compared to the thousands it once employed.

Gene McMillin made a wise decision when he gathered up Thelma and little Jeri and left Leadville and its mines to seek his fortune in other climes. For most of the people with whom he worked, the decision was to stay, and they kept their jobs at Climax.

Over the years after World War II, working conditions and salaries improved, and hundreds men and women had long and fruitful careers up in the rubble of Bartlett Mountain. For those who are unfamiliar with a miner's lot, it can be easy to believe they spend their years in Siberian drudgery and then die. In fact, most of them, dating back to the first muckers of the 1870s and clear up to the present, are a proud bunch of hard-working, hard-living Americans who have enjoyed full lives and earned an honorable living. They are, in fact, us.

Though Climax (along with most of the mining operations in the world) has committed some serious offenses against humanity and nature alike, it also provided a livelihood for a fair portion of Leadville's citizens for most of this century.

Terry Fitzsimmons, who holds a brief for the Climax Mine as well as an executive position for AMAX, shared with me a document entitled, *An Overview of Operational, Regulatory and Environmental Factors at The Climax Mine.* Terry specifically clarified the status of the Climax Molybdenum Superfund site as of 1992. He felt the following needed to be expressed:

1. I contend that while visually disturbing, Climax poses no acute or chronic risk to the environment.
2. All water discharged from the Climax Mine is treated and brought to stream quality standards before it is released. There are *no* discharges to the Arkansas River or Eagle River drainages. Ten Mile Creek is the only receiving stream for releases from Climax.
3. Panorama photos taken years apart show that "the hole in the ground" was there before mining commenced. It is a glacial cirque.
4. In the 1960s the Climax Mine acquired the land needed in the Ten Mile Valley for its expanded operations. In that expansion Climax acquired the mines you describe: the Oriental, the White Quail, the Rattler, the Wheel of Fortune. For the first time in nearly one hundred years the acidic discharges from those mines began receiving treatment before release and fish returned to Ten Mile Creek.
5. The bonding and financial warranty requirements for reclamation at the Climax Mine are set forth by law. Should one fear that the company might declare bankruptcy and become unable to meet its bonded liability, consider that since Climax is a subsidiary of AMAX, *all* of the corporation's assets (financial and physical) would be used as required to meet Climax's obligations.

There is empirical data in the AMAX outline showing that AMAX has, indeed, taken seriously the responsibility of cleaning up the mess at Climax that resulted in large part from an American philosophy of the past that made victims of us all.

As we struggle for the reunion at home, there is some hope. Climax, now part of the large, diversified corporation called AMAX, has developed a new understanding of the balance that is needed between the "greenbacks" and the green hills. They are beginning to know that America's greatest natural resources are the land and the people.

I once had a friend who loved to fight. He would on occasion go into bars in Wyoming or Montana and quietly say, "You know, there is really nothing wrong with coyotes." You can get the same reaction in Leadville by saying, "I really like the EPA," or "Climax really never polluted anything." Fights in Leadville have never been hard to find.

25

The Waters of Leadville

Music or not, "heavy metal" is not a popular idea in Leadville. For those who deal with such things as the chemistry of drinking water and the toxicity of pasture lands, "heavy metal" leaves little inspiration to song.

The mining district that developed on the east side of Leadville looks very much like an elaborate creation in the sandbox of the gods. There are two geological elements that dictated the layout of Carbonate Hill, California Gulch, Johnny Hill, and the rest of the areas of excavation up Stray Horse and Big Evans gulches: slope and the effect of gravity. Roads into the areas follow the creases of streams and angle up the sides of steep banks as notches cut into the earth. First there were wagons powered by teams of horses or mules; then a network of railroad spurs for rail cars driven by the rhythmic pulse of steam engines; and now with the decline in operations and rails and ties pulled, a few diesel trucks with whining gears and rattling "jake brakes" haul the ore down to a makeshift loading ramp near where the Malta depot once stood. The cliché of ants on an ant hill must have occurred to generations of observers from the top of Mosquito Pass. Engineers surveyed the hillsides and mastered the cutting of the roads and roadbeds at grades to allow vehicles to overcome the force of gravity.

Two other factors, however, are vying for the driver's seat: time and water. Time in geological scale diminishes the influence of humans and their mining enterprises to an instant. For millions of years, the slope and the gravity have drawn the waters from the mountainsides down to the watercourse of what is now named the Arkansas River. Time and the movement of waters created the gulches and canyons. In a human moment, we have altered the topography of this region radically more than have eons of nature's sculpting forces. To paraphrase an old butter commercial, "We have messed with Mother Nature." Significantly so.

An incredible amount of water flows in capillary rivulets and gathers in the brooks, streams, gulches, creeks, and finally the river of the surface systems. Beneath the alpine meadowland swells an even greater volume in coursing subterranean streams. As inevitable as are the snows, so are the waters.

The word "pristine" refers to the original state of a natural setting, but it also implies a state of purity. Throughout the rocks and rivers of nature there are naturally occurring pockets of elements that are toxic to life forms. If the first ancestral pioneers entering this continent had carried Geiger counters on their trek across the Bering land bridge on their way to Alaska and points south, they would have heard them ticking frantically on many occasions as they passed through or settled in regions high in levels of ambient radiation. And, doubtless, the more recent Indians who hunted and foraged the high mountain lands between what are now known as the Mosquito and Sawatch ranges, collected a minute flavoring of lead and zinc in their livers from drinking the sparkling waters pouring from the upper meadows of the Arkansas River system. Pristine doesn't necessarily mean one hundred percent anything.

When, in 1860, the prospectors began altering the flow of those waters for the purpose of extracting gold from the stream beds and surface soils of California Gulch, a process began with potentially disastrous implications for the environment of the immediate area as well as for a fair portion of the continent and even for the great waters of oceans. Well over a century before the rise of such persons of dubious fame as rock musicians, when the miners of Leadville began their rocking, they got right into heavy metal.

Hydraulic mining in the nineteenth century was a technique that employed large, steam-driven pumps to force great quantities of water through nozzles that looked like canons. (In some applications, rather than using pumps, water was tapped high up the mountain above the mining area, and high pressure was developed by the head of water flowing through a series of smaller and smaller pipes). The force of the water was powerful enough to blast the surface soil and dislodge more gold. The same civil engineers who built the access roads then became hydraulic engineers and channeled the voluminous waters into ditches and back into the surface system—water along with sand, gravel, and whatever not-so-precious elements had coexisted with the gold: most notably, lead.

The polluting effects of surface mining were only the beginning of the careless course of local history that eventually has led to "Superfund" toxic cleanup designation by the Environmental Protection Agency.

Leadville's second mineral boom came in the late 1870s, long after the rich deposits of surface gold had been depleted. This time the ore was mined from tunnels bored horizontally from the vertical shafts that dropped hundreds of feet beneath ground level. One of the most expensive items in the operational budget of deep mines in the silver belt has been the removal of underground water. Without the constant use of pumps, in a short time the shafts filled with water. A measure of the seriousness of economic threats and labor disputes over the years has been whether management determined them to be of sufficient influence or duration to justify shutting down the pumps, allowing the mines to flood. It was an expensive proposition to keep the machinery running when little or no ore was being produced, but the process of draining a flooded mine could take months, or, as in the case of the downtown mines after the strike of 1896, more than two years. (During the months of the strike, the mines filled not only with water but also with deposits of sand that had to be removed before any profitable activity could resume.)

Just ask Smiles Doyle, who spent much of his career as the state mining inspector. He knows the Leadville mines. He told us about the water level in the mines. The Matchless is down near the bottom of Big Evans Gulch. There the shaft is 365 feet deep before you hit the water level; the Canterbury Tunnel drains the water above that level. As you go up the hill toward the Ibex, the shafts are deeper before you hit the water. The gold is in the deep shafts where the tunnels are below the water table. Water, more than the depletion of minerals, is what has done in the Leadville mines.

Smiles Doyle, an Irish miner who was born up on Brooklyn Heights (the hill above California Gulch at the end of Harrison Avenue), worked at one time at the Empire Zinc Company in Gilman. He also helped build the Royal Gorge Bridge in 1929, not caring whether he was a thousand feet above the ground or a thousand feet beneath it. Ask Smiles—that is, if you can get a word in edgewise.

There was an engineering solution to the problem of underground waters: drainage tunnels. The idea was to bore a tunnel down slope from the mines that would allow the waters to drain. The first of these tunnels, the Blow Tunnel, was somewhat successful in unwatering mines on California Gulch. It was later purchased by the Yak Mining, Milling & Tunnel Company and extended, reaching the shafts of the Ibex complex on Johnny Hill in 1904. This project, renamed the Yak Tunnel, proved to be quite effective.

Over the years other tunnels were proposed, and some of them, to varying degrees, were completed. During the 1920s, John Cortelleni and other promoters of the local economy created a corporation to build the Canterbury Tunnel in an effort to remove water from the Prospect Mountain area and the lower mines of Big Evans Gulch and Fryer Hill.

John Cortelleni struck it rich in Leadville, probably many times, but the money he made by hitting pay dirt never built political mansions on Capitol Hill in Denver. The Cortellenis lived up on West Eighth Street; he was the mayor for twenty years. Cortelleni ventured into staking miners who remembered hitting veins of ore in shaft number two, or in the same "golden stairs" that geologically climbed the Ibex. Cortelleni was aware that every miner who had gone underground in Leadville knew a story about where there were nuggets as large as baseballs; consequently, when he would hit it big, he sank much of the money he made into another hole in the ground. The trouble with a guy like Cortelleni was that he knew that the stories really could be true, but you had to be lucky.

John never put it all back; he always drove a fancy family car. One of the last strikes he made was in the 1930s. The people of Leadville knew it because one day old John came driving up Eighth Street in a brand new, blue Pierce Arrow sedan. John could scarcely see over the steering wheel. He was sporting a snappy fedora and a big black cigar.

The Cortelleni strike just before the Pierce Arrow purchase involved about ten other miners. One of the ten was Bill Kerrigan's dad, who owned King's Grocery. Kerrigan came home that day, announcing that there had been a rich strike, perhaps as much as $60,000 for each investor. "Where is the money?" asked Bill and Eddie's mother. The response was typical, "Oh, Cortelleni knows where we can triple it!" Gambling towns are like that.

The problem with a tunnel was that to be most useful it needed to be dug as far down the slope as possible in order to undermine waters at maximum depth. Tunnels at higher elevations can be valuable in that you may hit gold, but you don't drain deep mines with them. The most practical location for a drainage tunnel was deeper than most of the mineral deposits. The Canterbury is just another hole in the side of the mountain now—its well-intentioned developers, frustrated by minimal returns, were forced to abandoned it. They struck only water. Tunnels can drain more than water.

Most of the mines are still full of water. But the tunnels were not so ineffective that they have not succeeded in spilling the poisons of the rock heart of the mountains into the watershed of the nation for the better part of a century. In the last decade of the twentieth century, the waters continue to flow from the shafts and tunnels of the sloping land and into the Arkansas River.

We can't say at what point people in authority realized the seriousness of polluting the water. As far back as 1881, there were those who argued that a little foul water was something the citizens of Leadville should gladly abide as a by-product of the privilege of having a local industry. That the mine-tainted waters might have effects beyond the wells, front yards, and pastures of Leadville and the surrounding area was not given much attention until the communities down on the plains that had purchased the water rights began realizing what they had bought. The Arkansas-Frying Pan water project was to have stored and routed much needed waters through the high mountains, west to east, down to the thirsty developments of Denver and its surrounding sprawl. It has been only recently that towns like Aurora have learned you can take the water out of Leadville, but it's not so easy to take the lead out of the water.

The discharge of the Yak Tunnel flowed for decades with little notice. Then for a few years there was a terrible "surge," and the old Yak literally spilled its guts for sixteen miles down the Arkansas River. The deposits of years of falling waters—rock, minerals, silt, and whatever else happened to be carried along with the steady flow of subterranean waters—built up dam-like obstructions within the tunnel. Pressure developed behind these "adhesions" until the inevitable persistence of water drawn by the might of gravity blasted through them with such force that the accumulated residue of decades spewed from the mouth of the tunnel and discolored miles of river rock downstream. Geologist Ben Arndt told me it was like turning on a water tap after it has been unused for a long time— you get something that looks more like a rusty nail than a crystal clear glass of Rocky Mountain spring water. No matter that the discoloration was the yellow-orange tint of ferrous contamination rather than the dark gray hue of lead, the Yak Tunnel had "come out of the closet" and became the focus of national attention.

Throughout mining history, the paper profiteers and entrepreneurial masterminds of exploitation have taken the silver and the gold, the lead and zinc, the molybdenum, the water, and, most significantly, the money out of Leadville. A nation has reaped the hard rock harvest of the ravaged hills and mountain sides of Lake County and has left little more than residue in its stead.

But now there is this matter of an environmental mess to be cleaned up, and suddenly what had been a national resource has become a cosmic blight.

Edith Seppi, long-time Leadville friend, civic activist, and historian, owns ranch land out on the flat where California Gulch flows to the Arkansas River. Her land has been polluted from both the early hydraulic mining and the later tunnels. Though there has been rechanneling, she can trace the original, meandering course of waters from the gulch by concentrations of lead and also by deposits of gravel just inches beneath the topsoil of her pasture. Other sections of her land that were not contaminated by California Gulch have elevated levels of lead and zinc as a result of irrigation waters via drainage tunnels and the Arkansas River. It seems that the complex water problems of Leadville come to focus on her property. She sees the need for a long-range solution to the problem that will require a major financial commitment on a national scale.

Edith and I spent a couple hours in the office of Neil Reynolds discussing a wide range of historical and contemporary issues related to Leadville's determined, yet haphazard course from the nineteenth into the twenty-first century. Neil is both an outspoken advocate and critic of his hometown. Just because he loves the place doesn't mean he has overlooked its faults. He describes the history of Leadville as, "a history of missed opportunities"—opportunities to develop a broader economic base than just that of mining, to annex sources of tax revenue, and generally, to deal with the future in terms of strategy rather than desperation. "It's like a television picture. We only need to fine tune it—we don't have to throw out the set and buy a new one. It could be so much better if we did a little adjustment rather than going off in a whole different direction."

I asked Neil what should be done about the environmental situation. As with most residents of this community, such a question evoked some strong opinions of the Environmental Protection Agency's handling of the problem. He believes the difficulty lies in applying eastern techniques to a western problem. Superfund moneys are being used to pay lawyers to assess the blame rather than correct the problem. "When, in the late sixties, someone realized you couldn't put your hand in the Ohio River or it would eat your hand up—they would go to Proctor and Gamble or whomever it was, and they could find the pipe that was draining into the river and they could demand it be turned off. They could shut the valve and that would help. The eastern part of the U.S. is much different from the West. The West has the resources; the East has the money—that's the way it's always been. The way the environmental legislation is drafted, we can punish Proctor and Gamble for polluting the Ohio River, so why can't we punish anyone who ever owned this land? Well, it doesn't work that way when you're dealing with natural situations; so why go through all of this—through the court, suing everyone and his uncle who has a sixteenth interest in a mining claim? Why should they have to be penalized and dragged into something like this?"

And his solution? Use the money to isolate what the problem is, build a treatment plant at the confluence of California Gulch and the Arkansas River, channel in the draining tunnel waters, and forget it. In other words, take the advice the miners have been giving at every EPA meeting since it all started.

Neil may be right, but perhaps we need to learn from the past and then practice our selfish interests on a larger scope. We, indeed, need to think globally and act locally. Caring for the future by understanding the truths of the past would help the EPA; it might also get us all into a common cause. It might be called, "Getting the herd headed in the general direction of west."

I asked two very different people about pollution and history. One was Bernard Smith, who owns ranch land down in the Arkansas Valley in front of Mount Elbert and Mount Massive. He said the water system there is so polluted from the mines that his grass is poisonous—he cannot raise cattle anymore. Bernard's family goes way back. The Smiths, along with their relatives, the Starr family, are some of the oldest families still living in Leadville. Bernard thinks that someone who deprived his family of the use of their land should be held accountable.

Then I talked to Vine DeLoria, Jr., a noted Native American writer whose family goes back a much longer way in the land now called the U.S.A. He wanted to talk culture. He said the white man should be proud; they took a river near Cleveland, Ohio, from the

Indians and in a short time the river caught on fire. Vine didn't seem to want to talk about the Arkansas.

There is an important point that needs to be made. The vast majority of the waters of Leadville are not troubled. Leadville, like any area of the country affected by the Industrial Age, has its water problems, but it also is a region of marvelous water resources. Throughout its delightful summer season, people from all over the United States and from foreign lands settle amid the trees of the Sugar Loafin' Campground in tents, and trailers, and travel homes—not to contemplate the ills of man but rather to take pleasure in and extol the blessings of nature. It has been that way since human beings first discovered the enchantment of the streams and forests and mountains of this region.

I'll tell you about the lakes of Leadville. Twin Lakes are the largest of them. At Twin Lakes there is probably one of the most impressive juxtapositions of mirror-smooth mountain water and spectacular mountain peaks to be found on this planet. My father courted my mother along the shores of those beautiful waters. The sixteen-mile trip down the Arkansas Valley was ideal for a Sunday outing.

We need to create a romantic vision of a perfect Sunday—romantic in the sense that art and poetry are romantic when they enhance the raw materials of reality with the touch of the human spirit. There are artists who, in trying to capture the essence of the West on canvas, have created images of such depth of color and intensity of gleaming light, and exaggerated proportions of mountain landscape as to project a vista of dreamlike unreality. It would seem that, by comparison, the real thing would be a disappointment. But it isn't. Granted, the painted peaks are sometimes more Himalayan than they are Rocky, and the clouds and canyons and foreground pioneers seemingly illuminated by the radiance of the gods—but there are real moments when the mountains tower like Titans and, aglow in late or early sunlight, become unbelievably rich in vibrant hue.

It is an early Sunday morning in the summer of 1905. In a rented buggy, my father and his favorite girl are poised on the crest of the last knoll before the dirt road drops down to the wide waters of Twin Lakes filling the vista below them. Mount Elbert and La Plata Peak—masses of jagged gray granite, trimmed by shadowed faces of winter's lingering snows—seem to rise and touch the infinite blue heavens of an entire universe that encircles the moment. Eddie Larsh and his best girl Lillian—with a basket of fried chicken, the warmth of the good sun, and the love in their hearts—owned the world for a little while on a perfect Sunday morning.

In a time when people were lucky if they got one day off a week, in a climate where the warmest season was a short-lived celebration, summer Sundays were really special. Eight miles west of Leadville, just off a circular route referred to as "The Loop," is an area called Evergreen Lakes—a cluster of five, not large, but beautiful natural lakes surrounded by trees. It was a popular spot for tourists as well as locals. A couple of big old wooden hotels stood out that way: the Evergreen Lakes Resort Hotel and the Mt. Massive Hotel at Soda Springs. People would come into Leadville by train, where they would be met by buggies and driven out to the hotels for vacations.

Sundays were not taken lightly in those days before World War I. In all the old pictures, the women are wearing fancy dresses and big hats, and the men are in coats and ties and bowlers. The first section of road heading out to the Loop was Leadville's version of a boulevard. It was a mile long and must have been half a mile wide. There were many who with curried horses, polished tack, and spotless buggies would don their finest threads and join a convivial promenade of fashion and style for a few turns about the "boulevard"—a roadway that was so immaculately maintained that "there was no place for a horse to stumble, not even on a straw." I picture it as a mid-summer, horse-and-buggy version of what Irving Berlin had in mind as an "Easter Parade."

And for some then, as now, Sundays were for fishing. Pollution and the EPA aside, any account of the waters of the Rocky Mountains would be sinfully incomplete without fishing stories. The waters around Leadville are still some of the best trout waters in the mountains.

I am reminded of a story about the fish my dad kept on ice in the window of the *Herald Democrat*. Before the Midland pulled its tracks in 1918, Leadville people could catch the train and ride up past Turquoise Lake and through the Carlton Tunnel to Lake Ivanhoe on the north side of Mount Massive. It was a great fishing lake, cold and deep. This lake is the headwaters of the Frying Pan River, a short, wild stream that spills on down below the railroad grade through Hell Gate on its way to Basalt and the Roaring Fork Valley.

Mom and Dad spent a Sunday afternoon fishing at Lake Ivanhoe in the summer of 1916. Dad was using an ordinary fly rod with a big brass spinner and a freshly dug angle worm camouflaging a sharp hook. Mom sat back and patiently watched; she wasn't much on fishing herself but always enjoyed going along. Dad was fooling with his line—he thought he had snagged a railroad tie—when the tie started to fight. It took over an hour but, with Mom's help, he landed an eighteen-pound trout.

Of course, that next morning he wanted to show it off, and he knew how to do it. He took a large pan from home and on the way to work stopped to see Old Man Cole at the Leadville Ice & Coal Company for some ice. He put the ice and the giant fish in the pan and set it right in the store-front window of the *Herald Democrat* along with a freshly printed sign that said, "18 pound trout caught by Ed Larsh on a #14 Rio Grande fly—Tennessee Creek." That day Dad was called everything but an honest man (the fish was almost as wide as Tennessee Creek itself) until he confessed where he had actually hooked the huge trout.

Fishing season used to start on May 25. Most Leadville boys over ten declared it a Tom Sawyer holiday—school was nearly over anyway. From those early days on, Dad loved the sport, and he was a good fisherman.

His Uncle Art was also a fisherman when he could get away from his mining ventures. In 1905, the year Dad graduated from Central School, the two of them decided to go fishing over at

Taylor Park near Tin Cup on the Western Slope. Art asked my dad to go along, explaining that he had staked out a claim over there and had to make some improvements on it every year as required to maintain possession.

In early July, Art and Eddie took the train to Granite, unloaded their packs and fishing poles, and hiked up Clear Creek to Vicksburg. The next day they climbed over the Collegiate Range and on the third day emerged at the east end of Taylor Park. They found the little tributary of Illinois Creek that flowed into Texas Creek, and from there they hiked to the log cabin Art and another prospector had constructed two summers earlier.

Dad used to say it was the best summer he ever had. The country was big and wild; they hardly saw any other people the whole time they were there. And, in the solitude, the two of them discovered what each had to contribute in creating a harmony of respect. And the fishing! In those cool summer waters there was such wonderful fishing! Within a few miles were so many streams it seemed they could fish a different one every day.

They stayed through July, and then one morning in August they saw the first warning sign of winter—the west side of the giant peaks of the Collegiate Range appeared with crystal white tops. Uncle Art announced they would break camp the next day and head for Vicksburg and then Leadville.

Dad said he had been homesick for a couple of days in the beginning, but when it came time to go home he didn't want to leave. He was sure he would never return. As they packed their gear and prepared to leave, Art, sensing the finality of an idyllic interlude, called Eddie over to the cabin and suggested they not take their fishing poles and, that way, they would be sure to come back the next summer. Eddie, with the first smile of the day, asked how they could hide them so no one happening by would be tempted to help themselves. Uncle Art suggested that they tie them to the top of the ridge pole of the cabin.

In 1955 I was back in Leadville visiting the folks, and Dad told this story—one more time. I asked him if we could take my Jeep and go over Cottonwood Pass by Buena Vista and see if we could find the campsite and maybe even the cabin. Certainly we could find Illinois Creek. My brother Jack was there, and the three of us decided to give it a try.

At first, nothing seemed familiar to Dad as we passed the turnoff to Tin Cup, then spotted Texas Creek. After checking a topographical map, it wasn't long before we were following Illinois Creek across the vast western plateau called Taylor Park near the back side of Mount Princeton. Dad didn't need the map any more. The land was the same. There were no visible signs of human "improvements"—no "golden arches" or condominiums in sight. Within our limited view of the world that afternoon, little had changed since August of 1905. Dad said he thought the cabin was just up beyond the next curve of the creek.

Our excitement was such that we could have been adventurers finally approaching King Solomon's Mines. We started hurrying as we rounded a little knoll, and there was the cabin.

The roof was gone, there was no door, the windows were like wooden "Vs." We stepped into the rectangular area that had once been a sturdy log structure and were standing within what one could almost call a sacred space outside of time: a zone that transcended exactly half a century and became the reality of a thirteen-year-old's memories of a favored uncle and fellow fisherman and a magical summer.

We had started to leave when Jack came up with the idea that, though the poles would have gone the way of the timbers, maybe the furls—the metal eyelets through which the line is threaded—might have survived. Jack looked at Dad; they both looked at me; and we all climbed into the middle of the roofless log cabin. The three of us spent half an hour sifting through the rotted rubble in the center of the cabin site searching for little circles of metal.

Fifty years is a long time.

We didn't find anything, but it wasn't really so important. None of us, especially my father, needed verification of the great fishing trip of the summer of 1905. It had survived fifty years in the vivid truth of Dad's savored recollection. It would have been nice to have come up with some furled metal evidence from the ruin but, as my old friend Wee Willie Wilkins used to say, "It' ain't a bad story the way it is."

The waters of Leadville are still flowing. The beautiful mountain waters still convey the essence of Nature through the arteries of a continent, communicating a message that transcends both history and bureaucracy. And what is the message of the waters of Leadville?

"Remember me. I call to you with Nature's powers and beauty. But, also, I am your golden rings and silver goblets, your guns of war, and the silks in your closet. I am your great granddaddy's stock portfolio, and I am the quenching cup to be sipped by your children's children. Ignore me and you ignore your own future."

26

The Sixth Street Irish

When asked how he managed to go broke after making a fortune, John D. Morrisey replied, "I spent my money on horses, gambling, women, and whiskey. The rest I wasted."

On a rainy summer afternoon not long ago, I was driving up West Eighth Street when I spotted Bill Kerrigan walking along in the late afternoon drizzle. I immediately pulled over and shouted at him, "Hey, Bill!," and he replied, "Ed!" Then the two of us were standing there in the middle of the street locked in a bear hug. I told him, "Kerrigan, you're just the fellow I need to see. We're writing a book about our hometown, and I'm going to include the Bohunks and you Shanty Irish in it—a book about Leadville's real people. I'm writing about our grandparents and parents and the people and stories we grew up with."

The Kerrigan brothers, Bill and Eddie, have been friends of mine most of my life. I knew their mother's family had come to Leadville with the early immigrants. I also knew both of them are proud to be Irish and love to tell a good story. Bill is an educator and for years was, in my estimation, one of the best school superintendents in Colorado and certainly the best Leadville ever had. Eddie has remained in Leadville as a local entrepreneur and miner. He served a term or two as mayor and has been on the city council for years. And, speaking of service, he also served drinks across the hardwood bar of his tavern, the RAM ("Ragged Assed Miner") throughout the Climax molybdenum boom of the 1960s and 70s—a man of many talents.

I asked Bill, out there in the middle of the street in the rain and, fortunately, little traffic, "So when did your grandfather first come to Leadville?"

He smiled, and I knew I'd gotten my last word in for a while. The East Side Irish are like that. If I'd had any sense, I would have waited until we were out of the road and the rain before I got him started.

"It was back in 1880 when my grandfather on my mother's side left Ireland and made his way to Leadville. He got his first job up at the Wolf Tone Mine, starting with a wage of two dollars a day. He was the first of my family to get here. Times were really bad in Ireland then, and he was determined to bring all seven of his brothers and sisters over to Leadville. You know how much money the miners made around here in those days—at most three dollars a day—and yet, in time, he was able to save enough to send each one of them money for their passage. In some cases he paid more than three hundred dollars to get from County Cork to Leadville, Colorado."

It was raining hard by then. I knew it because I was getting wet. Bill didn't know it because he was talking and he was Sixth Street Irish and didn't give a damn if he got wet or not. I was just about to ask him how three dollars a day could accomplish so much when he said, "I'll bet you're wondering how he did that on three dollars a day—especially remembering how he had a house full of little children to feed as well."

I nodded.

"'High-grade' and a large lunch pail," he said with a big smile, and we both stood there laughing until he started telling another story.

"High-grade" is a term that officially describes any sample of ore of exceptional richness. "High-grade" for miners refers to the gold nuggets that find their way into a mucker's coverall pocket or lunch bucket rather than into the management's ore bucket. It is a kind of inside joke that outsiders know about. There were assayers in Leadville who made fortunes paying miners a percentage, usually less than ten cents on the dollar, of the value of the gold high-graded out of the mines.

This is not to say Bill's relatives or his peers were thieves, secreting stolen gold right out from under the trusting eyes of the people who were "generous" enough to provide them with the opportunity for an honest day's labor. It was more like Johnny Larsh gambling down at the Pioneer Bar during those same years. You would not only be a fool if you didn't know where some of the aces were holed, you would also be the only player at the table who didn't. For the most part, the miners of Leadville were honorable men whose values were compromised by a dishonorable predicament. As part of the business equation used to determine what a day's pay would be, it was obvious that management considered any wages enabling a worker to more than barely break even while living a most austere existence were excessive. Whenever there was the possibility of a reduction in the inflated, boom-town prices in Leadville, such as when the railroad was about to connect the town with easier access to markets and lower freight rates, management immediately threatened to adjust wages down to conform to a lower cost of living. Consider what a message of hopelessness such a concept of economy sent to the workers.

So, you're down there in a tunnel, and timbers are creaking, and you've been busting your ass for nine and a half hours, and rumor has it they're about to cut your pay by twenty-five cents a day. Now what's that glimmering in the shadowy depths before you as you trace the vein? Just another piece of gold heading for the mill, or is it a dollar or two toward your family's food?

There's a story about a Leadville miner who got fed up with the high altitude and the rough winters, so he took his family back to Pennsylvania where he went to work in the coal mines. His wife threatened to quit packing a sandwich for him if he didn't stop high-grading a lump of coal in his lunch pail at the end of every shift. Old habits are hard to break.

But there was more to it than money. More than picking up a few extra bucks, it was a matter of dignity. It's a lousy system where people have to steal to maintain their dignity, but that was the world in which the hard rock miners found themselves.

Bill's grandfather was a refugee from the potato famine that had devastated Ireland for decades, and he was overjoyed to find any work at all. There were elements of the camp—particularly the Welsh miners who had been hired for their experience and others who had come to Leadville to claim their slice of El Dorado—who resented the Irish for their willingness to accept low wages and long hours with no complaint. The fact was, the Irish immigrants had seen such difficult times that they knew it best to first take whatever they could get, and then make the best of it.

There is no indignity to hard work, but there is indignity when payment for labor is insultingly low. Times were not so bad that people were starving but, considering the difficult and dangerous nature of the work and the lucrative margin of profit enjoyed by the elite few, distribution of the wealth was less than equitable. To give an idea of what three dollars a day would purchase in Leadville in 1880, consider that it took a man working a ten-hour day an hour and ten minutes' labor to buy a carton of eggs at thirty-five cents a dozen. A pound of coffee averaged about an hour's work, a pound of sugar about forty minutes, and a decent bottle of whiskey could cost a man two full days of drilling, blasting, shoveling, and keeping an eye out for two-ton bits and pieces of the mountain that could easily crush him. By comparison, at a conservative wage of ten dollars an hour, a miner in the 1990s can buy his dollar-a-dozen eggs in six minutes, his coffee in fifteen, and a bottle of Jack Daniels in less than an hour and a half. The ratio of work to purchasing power in those days was less than desirable, but, again, it was not impossible to get by—we have third, fourth, and even fifth generations to prove it.

The next time I saw Bill Kerrigan I made sure we were out of the rain. Jane and I met him at an Italian restaurant in Denver where Bill, with that great Irish twinkle in his eyes, said, "Ed, I've got something you may be interested in and, if you are, you can use it in the Leadville book. A few years ago, maybe forty, Eddie and I got together with Mike Donovan—you remember Mike, strong as an ox, used to compete in the mucking contest . . ."

"Sure," I told him. "I remember Mike and his brother Johnny."

"Well," Bill continued, "we wanted to be sure the Irish were remembered, so we put together the thoughts and remembrances of our folks."

"Are you interested?"

I grabbed it out of his hands and said, "Is the Pope Catholic?"

Sidelights on the Irish History of Leadville
by William Kerrigan, Edward Kerrigan, and Michael Donovan

In its earlier days, the city of Leadville had a large Irish population. The majority lived on the east side of town, with a particular concentration on East Sixth Street. The six hundred block was almost solidly Irish with people from all parts of the "Auld Sod." There were all types, variously described as Shanty Irish, Stovepipe Irish, Far Downs, Ordinary Irish, and Cleator Moors.

The latter group emigrated from Cleator Moor, a coal and iron mining town in Cumberland, North England. These people had lived in an Irish community, however, retaining their Gaelic ways and customs. They were Irish to the core and resented being called English. "Far Down" was the appellation given to the people from Ulster, in the north of Ireland. The terms "Stovepipe Irish" and "Shanty Irish" probably refer to the people who had stovepipes on their houses and those who didn't.

Although there was a clannishness among the folk from certain counties of Ireland, all areas were well represented, and no particular group predominated. The Irish, as a whole, got along well together, with a few sports here and there just to liven things up.

In those days the domiciles passed far beyond the present city limits. There were several houses in Stray Horse Gulch, above East Fifth Street. The lower end of Stray Horse was often referred to as "Cleator Moor Gulch," as a number of people from Cleator Moor lived there. There were more Irish people scattered through Adelaide, Graham Park, and Oro, the settlements northeast of Leadville, and south of the city in Stringtown and Bucktown.

Carbonate Hill, more familiarly known as "Chicken Hill," at that time was known as an Irish neighborhood. According to some accounts, the Swedes lived first in the vicinity of West Chestnut Street. (Some old-timers maintain that there always have been Scandinavians on Carbonate Hill.) There were numerous immigrants from County Cork on Chicken Hill and several in the Graham Park District. One segment of the Graham Park Corkonians had a reputation for boisterousness and had a habit of emitting blood-curdling war whoops on their way to town to celebrate a weekend. This led to their being nicknamed the "Utes." Mike Keefe's Saloon of East Sixth Street was the favorite hangout of the boys from County Cork. Keefe's regular patrons weren't quite as obstreperous as some of the other barroom hangers-on of that era.

The oldest of the pioneer Irish families are the Starr and Smith families, members of which are still living in this area. The first Thomas Starr settled in California Gulch in 1860. He operated the Starr Placer, using hydraulic power to wash the gold-bearing gravel down from the hillsides. This was a profitable operation at the time. According to tradition, the first Catholic Mass said in Lake County was celebrated by Bishop Machebeuf in Tom Starr's blacksmith shop, the largest building in the California Gulch settlement.

There is an account in *The Carbonate Camp Called Leadville* describing how Thomas Starr carried a sack of flour on his back from Fairplay across the Mosquito Range down to California Gulch and shared it with his neighbors, an incident which illustrates the fortitude and open-heartedness of the Irish pioneer.

His son, Thomas, was a lifelong resident of California Gulch, as is his grandson, Thomas Starr, who lives a short distance from where the old Starr home was located. The old house was torn down some years ago when placer mining had a short-lived revival in that area.

Henry Smith first settled in lower California Gulch, somewhere in the vicinity of Front Street about 1866. He homesteaded the Smith Ranch south of Malta in 1870. His son James lived and farmed on the ranch all his life. His grandson, Dr. Bernard Smith, the efficient veterinarian, has a residence on the grounds of the ranch.

An old custom, rarely observed anymore, was the Irish wake where a deceased person was paid his last respects in the family home by friends and neighbors. The casket and formal offerings were placed in one of the larger rooms where all who entered would pause for a last glimpse and a prayer for the soul of the departed and then offer their sympathy for the members of the family.

These affairs generally lasted into the late hours. Those who had come to offer their condolences sat around on chairs in the parlor, dining room, and kitchen talking quietly about their experiences shared with the deceased. If anyone happened to mention the descendant's shortcomings, they invariably added the appropriate remark, "God rest his soul."

A large pot of coffee was kept simmering in the kitchen. At a late hour, all of the gentlemen retired to the kitchen, a bottle was passed around, and the conversation became a little animated. Most of these wakes were quiet, solemn affairs, but there were a few at which a liberal quantity of spirits was consumed, and things got somewhat out of hand.

Old-timers used to tell of the early Irish wakes in Oro, where the mourners wailed in Gaelic, a weird, old-country custom. This observation is difficult to verify, but it does make a colorful story.

When the first St. Vincent's Hospital was erected squarely in the middle of East Tenth Street, there were threats from the citizenry to dismantle or move the building by force. The "Clan-ne-Gaels," as the Irishmen were dubbed—in the same way some writers refer to the Italians as the "Costa Nostra"—were influential in forming the military organizations which protected the hospital building. One such group, the Mulligan Guard, was well armed and ready. The hospital wasn't moved.

Other organizations, the Wolf Tone Guard and the Rocky Mountain Rifles, protected the hospital premises at various times from claim jumpers and land-grabbers. The Wolf Tone Guard was named for the great Irish patriot, Theobald Wolf Tone, who lead an abortive revolt against the English in 1798. The Rocky Mountain Rifles, a unit of the Colorado National Guard, led by Major John Quinn, was called out to patrol the Cripple Creek area during the Cripple Creek Strike of 1893. Most of the "Rockies" were Irish and a majority were members of the miners' union. Consequently, they refused to participate in an action against their fellow miners. The governor of the state of Colorado summarily disbanded the entire unit.

Most Irish immigrants had a willingness to work but as individuals differed in the way they utilized their resources. Some were lucky spendthrifts, others fought the battle of survival valiantly and lost. And there were those who accumulated sizable fortunes from ambitious ventures and careful investments.

The three Gallagher brothers, so the story goes, discovered the Camp Bird Mine on Carbonate Hill when one of the three stubbed his toe on a rock which happened to be rich in silver ore. Most mining men don't place much credence in this story. The loose rock, leading to the rich lode, is one of the most popular mining legends. A more likely version of what happened is that the Gallaghers first decided to dig along side an established claim. The owner, not liking the idea, advised them to do their digging farther up on the hill, which they did.

Whatever the circumstances of their discovery, Charles, Patrick, and John Gallagher worked the Camp Bird and the adjoining claim in 1866 and 1867. Evidently, the venture yielded some good returns. The Gallagher brothers sold the two claims to the St. Louis Smelting and Refining Company for $250,000. They divided the money and went their separate ways. Some years later they were all flat broke.

Town men, Peter Linnerty, John Taylor, and Richard and Patrick Dillion, found a rich vein of silver in the Little Chief Mine on Fryer Hill. The partners had already made a profit of $100,000 when they sold out to J. V. Farwell and Associates of Chicago for $100,000. The Dillion brothers squandered their fortune in less than two years. Another prospector, John D. Morrisey, who had made a fortune in mining, "blew the works" on all the available vices and literally drank himself to death. He died a pauper.

The three miners who discovered the Little Jonny Mine are a good example of the many who tried and failed. On one of the coldest days of winter, Thomas Kelly, John Curran, and Michael Donovan shoveled through six feet of snow to find a solid surface and stake their claim. The Little Jonny Mine was named for John Curran, who was a man of slight build and stature. The three miners didn't find anything of value as did the prospectors of Fryer Hill where the minerals lay almost on the surface. Six months later, Thomas Kelly died from exposure; John Curran died not long after. Donovan, who survived, sold his share for $2,500. The heirs of Kelly sold his holdings for $1,200, and Curran's sold his interest for $3,500. Gold was discovered in 1890 at considerable depth in the Little Jonny Mine. Subsequently, the "Jonny" became one of the greatest gold-producing mines in the history of the Leadville Mining District.

One of the more noteworthy miners was Peter McBreene, who made a fortune in mining. McBreene helped to establish the Leadville Savings and Deposit. He owned the building at Fourth and Harrison in which the business was located. The bank failed because some of his associates in the enterprise misused the bank funds. At an age when most men are satisfied with a life of semi-retirement, Peter McBreene assumed the personal responsibility of paying off the bank's deficit. He went back to work in the mines to reimburse all the stockholders who had lost money through the bank's failure. During the strike of 1880, he reopened the old Maldon Mine, paying the miners according to the union scale. It is sad to note that men of integrity like Peter McBreene are just mentioned in passing, while the notorious characters have achieved immortality in the lore of the West.

John McCombe was truly a self-made man. He was not only tenacious but displayed a lot of good, hard common sense. Born in 1851, in County Kings, Ireland, he immigrated to the United States in 1873, landing at the Port of New York with four pounds, six pence in his pockets. McCombe worked at various jobs in the United States and Canada after his arrival. In 1877, he decided to go west. The young traveler, after reaching Colorado Springs, walked to Leadville with his blankets on his back and ten cents in his jeans.

He was employed for a period as a prospector in the Leadville area, and in the spring of 1878, the young miner began prospecting on his own. He located several claims, which he sold at a good profit. It is estimated the McCombe earned over $100,000 from these ventures. Unlike some prospectors of his time, he invested these savings carefully. McCombe returned to Ireland and brought back an Irish bride. Upon his return to Leadville, he opened two more mines, bought a home, and settled down to a life of comfort.

Thomas Walsh, one of the managers of the Grand Hotel on East Chestnut Street, made considerable investments in mining. He received a substantial return from the profits of the Evelyn Mine in Graham Park, which he named for his daughter. The bulk of Walsh's fortune was obtained from the profits of the Camp Bird and Golden Smuggler mines in the Ouray area. These two mines made him a millionaire. His daughter Evelyn married Edward Beale McLean, the wealthy publisher of the *Washington Star* and *Cincinnati Enquirer* newspapers. She lived in Washington, D.C., for several years after McLean died. Mrs. McLean purchased the fabulous Hope diamond, which was reputed to have a curse on it. Indeed, her life was marked by tragedy. After Evelyn Walsh McLean's death, the Hope diamond was given to the Smithsonian Institute, where it reposes in all its baleful magnificence.

Of all the immigrants seeking to escape the poverty and restrictions of life in the old world, the Irish were among the most ambitious and adaptable, proving themselves able to cope with new environments and the changing conditions of life in the growing West.

Any account of the Irish would be incomplete without mention of Father Horgan, a Leadville legend. He was priest for the east side Catholics at the Annunciation church. He and I both were convinced that he owned the church—towering steeple and all.

Father Horgan was a big man. When dressed for the street, he wore a long black robe. Suspended on a chain beneath his white starched clerical collar was a large silver cross that seemed to be in constant motion. He was one to add a dramatic element to the words of his booming voice by making great gestures with his arms.

One day I was kicking a rock down West Seventh Street, and Father Horgan stopped me. He wanted to know what I thought I was doing. There we were, this huge holy man—when he was younger he had been a boxer—towering over me in his black robe and with that great silver cross swinging about. I could have answered that I knew what I was doing—I was kicking a rock. But I was afraid he would ask me why.

Father Horgan had a way about him that made me want to avoid him whenever possible. I had heard stories about him from my Irish friends, who were fearless in the streets and school yard and yet were in awe of him. There was a story about a fight he had with Father Frank Trunck, the priest of the Austrians' Catholic church, St. Joseph's. Father Frank had a style and legend of his own. When he answered his phone he would simply say in a loud voice, "Trunck!" Many people thought he said "drunk," and some weren't too surprised by the thought.

One day the two priests were out at the Catholic cemetery and got into a dispute over the boundary between the Irish and the Austrian sections. There was a plot of ground in the no-man's land between sections, and one day the two holy men were out there throwing a wrought iron gate at each other and discussing the real estate in less than gentle terms. "Jesus and the Two Thieves," a large sculpture, was eventually erected on the spot. There is no record of which priest was favored.

Religion was a major factor in Leadville. For some reason, I think of Mary Lou Williams, whom I dated for a few months right after World War II. She was a beautiful Irish girl who lived with her family up on Chicken Hill. I would pick her up and we would drive past the Catholic Church on our way out to park by the D&RG depot. Mary Lou, who for some reason in those days insisted on being called Merry Mary Lou, would always cross herself as we passed the Catholic Church. After a while, in the interest of sociological research, I tried driving out Hemlock and past the C&S depot—avoiding her church and thus creating a small controlled study. Unfortunately, it didn't seem to have an effect on her behavior one way or the other.

The Williams family lived up on East Second and Toledo Avenue near the Penrose Mine. East Third separated the Swedes from the Fifth Street Irish. The Irish were scattered all the way out past Tenth Street where St. Vincent's Hospital and St. Mary's Elementary School anchored the east side. The hospital had nuns and so did St. Mary's School. Father Horgan stood as a sentinel at Seventh and Poplar when he was scourging the town for delinquent souls. I don't know why, but I was convinced kicking rocks was some kind of Catholic sin.

The west side Catholics had different names such as Jackopic, Stalcar, Damjanovich, or Yelenck. They had their own church and Father Trunck, and they didn't belong to the Knights of Columbus. The Kellys, Ryans, Doyles, Donovans, and Kerrigans didn't belong to the Slovenian Lodge. Most of the Bohunks worked at the smelter while the Irish worked in the mines or at the courthouse. The Austrians made dandelion wine. The Irish made a lot of noise. They were both always busy on Sunday mornings. If the Irish went down on West Third, they were asking for trouble. If the Austrians went up on East Sixth, they had better be just passing through.

Leadville would not have been the same without the Micks. Up the Irish!

27

Leadville Inspiration

It's funny what memory will do to the past. I started at the Ninth Street School in 1928. Of all my memories of my early days in first grade, I have the clearest recollection of a conversation between Henry Stauffacher and our teacher, Miss Shaddle. Long before some opportunistic linguist coined the term "positive reinforcement," Miss Shaddle was practicing the technique while walking up and down the rows of her classroom. She leaned over the small desk where Henry sat and commented on his artistic endeavor, "Why, Henry. What a nice horse you have drawn."

Henry's reply might have set educational psychology back for decades, at least as far as Miss Shaddle was concerned. He turned and looked up into her smiling face and said, "You'd better watch out or it'll shit all over you."

One of my most vivid memories of high school is of the walk from the school on the side of Capitol Hill on West Ninth down eight blocks to where the woodworking shop was located at Central School. Principal L.W. Thompson told us, to the minute, how long it was to take us to make the journey and was quite specific about the route we were to take. Upon threat of expulsion, Harrison Avenue was to be avoided because of our potential for disrupting business activity, and State Street was off limits because of the nature of the business activity conducted there.

We were, however, good boys and, in daily compliance with the dictates of our esteemed principal, would march forth from the halls of academia to the shops of craft consistently within the time prescribed. We didn't even stray from our charted course—that is until we got to Third Street, where *in a daily ritual of physical conditioning we would dash a block east and then south on Harrison so as to allow for a casual stroll toward Central School on State Street, past the saloons and, most importantly, past the infamous "cribs" where dwelled the ladies of pleasure. They would taunt us with their nasty talk, their seductive ways, and generous glimpses of intimate flesh. It was almost enough to make us want careers in the industrial arts.*

It was all in fun. The prostitutes had their clients, and we had our school books and the stopwatch scrutiny of Principal L.W. Thompson to keep us on the narrow; he had failed in his attempts to keep us on the straightest path. As the school year progressed we got to know many of the women by name—Doris, Irene, Wanda, and Kathleen. They became a regular part of our schedule and, in time, they knew our names too.

That casual familiarity almost spelled the end of a budding romance for one of my cohorts, J. J. Coble. One evening his girlfriend Alberta dared him to walk her down State Street. He gave in, reluctantly. As he feared, Alberta was less than favorably impressed when they were greeted by a seductive chorus of immodest voices singing out, "Hey, J. J., who you got with you? J. J., don't you love me no more?" And, of course, he didn't help his case by answering, "Now you cut that out, Irene. You, too, Doris." The curriculum of Leadville was broad based.

I asked Alberta to tell us about her folks and her times in Leadville. There isn't enough space in this book for her to tell us about J. J.

Alberta Mangold

John and Catherine Bondy were latecomers to Leadville, arriving in 1896 from Ishpeming, Michigan. With them were their three children—Albert, William, and Ester. My mother Ester was three at the time. In 1897, a daughter, Mayme, was born. A son, John, arrived in 1899, and another daughter, Elizabeth, arrived in 1902. The birth of Elizabeth resulted in her mother's death.

My grandfather John was a diamond driller forced to work long hours away from home. He tried unsuccessfully for over a year to keep a housekeeper around to help bring up the children. John eventually decided he was unable to care for his kids and that the four youngest would be better off in an orphanage. He took them to Denver and placed them in a home for children. They were there for a short time when tragedy struck. Baby Elizabeth died of what they called membranous croup—probably a form of diphtheria. Upon hearing this, John returned immediately and took the other children from the orphanage. Before returning to Leadville, he took his starving brood to a restaurant for a huge breakfast, the likes of which my mother said she never forgot.

Mother completed grade school and was told by her father that her education was finished; it was time to go to work. After several jobs, mostly doing household chores, she was employed by August and Emma Hahnawald to take care of their children. The Hahnawalds owned a bakery and were quite wealthy. Upon selling their business in Leadville, they moved to Denver, taking my mother with them. There she met my father, Albert Sidney Mangold, who had come to Colorado from Pittsburgh for health reasons. They were married in January, 1918.

Mother used to tell of having smallpox as a young girl and of men coming to the house, putting her and her mattress on a wagon and taking her to the "pest house." There a woman would bathe her and oil her face. The woman took such good care of her that Mother never had any scars. Lucia, my younger sister, says she remembers Mother saying the woman was a prostitute and that prostitutes were the "angels of mercy" in times of plague and pestilence. Mother told of my Uncle Johnny losing his hair from typhoid fever and how they massaged his head with cuticura (ointment), causing a beautiful head of curly red hair to grow back.

When I think of J. J. and Alberta I don't worry much about Leadville's future. They had twelve children, all Catholic, and I know some of them will cycle back to the old hometown—with a legacy of oral history.

J. J.'s family came to Leadville early. His grandfather knew my grandfather back in the 1870s and 1880s. My dad knew Bill Coble, J. J.'s dad, when they were kids in the first decade of the twentieth century. They played together up on West Seventh along with the McKenna kids. Then the Cobles moved to a warmer clime, down the Arkansas to Cañon City.

Thirty years later, when Bill Coble moved his family back to Leadville to work as an agent for the Denver & Rio Grande Railroad Express, he and Mrs. Coble had two sons—Bill, Jr., and James Joseph. J. J. was a freshman and I was a sophomore at Leadville High School the same year. He was a good, tough athlete and a full-of-hell Irishman; we became dear friends immediately.

About that time J. J.'s father bought a brand new 1940 Packard sedan—beautiful. Mr. Coble made a serious mistake by leaving that car and the car keys at home while he was at work. J. J. and I would take turns, starting up at the corner of Eighth and Leiter, going as fast as we could in the great Packard and then sliding into their graveled driveway.

A few months later, J. J.'s dad was looking at his car and said something like, "My God, I've only got eight thousand miles on these tires, and they're already worn out." J. J. never told his dad that a couple of those thousands of miles were going sideways.

J. J. titled his account of Leadville sledding "Nine Months of Good Sledding, Three Months of Slush."

J. J. Coble

Growing up in Leadville, you were forced to make your own amusement. There was always the adventure of hiking to the mines on Johnny Hill and looking for samples of ore. You could go to the local theater, sometimes twice a week if they changed the movie. A third choice might be to venture on down to the local hang-out, Peck's Pool Hall. There was always someone with an idea around as to how we should spend the evening, be it a beer, a movie, or a trip up the hill for some fast sledding.

The most exciting evenings were when we went sledding. All you needed was four or five bodies, the Cadillac of sleds—a six foot Flexible Flyer, warm clothes, gloves, and a flashlight. The girls in Leadville did not care for this sport, although once in a while one or two would come along. One trip up and down was usually enough to last a lifetime for those who dared to accompany us.

We would normally meet at Peck's around 6:00 P.M. with anywhere from six to twelve guys pulling three or four sleds. We would walk up Fifth Street toward Johnny Hill, sleds in tow. During a good snowstorm it would usually take us two or two-and-a-half hours to reach the top. The road was narrow and full of curves. Sometimes a few ore trucks would be hauling at night, either carrying ore to the mill or doing a little high-grading. Some of the drivers would attach a bell on the truck to let us know they were coming. When you reached the Jonny Mine #1, you felt as if you were on top of the world, for you could see the lights of the town far, far below.

The Flexible Flyer could accommodate four people comfortably—two lying down and two kneeling. The person lying on the bottom would steer and the person on top of him would hold the flashlight. The trip down was rather scary—curve after curve, through the four trestles, and on down Stray Horse Gulch, down past the town of Adelaide, down past the Mikado, past Finn Town, past the mine called Midas—all the way hoping not to hear a bell or see the headlights of an oncoming truck. If, in fact, you did, it was into the ditch with everyone gasping for air. The ride would eventually end in Leadville—two hours of hiking and pulling the sled uphill—all for a five minute ride back down. With that the evening was over and it was back home by the coal stove you went to await another night of adventure.

It was 6:00 on the evening of January 29, 1939. Down at Peck's, the topic was "Let's go sledding." In the group were ten fellows. Six of us, including Earl McKenna, Ed Larsh, and myself chose to go to the Liberty Bell Theater for a movie. The other four decided on "the hill." The sledders were Aloysius Blamey, Kern Hall, Emil Paschel, and Joe Saseck. Out they went into the night and into the snow, pulling the Flex up Fifth Street. About halfway up, they decided they had gone far enough. The temperature had dropped to about seven degrees below zero, so down the hill they came.

About two-thirds of the way down, on the corner of Fifth and Alder, a man driving home through the storm didn't see the boys or the sled. There was no way to stop. The sled ran into and under the car. Kern Hall died at the scene. Emil Paschel and Joe Saseck died several days later. Al Blamey, who was riding or kneeling on the back, was thrown off and fell into the snowy ditch and survived.

When the movie was over, we found out what had happened and went over to Fifth and Alder. Imbedded into the telephone pole there was a slat from the Flexible Flyer.

Stray Horse Gulch has other stories to tell, but none about Flexible Flyers after that night in January of 1939.

Jean McDonald was Catholic. She went to St. Mary's Elementary School, so I didn't know her until we arrived at the public Leadville High School up on West Ninth as sub-freshmen. She was beautiful and still is. I had a crush on her that I carried clear into our senior year, when I finally gathered up enough courage to ask her to a school dance. She very graciously said no.

I remember the night we graduated—fifty-three of us sitting up on the stage at the Tabor Opera House, June 1941. Jean gave an address as class valedictorian. I didn't see her again until our fortieth class reunion.

Jean McDonald

In the 1890s my grandfather, Dr. Roderick J. McDonald, along with his wife and two sons moved to Leadville to set out his shingle as a medical doctor where there was a desperate need for his services. There was no such thing as a weekend off, or even a day off—on call twenty-four hours a day, seven days a week. He would make his calls in a horse and buggy or a horse and sleigh during the winter months. His practice consisted of setting broken bones, delivering babies, treating communicable diseases, emergency appendectomies, mending miners' broken bodies, removing warts, etc.

During World War I, his health started to deteriorate, so in 1918 he asked his son, Dr. Franklin McDonald (my father), to come to Leadville and help him after he was discharged from the army. Franklin had finished medical school before going into the army and had his sights set upon going into practice in Detroit after the war. But, he took his new bride to the two-mile-high city, where he worked with his father until R. J. died.

In that time, my father became so involved with the good, hard-working and loving people of Leadville that he chose to devote his life and talents to them. The depression years were hard on the miners, grocers, clothing salespersons, hardware owners, and shoemakers, as on all Americans. There was little or no money to pay the grocer, much less the doctor. Illnesses, accidents, and births continued as usual, however, and Dad was always available whenever and wherever he was needed. The patients were always apologetic that they could not pay, so they did the best they could by bringing venison and trout to him. I could not look at a trout, much less eat one for twenty years.

Dad's office was in the front part of the house where we lived, so we didn't have much privacy. It wasn't unusual to have an accident victim carried into our dining room while we were eating dinner. Seeing a bloody body in someone's arms really took our appetites away.

One of the highlights of Dad's life in Leadville was the time that President Harry Truman's train was scheduled to stop at the station at Malta—just west of Leadville. As county Democratic chairman, Dad was invited to meet the president during the train's brief stop. After the introductions, the president asked Dad if he would like to join him in a drink. (This was 9:00 A.M.!) So the two of them had a shot of whiskey and a few minutes of conversation before the train departed. What a thrill!

My most vivid memory of growing up in Leadville was the caring people who lived there. They were always there for one another. If there was illness in a family, someone was always bringing food to help. When a woman had a baby, neighbors took turns caring for the other children and the husband until the new mother regained her strength. If there was a death in the family, friends were streaming into the home with food and loving sympathy. I learned such a great lesson from my mother doing all of this that it has become a big part of my life caring and helping. Leadville was a city of LOVE!!

My sister, Thelma, was valedictorian on the same stage of the Tabor Opera House seven years earlier in 1934—at the age of sixteen. She has been a major influence on my life since I was a tiny baby when she started taking care of me—she was five.

Thelma Larsh McMillin

Ruth McMahon was my best friend; I was fourteen, and so was she. She lived in a little white house on the hill on West Seventh Street. I lived on the same hill on West Sixth. There were, however, more differences it seemed, than there were similarities between us. She had gone to St. Mary's School, being Irish Catholic, and was in the seventh grade. I had gone to Ninth Street Public School, not being Catholic or anything else. I was in the ninth grade at the high school, having skipped two grades. Ruth's dad was a politician up at the courthouse; my dad was a printer at the *Herald Democrat*. Ruth was five-feet-two and weighed 140 pounds; I was five-feet-six and weighed 105.

I didn't write in my diary every day, only on special occasions or important days. The first entry was on my birthday, the diary being a present from Mom and Dad, January 17,1930. On December 21 of that year I wrote: "Today Ruth and I took a package of food that Mrs. McMahon made up to Mrs. Tabor. Mr. McMahon asked us to deliver the package yesterday. He said Mrs. Tabor would let us in, once we knocked and told her it was a present from John McMahon for Christmas. Mrs. Tabor's cabin is way up the road toward Mosquito Pass. It took us almost an hour to get there as the snow was not packed all the way. Mrs. Tabor at first wouldn't let us in, but we looked through the window and knew she was there. Ruth told her who we were so she asked us to come in. The cabin was cold so I asked Mrs. Tabor if I could put some coal in the stove and she said, 'Sue brings me a sack of coal every Saturday.' So I did anyway. Mrs. Tabor said she liked us because we weren't after the Matchless like everybody else who came up and tried to have her open her door. She never opened the package. We left very soon, but first I asked her if we could come back and she said, 'Yes, my dears, but don't bring anyone else.' I intend to go back, but first I am going to ask my teacher to tell me all about Mrs. Tabor who everybody calls Baby Doe."

In another entry, a few months later, I wrote that Ruth and I went back. We could see her but she wouldn't answer the door. A year later, Eddieboy and I talked to Baby Doe when she was walking down West Seventh. It was spring time, and I can still remember her saying as she presented us with a bouquet of dandelions, "Look at these; they are as pretty as a rose."

Frank ("Patches") Pacheco, a Spanish-American who as a child was part of the Hispanic immigration into Leadville in the 1920s, lived up on East Second Street with his mother and his sister. He graduated from Leadville High School in June 1943, the same year as my brother Don. That July, Frank joined the Navy and served for three years on an aircraft carrier. He returned to Leadville after the war with an honorable discharge and the G.I. Bill of Rights.

One night in 1947, Jack Neelan and I were in the Pioneer showing off as "big time" college football players. Three things happened that night revealing dramatic changes that had occurred in the process of growing up during the time of the war.

First of all, this "Mexican" kid was in the Pioneer, and he had no reason to be fearful for his personal safety. The second was Neelan and I walked over and bought him a beer. The third was Frank Pacheco was on his way to Western State College with the G.I. Bill.

Frank S. ("Patches") Pacheco

For me, Leadville is a place filled with memories. I can remember when we would go with my mother to town and on occasion would see Baby Doe Tabor, dressed in rags and her feet wrapped in gunny sacks and begging for money. My mother would always give her some change and instruct us not to make fun of her and to treat her with respect.

I can vividly recall my mother's words of wisdom. "Get along with people, regardless of their backgrounds. And you must always strive for a better education. You are never too young or too old to learn." In as much as Leadville was populated with many ethnic groups it was a must to get along with each other. For some it was more difficult than others—but, taking my mother's advice, I had little problem.

Memories of Leadville hold a special charm for me. They chronicle a rugged terrain of our country, whose geological wonders are surpassed only by the brand of people who have lived there or still remain there, sustained by a spirit of "live and let live."

Both of my parents were born in New Mexico and were decendents of the Spanish Conquistadors. They came to Leadville by way of Durango, Colorado, in search of employment. My father was a miner by trade and work was plentiful in the mines, mills, and smelters. In 1926, my mother and father were divorced and life for us took on a new dimension. My mother was a proud woman and determined to raise my sister and me in a decent home. Working as a maid at the Vendome Hotel as well as being a seamstress, she provided us a good home and security despite the difficult times during the depression.

In 1947, the influx of returning servicemen made it difficult to find steady employment. It was a case of finding work or enrolling in college. I applied and was accepted at Colorado University in Boulder. During my first semester I came home every weekend I could. I loved my hometown and its people. I still recall, toward the end of the semester, I came home on a weekend and met Ed Larsh and some of his friends from Western State College at the Pioneer Bar. In the dialogue that followed, they convinced me to transfer to their college. At the end of the semester I made the change and remained at Western State until graduating in June of 1950.

Prior to my graduation, I married Katherine Tubbs from Seymour, Wisconsin. We have three children, two daughters and a son, and six grandchildren. I owe my values to my mother. It is my hope I will see my grandchildren follow in the same footsteps. I have had a home in Denver for years, and in my work I have lived in several foreign countries. But when anyone asks me where my home is, I always say Leadville, Colorado.

Gerald McMillin asked me if I had any Leadville stories from Dr. Billy Rose. I said I didn't, and he told me he'd try to get hold of him for us. Arriving in the mail a couple of weeks later was a tape of recollections recorded by Billy, the grandson of the first dentist in Leadville. Billy Rose is a friend and, like a lot of people from the old home town, a hell of a storyteller.

Dr. Billy Rose

The Rose family started in Leadville in the summer of 1879, when my Grandpa came over Mosquito Pass from Missouri with a small bag of dentist tools. In Leadville, twenty thousand people came that year. There were no rooms, no facilities. My grandpa was able to rent a cot in a tent on a shift basis. He would have it for eight hours, and then someone else would take it over, no sheets.

The price of food was very high, and his small grubstake was running out so he opened up the first dentist office in Leadville. It was down on Harrison Avenue between Second and Chestnut on the sidewalk. He got himself an old folding chair and a carbide lamp and went to work everyday about 5:00 in the evening. He would have two quarts of whiskey which he used to sterilize his few tools, and he also used it to help the miners handle the pain. He had two sons, W. S. Rose and J. H. Rose, both of whom became dentists. Then I became the third generation to practice dentistry in Leadville— ninety straight years of dentistry from 1878 to 1967.

At one time there were twenty-seven passenger trains in and out of Leadville every day. The traffic on the streets of Leadville before automobiles was horrendous. The large ore wagons would be pulled by four, six, or eight horses, and many times they would be so close together you would have to wait four or five minutes just to cross the street. At that time, there were in excess of twenty thousand horses in Leadville. The horse was used to get the men to the mine, or they would have to walk.

When zinc was discovered at the Wolf Tone, the mine was owned by Sam Nicholson; they hollowed out a stope that was approximately 200 feet in length and 90 feet wide and about 150 feet high, and that was solid, crystal zinc. When it was lit up it looked like a Christmas tree on the inside, they tell me. And somewhere along the line the society people in Leadville decided they should have a banquet, and Mr. Nicholson put it on down in the mine about five or six hundred feet underground in this large stope. The Miller Bakery and Confectionery Company catered the dinner, and there were somewhere around 100 to 150 people, including my mother and father and my grandmother and grandfather. The ladies wore all their finery, fur coats, and long evening dresses. They got in sleighs and rigs and were driven up to the Wolf Tone Mine, where they went down in the cage that had been lined with red plush velvet. They had orchestras down in the mine. They had dancing. It went on quite late in the evening. It was in the winter time, and they had to come back out of the mine, get dressed up in their robes, and ride back down to Leadville.

Ice skating and bobsled riding were the popular sports in Leadville at the time. You pulled the bobsleds up as far as the Jonny Mine and then would ride down the hill across Harrison Avenue going fifty to sixty miles per hour and go clear past the smelters . . . making about a seven-, eight-, or nine-mile ride. You got one ride a night, and it was a good one.

On one of those rides (my father owned a bob), there was a fellow named Wade Dale sitting on the sled behind him there were about fifteen men on this bob sled. They were crossing the railroad tracks on Third Street, and for some reason Wade put out his leg and got it caught underneath the rails and completely tore it off at the hip. They took him to the hospital and did what emergency work they could do for him, but he was left with one leg. He was despondent and went out to California and started the Dale Coffee Company, a very prosperous operation. It was a forerunner of the present Safeway Stores, originating from an accident up in Leadville.

I, too, had a bobsled in my younger days. Once we were coming off Seventh Street Hill and tried to turn at the bottom of the hill on Spruce Street. We were going a little bit too fast, and our bobsled went through a window and wound up in the living room of the Gallagher home. It was a very embarrassing situation.

In the early days of automobiles in Leadville it was quite a deal. If you went to Denver, you had to go down to Buena Vista, Salida, Cañon City, Pueblo, Colorado Springs, and then Denver. That was a long, long trip, well over two hundred miles. We used to leave at four in the morning, and if we would get to Denver by eight-thirty or nine that evening it was a fast trip. The roads were not paved. They were just two ruts that you drove down. You'd come to a place where a farmer had a fence, and you'd have to get out, open the gate, drive the car through, and close the gate. Then you'd go across the field and do the same thing again.

Tires were a big problem. On the average you figured on changing ten tires between Leadville and Denver. At that time you had maybe a spare or two. I remember my father had four spare tires, two on the back and one on each fender in the front. And many, many times I can remember we had to patch the tires and pump them up by hand. Along about that time someone came up with an engine air pump and my dad had one put on our car. He loved it when we would come upon some motorist laboring away pumping up a flat tire. We would pull over and he would get out the hose, crank up the engine again, and pump up their tires for them. Probably a third of our time getting to Denver was spent pumping up other people's tires, but it was a good, humanitarian act.

I also remember when my father bought our first car from Charlie Edwards. Charlie brought the car up from Denver. It was an Overland. We were all standing out on the sidewalk on Poplar where he said he would pick us up and take us for a ride. It was my grandmother, the two girls, my mother, and myself, and we were all standing there outfitted in dusters and goggles. Doc [my dad] came up the street and he saw us, but he drove on by. We were all crushed because he didn't stop and pick us up. We found out later he didn't know how to stop the car. He finally drove it up Capitol Hill and made it stall at which time he set the brake, removed the back seat, and took out the book of instructions. That's how he learned how to drive. Later on he came by and took us for a ride. That was our first experience with the automobile in Leadville.

I recall an incident that happened to my grandfather when he was the mayor of Leadville. In the early part of his career, the sewer question came up. The sewer had been put in by A. V. Hunter, and he had a twenty-year franchise. The franchise was about to expire, and he wanted it to be renewed. He went around to all of the alderman and bribed them to vote in his favor. My grandfather got wind of it and, knowing the people of Leadville to be against it, he decided that he would vote Hunter down. He didn't have the votes to do it, but he had tactics otherwise. In the course of the meeting, when the question of the sewer came up, my grandfather called a recess. While the council was out, my grandfather hung a hangman's noose over the front edge of his desk. When they reconvened, he said "Gentlemen, now we will vote on the franchise on A. V. Hunter and the sewer." The new contract was not approved.

On his tape, Bill Rose touches a lot of other bases: "Ma and Pa" grocery stores; the whores in the cribs on State Street; the assayer, Ed Mandy, who made hundreds of thousands in the "high-grade" industry; the badger fights from a first-hand perspective; gamblers and prize fighters; the story of a Denver "revenuer" who died of a heart attack when a bootlegger fired a shot into the air (the paper next day reported the coronary, not the gun shot).

Somewhere between the whiskey-bottle dentistry of Bill's grandfather and the high-speed, modern techniques of Bill's era, as a kid I found myself in the second floor office of Doc Rose in the Delaware Hotel, gripping the arms of a dental chair with white knuckles and doing all I could to keep from hollering. (Doc Rose would give you hell if you screamed while he was working on you.) The only good thing about the experience was that, as you sat there with eyes staring up at the ceiling and Old Doc Rose's fists in your mouth, he told such wonderful stories of Leadville's early times. Just think of it, in a tooth-pulling tradition that spanned ninety years, the Rose family was there from the earliest train to the last. Grandpa Rose might have been pulling teeth out on the sidewalk when Ulysses S. Grant and his entourage arrived on the first train. Doc Rose was grinding away at tooth decay through Prohibition and the Great Depression, and Bill Rose practiced right into the modern age.

Thanks for the tape, Bill.

Donald Griswold arrived in Leadville the first day of September 1933. He had been hired by L. W. Thompson to teach Latin at Leadville High. The first day he was in his new home, a couple he had known from his hometown,

Mr. and Mrs. W. P. Stirling, insisted that he come down to their new house at Twin Lakes for dinner and that they come into town and pick him up.

Donald Griswold

When the Stirlings saw me standing in front of the Vendome Hotel, they recognized me immediately. I suppose the shy, quiet, studious young boy they remembered had not changed that much since I had last seen them. I was ten years older, now six-feet-three-inches tall, but still shy, quiet, and now not only studious but soon to become a teacher of Latin and English.

As we passed the old sway-back barn near Hayden's Ranch and wound our way to the top of the hill where Mount Elbert seemed to guard the icy blue waters of Twin Lakes, I asked if we could stop. I was in awe of the natural physical beauty. Later Jean and I would often go and picnic there in those best years of our lives that were to follow.

The Stirlings brought me back to Leadville in time to watch the Labor Day Parade. You can imagine my surprise when I realized the celebration was a mock funeral for the purpose of "burying" prohibition. As I watched the so-called mourners and the removal of a wooden box, covered with weeds and dropped at the ball park, the thought crossed my mind, "You don't suppose most Leadvillites are beer guzzlers or hard liquor drinkers, do you?" As I took up my duties at school I soon learned Leadvillites were hard working, friendly people ever ready to lend a helping hand.

As the school term progressed in the fall of 1933, Principal Thompson gave me the responsibility of assisting the seniors in publishing an economical yearbook. After making plans and some suggested lay-outs, I went to the *Herald Democrat* printing office and was told I would be working with printer, Ed Larsh, who was called to the front office. He took me to his work table in the rear of the building, and we reviewed the plans I had made with the yearbook staff. Larsh found them acceptable, made some suggestions for cutting the cost, and then asked me, "How come you know so much about printing?"

I told him I had started learning the trade at the age of twelve and that now I was a member of the International Typographical Union. Larsh stepped back, pulled a card from his desk and said he was a member of the union also. The work of printing and publishing the high school annual proved to be professional and economical.

A few years later the son of printer Larsh entered high school and was a student in one of my classes. Fifty-two years later, I tried to remember Dr. Larsh as a student, but I couldn't. I only remembered an English class on April 1, 1940.

I always tried to be a model Latin teacher. I dressed in conservative suits and always wore a tie. I neither drank nor smoked. I was always prepared for my lessons, books in hand—decorum was essential. I was still tall, bashful, shy, studious, and quiet.

Eddie Larsh and a new student in town named Kathleen came up to the front of the room where I was busy conjugating a verb. Eddie said, "Kathleen isn't feeling very well." Kathleen was a good student and one of the loveliest young ladies I had had the pleasure of teaching. As Eddie got my attention, she fainted right into my arms. I had no choice but to carry her from the room—her long black hair draped from one arm and her long legs from the other. Eddie was quick to open the classroom door. With a crimson face and Kathleen in my arms I stepped into the hall. The whole class followed right behind us. On cue from another boy, the class called, "April Fool!"

I married Jean Harvey, who was also teaching at the high school. Her father was William Harvey, who had taken over the Western Hardware Store from his father in 1907. The building still stands on the corner of Fifth and Harrison. The original hardware store was started long before the turn of the century and provided service for almost three quarters of a century.

Teddy Lane worked at the Western Hardware Store for forty-five straight years. The entire length of both sides of the store was counters, behind which were hardwood cabinets with drawers from the floor to the twenty-foot ceiling. Each side had a ladder on runners. Teddy Lane could push the ladder to the exact spot, climb the ladder, and go right to any nut, bolt, or screw you desired.

The Western Hardware Store supplied the mines from the Little Pittsburg to the Resurrection as well as the needs of the miners and their wives. The business was hardware. If you couldn't buy a particular vessel or container made out of sheet metal, Dick Bennett and Steve Malin would make it for you. The Western Hardware was itself a fixture in the center of town; it was where Stray Horse Gulch started up Johnny Hill and where a western handshake could seal a thousand-dollar contract. The essence of the Harvey's store was integrity.

Through Jean I got to know the real people: the Harveys, the Kitts, the McDonalds, the Thompsons, the Kellys, the Cortellinis, and hundreds of others. I am reminded of a saying by Confucius when I think of people like the printer, Ed Larsh, and the hardware man, William Harvey, "One courteous family can lift a whole state into courtesy."

Jean Harvey Griswold died in December 1991. I remember her as my teacher but more so as a lady who exuded a caring goodness. I remember Don Griswold as a teacher who was shy, quiet, studious, and a terrific gentleman. I remember them together as a class act.

The medium was the message.

The Kerrigan brothers, Eddie and Bill, were pallbearers for Charlie Fitzsimmons in 1988. Both of them told me I needed to call Terrance, his youngest son, and get the "Leadville Cocktail" story. Terry, who is the public relations director for Amax Metals (the mother company of Climax Molybdenum), was someone I had known well but hadn't talked to for over forty years. I gave him a call and said, "Okay, what's this story about the 'Leadville Cocktail'?" He said it was one of the best tales he had about his dad.

Terry Fitzsimmons

The Leadville Cocktail Story

Fifty sacks of high grade ore, the value of which was placed at $50,000, were brought into Leadville from the property on the Ibex Mining Company on Breece Hill. The rich ore was the second largest shipment which has been made from No. 2 shaft where some of the richest veins ever opened on the Ibex were encountered by leasers early in February.

Steady work which has been going ahead on the high grade vein uncovered the second packet of rich ore.

The eight Austrian leasers who discovered the gold in February are still operating the lease.

—FROM THE LEADVILLE HERALD-DEMOCRAT, APRIL 11, 1920

The famous Ibex Mine on Breece Hill was one of America's great gold mines, and the tunnels and veins of gold and silver connected with the equally famous Little Jonny Mine.

In the 1920s, some mining companies in the Leadville Mining District preferred to lease portions of their underground workings to "independent miners" or "leasers" to reduce the high overhead costs of payrolls and supplies. The leasers paid their own costs and also paid a royalty to the property owner based upon the value of any ore the leasers shipped from the property.

The eight Austrian leasers who re-discovered the Little Jonny's Golden Stairs were the Pudnick Brothers. After receiving $50,000 in paper money, they went down to the Silver Dollar Bar to divide up their profit. They sat down around a large poker table, ordered a round of drinks, and the oldest of them started dealing out the bills. The problem was that none of the brothers could read or write or was proficient in math. It became obvious to the Pudnick brothers that they needed a little help.

One of them went over to the bar to where my dad, Charlie Fitzsimmons, was sitting and asked if he might give them some advice. Before the day ended my dad had become the trusted accountant of the Pudnick Brothers. That day Dad opened a bank account in the lease name, deposited the cash, drew eight checks in equal amounts to cover agreed upon individual shares, and kept a remaining balance in the account to cover future lease expenses.

Their money management problems were solved, and from that time on the Austrian miners turned over the lease settlement payments to Dad for deposit and similar distribution.

The Pudnick brothers leased from the Ibex Mining Company for several years and prospered. In time, the high-grade ore was mined out. It is assumed that the brothers returned to working for a day's pay in the many mines then active in the Leadville district, and little else is known of them.

Thirty years later I got the rest of the story. My dad was one of the most honorable people one could hope to know. In the throes of a raw town like Leadville, however, circumstance can dictate compromises.

The Pudnick Brothers had wanted to pay Dad for the help he gave them during that time back in the 1920s. Dad knew it was such a simple thing and required so little time that he refused. But from time to time, over the course of the years they worked their lease, as a token of their appreciation, one or more of them would give Dad a small gold nugget taken from the mine.

This posed a problem for Dad, since this was "high-grading" or taking values from the property without paying the mine owner the royalty to which he was entitled. Dad could have refused the nuggets or he could have turned his trusting friends into the law for high-grading. He did neither. Dad's solution was to tuck the nuggets away and never sell or otherwise use them for personal gain.

In addition to being honest, he was also very creative—he started serving cocktails. For a long time it seemed that "Leadville Cocktail" was reserved exclusively for friends or relatives from out of town.

Mom's finest glassware was brought out. The ingredients varied. Frequently Dad would serve champagne. Other times he would mix a rye Manhattan. Wine was sometimes used and even beer found its way into the long-stemmed crystal glasses. The cocktail became unique only when the final ingredient was added and sank in a stream of bubbles to the bottom of the glass. It was a small native gold nugget!

In other instances, such as when a friend was in the hospital for kidney stones, Dad would bring in a gold nugget in a test tube and assure the patient it was the very kidney stone which had caused the pain. There were other times when gold nuggets were given in a jewelry box to a friend who needed something to lift morale.

After several years, it seemed that Mr. Fitzsimmons had run out of the special ingredient needed to concoct his "Leadville Cocktail," but that was not completely true. He had six more cocktails to serve. Eddie Kerrigan told me the story of the last cocktail—Terry wanted it that way.

When Charlie Fitzsimmons died at age ninety-four, he left a will with specific instructions as to who were to be the pallbearers. Bill Kerrigan and Eddie were among the six Leadville men named. After the funeral, family and friends gathered for a drink. In front of each of the six who had carried Charlie to his grave was a crystal glass and reposing in the bottom of each was a genuine, Leadville, high-graded gold nugget. At the funeral, Terrance J. Fitzsimmons, youngest son of Charles Fitzsimmons, gave a toast as he finished telling the story.

That explains the "Leadville Cocktail" and the reluctance to serve it to residents of Leadville until more than fifty years after the episode with the Pudnick lease. And we say to you, Terry, old friend, thanks for sharing one of the great stories of Leadville, U.S.A.

And to you, Charlie: Way to go! Slánte!

In a pattern that can't be just coincidence, four boys I grew up with in Leadville went on to earn doctorates in education and become school district superintendents. I asked each of them about the influence of Leadville on their lives. (Bill Kerrigan's story is in the chapter on "The Sixth Street Irish.")

Jim Raine

The old days (a relative term) in Leadville represented times when cultures and sub-cultures set the tone of the environment significantly more than we experience today. The old days in my frame of reference were the late thirties through the fifties. The Leadville culture of the era continues to fascinate me.

If you were of Slovenian heritage, which my mother Angela brought to our family, you lived on the west side of town; attended St. Joseph's Catholic Church; celebrated weddings, dances, and religious holidays at the Slovenian Hall at 527 Elm Street; and gave the east side Irish, Italians, and Swedes a wide berth when crossing Harrison Avenue. My dad, Mickey, whose ancestry was English and Scottish, met my mother while they both worked at Climax. Mickey was an outsider to the Slavic culture but soon became immersed and accepted. He originally worked at the Frank Zaitz Mercantile Company, which was a "shopping mall" before its time. Dad eventually became the Lake County Assessor following a long career with Safeway.

I grew up feeling that the people of Leadville were friendly, caring, sharing, competitive, somewhat introverted, and very traditional. The west-siders were employed at the AS&R Company in Stringtown (commonly known as "The Smelter"), Zaitz Mercantile, or one of the mines south of town. Frank Zaitz was the "godfather" of the Slovenians and Croatians. He sponsored people from the "Old Country" by finding jobs for them. They owed their souls to his company store, which extended credit for the necessities of life. During the time my dad worked for Zaitz, we bought everything we needed from the "store," including food, coal, clothes, cars, and our home.

There was a dependency that existed that fostered security on one hand but stymied creativity on the other. This was an element of that culture that probably would not be valued today. But in those times security was vitally important.

The sub-cultures were also involved in struggles. I recall that some of the west side people were Croatians, a nationality that the Slovenians criticized even though they both came to the United States as European neighbors. The encouraging fact is that the Slavs and the Croats in Leadville could set aside their differences when it came time to deal with problems that were external to their environment.

I learned while growing up that the many sub-cultures of our town could be more tolerant and unified once one left the city limits. When I left home to pursue a college education, I found myself thrown in with a lot of other Leadville students. I wondered about my place in this group after having grown up as a west-sider, because many of the rather large group of us that enrolled at Regis

College were east-siders. Surprisingly, we created one new culture, which was a Leadville culture, even though we represented almost all of the nationalities in our town. That group is very much intact today, although the necessity of such a group is no longer there.

The group of Leadvillites who attended Regis College as well as others who sought higher education from other institutions were representative of the importance our culture placed on education. Many of our parents left school at the sixth grade, and few finished high school. They must have known that the dependency on that culture wouldn't last, and that education was the only way to achieve a better life.

Several of us who entered the field of education became leaders in the public schools of Colorado. At one period of time, seven of us were serving as school superintendents. We evidently had either a thirst for knowledge, a desire to excel, a need to escape from the dependency of our earlier culture, or all of the above. There is no doubt that our families and our culture created the incentive to move ahead and find success.

The strength of the Leadville culture, especially the Slavic culture that I remember leads me to share an experience that verifies the friendliness and trust I experienced while growing up with the Leadville connection. In 1987, our family planned a trip to Yugoslavia. My mother no longer had living relatives there, but her friend, Catherine Savoren, suggested that we might visit some of her family. Mrs. Savoren gave us a letter of introduction, written in Slovenian, and the address. We found the village of Semic, which was very small, off the paved roads in the north central part of Yugoslavia. The village was so remote that language was a barrier. Few tourists visited Semic! A stop at the local Catholic Church and directions from a person walking on the road took us up to a small farmhouse.

The woman of the house, Tonchka, was skeptical of us at first, but after reading the letter which said we were from Leadville, she smiled radiantly, invited us in, and called Ludwig, her husband, from the field. Although neither of us knew the language of the other, we spent the next three hours communicating the best we could.

We had lunch, drank their local wine, took photographs, and visited as much as we could. The only universal term was "Leadville," and that concept held our bilingual conversation together. We had a marvelous time. In fact, our children viewed that afternoon as the highlight of the trip because of the spontaneous hospitality of our hosts.

After returning home, we took a bottle of Slivovitz, a gift from the family we had visited, and our pictures to share with my mother and Mrs. Savoren. Mrs. Savoren looked at the pictures and immediately said, "These are not my relatives!" Stunned, we wondered what had happened. Who then were these people? Why did they treat us so well?

It seems that in error Mrs. Savoren had given us the address of another family with whom she corresponds. The town we should have visited was some eighty miles away. The letter she had written must have been very confusing because it was directed to another family and doubtlessly made no sense to the family we visited. But our hosts for that day became instantly hospitable, friendly, trusting, sharing, and caring when they recognized the Leadville connection. You see, it worked thousands of miles away.

Walt Jackson

An important characteristic of the Leadville I grew up in—a characteristic that doesn't seem as prominent today as it was then—was, for the lack of a better term, the self-sufficiency of the people. It seems to me, that people had a "trade," but in addition to their trade, they possessed a wide variety of skills and were able to do many things that people automatically hire done today. I can remember my dad doing his own carpentry work and having the plumbing, electrical, cementing skills required to build and maintain our house. At the same time, however, there was a willingness to share expertise and to help when needed. The readily available services and the willingness to help created a real sense of community, a feeling that no one was alone, and that the problem could and would be worked out.

One example that represents a scenario that in one form or another has replayed itself many times in Leadville is the following: I had been gone from Leadville for a number of years—the army, school, work, and other odds and ends. We had just finished school in Indiana and were ready to move back to Colorado. Naturally we were without money, but needed to move our belongings with us. Needless to say we didn't find many takers to lend us money. So, I called Hugh Smith, president of the Commercial Bank in Leadville (collect at that) and explained our plight: we wanted to borrow money to buy a truck to move us back to Colorado. Hugh explained to me that we had been gone quite a long time, no longer had a bank account, didn't have a job, and had no prospects in sight. But he did remember my family and me. Hugh told me to write the check, the Commercial Bank would cover it, and when we got back to Colorado to come to the bank and do the paper work. How about that!

Ed Kutzleb, Bill Kerrigan, Jim Raine, and I still meet at the "Leadville Superintendent's Conference." Every year we talk about how we, as well as other Leadville folks, ended up in administration. Part of the answer is reasonably clear to me. The education I received in the Leadville School System was excellent. The support I had from family and friends was outstanding. And perhaps the most significant factor of all was the environment that existed when I was growing up that provided the opportunity to share, cooperate, lead, follow, create and organize activities, work and effectively make use of available time. Such an environment fosters perseverance; calculated risk-taking; and an attitude that if something is going to get done you have to work at it, you have to be willing to help yourself, and in some cases if it is going to get done, you have to do it yourself.

When Walt was school superintendent of Summit county, his office was in Frisco. On more than one occasion, when Jane and I were passing through on our way to Denver from the Roaring Fork Valley we would stop. One day, after five, we were having a beer at one of Frisco's bistros, and Walt told me this Chicken Hill story.

Walt's dad was a custom craftsman in the art of welding—running a business out of his own garage. Mr. Jackson was a man who had his priorities very straight. One afternoon during the heydays of the mines, the foreman of the crusher from Climax Molybdenum Company came wheeling up Third Street and pulled into the Jackson's driveway. In the back of his truck was a complicated gear mechanism that was broken. The part was essential to the main operation of the crusher, and with the crusher down the entire system of Climax—from the moly to the mine cars to the hardened steel—came to a halt.

The foreman said to Mr. Jackson, "Can you fix it?"

He replied, "Yep."

"When? I need it right now."

"Come back the day after tomorrow," said Mr. Jackson.

The foreman left and returned two days later. He parked his truck and went into the welding shop to discover Walt's dad welding a sprocket gear for a twelve-year-old who stood there marveling at the blue flame controlled by the master.

"What in hell is going on?" demanded the foreman. "Here you are fixing the gear off this kid's bicycle and you haven't fixed my gear that's holding up production at the biggest molybdenum mine in the world. How come?"

Mr. Jackson closed the valves on the oxygen and acetylene tanks and turned to the red-faced foreman and said, "Well, I guess I think this kid is more important."

That's the way Mr. Jackson's kid runs the Durango School District.

Ed Kutzleb

During the late 1970s, individuals in attendance at gatherings of public school superintendents in the State of Colorado were amazed by the answer to the question: What city in the state produced the greatest number of practicing superintendents? When Leadville is identified as the locale from which seven natives successfully negotiated the hurdles associated with laying claim to the superintendency of cities throughout Colorado and Wyoming, the first response is usually one of doubt or disbelief.

How could a little town situated in a hostile mountain environment ever spawn that many successful chief school district executives in one generation? The "big city boys" would say Leadvillites were fortunate if they could even find their way out of the mountains and into civilization. To accept that so many had blazed a trail to the top of the educational hierarchy in public schools was a little difficult for some "flat-landers." The facts are there, however, and have been documented on various occasions. In alphabetical order, the roll call is as follows: Don Bartell, Bill Conklin, Walt Jackson, Bill Kerrigan, Ed Kutzleb, Jim Raine, and Steve Schuster. All are native Leadvillites, and all served as CEOs in school districts throughout the state of Colorado, with the exception of Bill Conklin, who spent his educational career in Wyoming.

To this crowd, add John Swenson, who at that same time was Chief State School Officer of Colorado and president of a Denver area community college, and Ed Larsh who was a top administrator with the U.S. Office of Education and recipient of the "Alumni of the Year" award at Western State college in 1990, and you've got a group of hometown boys who have influenced education in the Rockies.

What was it about the Leadville environment that nurtured and motivated so many into such a challenging and demanding path of life?

The hardships created by the Great Depression had to be an important element that contributed to the molding of our positive character and attitudes. My dad, Elmer Kutzleb, was employed by the Zaitz Mercantile Company, as was Jim Raine's dad. He walked to work and home six days a week (and quite often on Sunday for no extra pay). The walk from our home at 120 East Twelfth Street, which is located "on the other side of the tracks" not far from "poverty flats," to Zaitz was a diagonal route. The route came close to bisecting the entire city.

Nearly everything our family needed in the way of consumer goods was purchased or, more accurately, charged at the "company store." I recall many depressing discussions between my mom (Irene Gilroy Kutzleb) and my dad regarding the meager amount of money that was left after the "company store" took its monthly toll. My mom helped out by keeping books part time at Durning's

Coal and Feed Company. There were many sacrifices that had to be made for many things, but somehow our folks made certain the essentials of food, clothing, and a warm and loving home were always made available to us. I believe this was accomplished to a large extent through a commitment to hard work and pride in a job well done. The "Leadville work ethic" had to be a trait we all learned and used to our benefit throughout our professional careers.

My dad was a living example of that "ethic" in practice as demonstrated in the winter of 1935 when he had the distinction of being the last one to see Baby Doe Tabor alive. Every month or so, the former queen of Denver and Leadville high society, would clothe herself in worn and tattered garments, wrap her feet in old burlap feed sacks, and walk from the Matchless Mine to Zaitz's store. When her shopping was finished, one of the drivers would take her back to her cabin. In February of 1935, she completed what turned out to be her last shopping trip. My dad was selected to drive Mrs. Tabor and her groceries back to her property. Quite some distance from the entrance to the mine, it became impossible to break through the large snow drifts. The truck mired down in a large drift and could go no further. My dad first carried "the queen" and then her supplies to her cabin, built a fire, and made certain she was safe. She asked that he return in April, and he assured her he would and then departed to the disabled truck.

A few weeks later, Baby Doe was found dead in her cabin. My dad's picture appeared in the *Denver Post* on March 8, 1935, accompanied by a story commending him for his persistence and determination in getting Baby Doe home safely from her final trip to town.

Going the extra mile to make sure the job was done right was a characteristic of Leadville people in which they took a great deal of pride. Again a lesson we all learned first hand at a very early age and undoubtedly contributing immeasurably to our later success.

"The Leadville work ethic" was often instilled at an early age through the many part-time jobs available to youngsters who were sufficiently motivated to accept some rather harsh working conditions along with some rather meager rewards. The various delivery services provided by businesses throughout the community were the prime source for part-time jobs. Many of us started our delivery jobs carrying the *Leadville Shopper* to homes all over the community once a week. The *Shopper* was a family venture run successfully by Ed Larsh's dad with the help of his entire family and the assistance of a few delivery boys.

Later I got a daily route delivering the *Herald Democrat*. It was important that the route be completed and the papers delivered regardless of how late they came off the press or the weather conditions.

Advancing up the delivery service ladder to that of a truck driver for one of the many small grocery stores was a prized and often envied accomplishment. My dad left the Zaitz Mercantile in the early 1940s and purchased a small grocery store in the 500 block of Harrison Avenue—he called it "Elmer's Grocery." I had the good fortune of taking on Dad's delivery truck and thus gaining admission to an elite fraternity. Some of my fellow drivers included Johnny MacLennan, who drove for Cumming's Grocery, Leonard "Patty" Roach, who drove for the Vienna Grocery, Max Cornella, who drove for Cornella's Grocery, and one or more of the Kerrigan clan who helped their dad operate King's Grocery.

Elmer's Grocery was truly a mom and pop business. Only now am I beginning to appreciate the combined risk and commitment assumed by my folks and others who operated small businesses at that time. To one day announce to his family, as my father did, that he intended to abandon the security of a steady monthly paycheck for the uncertainty of becoming an entrepreneur in a mining town took some courage. It was a risk that not everyone would take.

These are only a few of the characteristics that come to mind when reflecting on the uniqueness of Leadville natives. Many others, such as a firm belief in the value of a formal education, the unwavering commitment to a Christian way of life, and the open acceptance of your fellow man regardless of his background are but a few of the additional characteristic that predominated during my growing up in the "melting pot" called Leadville.

28

A Golden Afternoon

As part of our commitment to the oral history of Leadville, Jane, Robert, and I realized we needed more personal stories of the town and especially authentic, first-hand tales from the mines. We needed a place to meet, a place to share the stories. We all knew where the Golden Burro Bar and Cafe was on Harrison Avenue across the street from the Herald Democrat. *I didn't know Carol Luoma, the present owner, but Ed Kerrigan did, and he asked her if we could meet at the Burro. We met there maybe four or five times. Some different people would come each time—a few would drive up from Denver; others came from Salida; some from Leadville; Gerald McMillin came from Florida; Robert came from Grant.*

Over the course of the year, we got to know Carol Luoma. We talked Leadville; we connected; we shared names from the past. Carol, the daughter of Iona and Wilfred Brink of the Chicken Hill Brinks, sat in and told us about her father who was a miner/mechanic at the Resurrection and other mines up on Johnny Hill. We kept saying that we wanted to meet him because we knew that "Viv" had a lot of stories to tell. He had a cabin at Turquoise Lake near the Kitts, and he worked with Ray Kitt at the Resurrection.

Carol finally arranged for us to meet Viv, but he became ill the week before we were to do so. Carol called a few days later and said that Viv had died. Ray Kitt described his friend Viv in a simple way. "He was born, raised, lived, and died on Chicken Hill. He was a good son, a good husband, a good father, and a good friend." Oral history is as fragile as the human life.

Around the table one Saturday afternoon in January 1992 were Edith Seppi, who came to Leadville in 1942; Jane Larsh; Robert Nichols; and four others who were all born in Leadville. Ray Kitt lived up on West Ninth, Carl Miller up on Chicken Hill, Eddie Kerrigan in the heart of the Ninth Street Irish neighborhood on East Ninth and Poplar, Lee Schraeder on East Ninth, and I had lived up on West Sixth.

One of the most rewarding aspects of "circling the bases," beginning at home and making your way back home again is the connections you establish. Each element, each story or fact or idea, is a part of a larger message, and it is the chore of oral historians to discover as much of the "whole" as the sum of the parts will reveal.

On that memorable Saturday afternoon in the Golden Burro, sitting at a table surrounded by a cross section of Leadville's character as well as its "characters" (some of whom who had known each other all their lives and yet had never sat down together in one room), a special sense, almost magical, enhanced the hours. Each story was told with candor and eagerness and was listened to with genuine interest. There never was never a sense of competition or one-upsmanship, simply the shared pleasure of memories, and no one even noticed the tape recorder after the first few minutes.

Join us! Sit down. Have a cup of coffee and listen in.

Kitt: My mother's mother, Elizabeth Playford, came from Wroxiter, Canada. I'm not certain when my grandfather Tracy came to Leadville, but it was in the early times; he was from New Brunswick. My dad's father, Albert Kitt, came from the Township of Barrow on Furnace in the Yorkshire District of England. He migrated to the United States in the early 1870s and, along with his brother, came to Leadville in 1876. Grandma was from Cornwall, born as Elizabeth Eddy Hicks.

Are your people called Cornish?

Kitt: Yes, but more frequently, "Cousin Jacks."

Kerrigan: And not a spark of ambition in the bunch of them.

Kitt: It took the Cousin Jacks to teach the Irish how to operate a wheelbarrow and shovel; after that the Irish did all the work.

So, Ray, tell us about the timbermen.

Kitt: Both my grandfathers were timbermen. Grandfather Kitt learned his craft in the coal mines of England, and Grandfather Tracy—his name was Amasa ("Ace") Tracy—picked up his skills from the timber business. His home was once a place called Tracy Mills up in New Brunswick.

The two of them became competitors in the business, both being hired as contractors in Leadville—the men who, using various sized timbers would shore up broken ground to prevent cave-ins and slides. Normally the miners would do their own timbering, but if they hit a particularly bad piece of ground then they would hire one of my two grandfathers—they each had a crew of men—who would go in and get the job done. It was dangerous work, and both took a lot of pride in what they did.

This created a manner of bitter competition between the two—they hated each other's guts. Underground there was no monkey business—it was all serious. But when they met on the Leadville streets, they gave each other a wide berth or fists were liable to fly. No one ever won because the fight never stopped. This competition between Tracy and Kitt went on all the years that they lived in Leadville. And then later, when my dad and my mother got married—my mother being a Tracy and my dad a Kitt—old Tracy didn't like it at all. Albert Kitt was already dead, but I'm sure he was spinning in his grave.

We thought for all those years that the problem was the competition between Kitt and Tracy in the timber business, but later my mother contacted a great-aunt back in New Brunswick, Canada, who was the family genealogist, and found out the dispute probably began up there. Grandfather Tracy had an older brother whose daughter was married to Grandfather Kitt in his first marriage. The marriage ended in divorce, and that started the whole thing. Grandpa Tracy was a hard-shell, stiff-necked Baptist who didn't believe in divorce. Years later I asked my mom if she ever thought about divorcing my dad and she said, "No, I haven't, Ray. I've considered murder a couple of times, but never divorce."

Was your dad a timberman?

Kitt: For a while. Grandfather Kitt died, and Grandma married a man named Shimmin. Dad and his brother Harry worked with

"Pa" Shimmin in the Penrose Mine, which was literally in their backyard of 407 East Fifth. Dad was in his late teens.

One day they were timbering a small tunnel that was following a vein of ore. Dad was down on the station level and Pa and Harry up in the "dog hole." Pa would call down the measurements, and by the time Dad could get the timber cut and up to them it would be too long—the "back" [the roof] was coming in that fast.

On that particular day, Dad went up to the surface for more timber and decided to eat his lunch. While sitting there on the lumber pile on that warm spring day with the squirrels running around and the good feel of the sun upon him, he thought to himself, "What in the hell am I doing in that hole in the ground?" With that he took his carbide lamp, hard hat, belt, and even his lunch bucket and threw them all down the dump. He walked home and never went underground to the day he died—and even then he had made arrangements to be damn sure he was buried above ground in a mausoleum on the top row.

Pa Shimmin could never understand Dad's decision to quit, and this caused a strain on their relationship that lasted for years. Pa was a Manxman from the Isle of Mann. He had a couple of buddies from the Old Country, and they would occasionally walk to town and have a few beers and then go home, minding their own business. But once in a while Pa would get crosswise with somebody and nearly come to blows—usually over some trivial matter. Before it would get physical, Pa would withdraw, go home, and under some pretense get Dad and Harry to go with him back to the debate. On his arrival at Swanson's Pool Hall, he would announce, "I brought me boys. Now we'll see who's right and who's wrong!" Everyone usually took this with great humor, and peace would prevail.

What did your dad do after he gave up his heritage as a timberman?

Kitt: Dad loved horses and was very good at training and breaking them. He was particularly good with teams: two, four, six, eight horses at a time hauling ore from various mines off of Breece and Fryer hills to the mills. He frequently worked with Jim Glover (Mary Glenn and Dorothy Hayes's uncle) as it was to each other's advantage to have a buddy in case you got into some kind of trouble—breakdown or whatever.

The trip down the hill was always an adventure; there were plenty of opportunities for something to go wrong. Some of the hills were so steep that the wagon brakes and the teams couldn't hold back the load. Then they'd have to "rough lock" the wheels, which was to wrap a length of chain around the rim and lock the wheel so that the chain was on the bottom and the wheel wouldn't turn. Sometimes they'd have to repeat this process numerous times between mine and mill, but it sure was better than a runaway.

The loads would average about eight tons and often had to be shoveled on and off. A normal day would be at least twelve hours, or often longer, and six days a week. Two or three dollars a day would be good pay.

One of the first things I remember Dad teaching me was, by using leather thongs, how to hold the "ribbons" (the reins) for a team of horses. Four-in-hand was the term. I later hauled ore for Johnny O'Connell, but it was in a truck with a heater, soft seats, and air brakes.

Lee, your dad was in the ore hauling business, wasn't he?

Schraeder: Yes, he was. My roots in Leadville go back to my grandfather, Thomas O'Mahoney, who arrived in 1879. He was an educated man with an AB degree from Notre Dame and law training at the University of Michigan. When he first came to the area, he lived in Malta where he cut and sold firewood. He married Catherine Shiel, who was a school teacher, and they moved the four miles up to Leadville where she taught classes to people who were interested in becoming United States citizens. Their daughter, my mother, in later years (the thirties and forties) did the same thing while serving as clerk of the District Court. She was instrumental in helping many, many people with their citizenship. There are people in Leadville now who, when I go to see them, say, "I've got my naturalization papers here with your mother's signature on them."

Kerrigan: My father was one of them.

Schraeder: She helped plenty get their papers. My grandfather,

Thomas O'Mahoney, was elected to the Colorado House of Representatives from Lake County in 1891 and served through the Eighth and Tenth General Assemblies. In later years, beginning in 1896, he was elected county sheriff, police magistrate, and, from 1916 until his death in the twenties, he was county judge.

My dad, Harry Schraeder, was Lake County sheriff for twenty-five years. He came to live with his grandmother out in Poverty Flats when he was a young boy. I'll tell you how he got into the freight business. As a young man, he got a goat and a cart and started hauling tin cans from Leadville to the smelter. When he saved enough money, he bought himself a team of horses and a wagon with a big tank on it. He'd go out to the Arkansas River and get a load of water which he would deliver to people in town—he established a route. Once they got water piped into homes that business was gone, but by then he had enough money to buy more horses and ore wagons and started moving ore from the mines to the smelter. At one time, down behind the old Liberty Bell picture show on Sixth, from the alley down to Pine and clear from Fifth to Sixth and East Harrison Avenue, he and a guy named Harry Gilmore owned the whole square block and had their barns, their horses and wagons there.

Do any of you remember Gilmore's Barn?

Kitt: Sure. My dad worked for Gilmore.

Schraeder: Both of those barns burned to the ground in 1933.

Lee, did your dad drive a team?

Schraeder: No, by the time he was in the ore freighting business, he had mule skinners who worked for him.

Kerrigan: Now there was a rugged bunch.

Schraeder: They sure were. You know they lived right there in the barn. Each mule skinner had four horses, and each horse had a stall, and then the next stall would be the mule skinner's. They lived right with their horses.

Kerrigan: Can you imagine the excitement of bringing a full load of ore off Johnny Hill? A load of ore and four miles in front of you coming down that hill. They had to know what they were doing.

Schraeder: And they did. When I was a kid in the second grade—of course I went to St. Mary's School—the teams would come down either Fifth or Seventh. I'd know which one they'd be coming down. When I got out of school, I'd run two or three blocks over and sit on the curb and wait. Then down would come the teams with the horses snorting and breathing heavy and the wagons sagging with the load. One of those mule skinners would hoist me up next to him on the high board seat. There would be those four huge animals and the great wagon and they would hand me the reins as we rolled through town. There wasn't anything greater for an eight-year old in Leadville. I felt like a king on his throne.

Each Saturday, one of the mule skinners, his name was Brice Vinyard—he lived down in the barns—would come to our house at 220 East Ninth Street and get me, and we'd go down to the old Court Exchange Restaurant. I would sit there at the counter with ten or fifteen mule skinners, and we'd have breakfast. I learned some language there that you never heard up at St. Mary's. My folks, like yours, understood community education.

After we finished breakfast and stopped off at Peck's Pool Hall for a candy bar, we would go to the barn where the horses were to be curried, stalls cleaned, harnesses polished, and wagons greased. I was really living! There were always wagons we had to take down and run into the river so the water would swell the spokes and make them tight.

The mule skinners had their games, too. Great games of mumblypeg—they'd take a knife and flip it, and if it hit and stuck on the point, it was worth three points and all. And they were experts with those blacksnake whips. They could pick flies off the rear end of those horses fifteen feet away, and the horse wouldn't even flinch. And when they were just playing around, they would take turns snapping cigarettes out of each other's mouths.

We'd spend all day Saturday with the horses, the tack, and the wagons. What a great way for a kid to spend a Saturday. Let me tell you that these mule skinners were so tough that their spit bounced. There wasn't any of them who was married, and they were all heavy drinkers. They chewed tobacco and were always spitting and cussing—they pretty much kept to themselves.

One of those guys lived in Cody's barn up on West Sixth Street. His name was Sam Carny—you probably remember him, he was one of the famous ones. Sam had this big chew of tobacco and kept a pint of whiskey right in the wagon with him all the time—and that whip. I don't think he ever said a sentence, this is the honest-to-God-truth, I never heard him say a whole sentence without at least four or five really good swear words. He was a tough son of a gun.

Kerrigan: You talk about chewing tobacco. Carl and I had the experience of Hy Hefley down in the mines. Hy mixed his own "snuse," and it had rum in it. It was snuff that you soaked. He'd even chew at night. His wife wouldn't sleep in the same room with him because he had a chew. I ate lunch with him one day, and he had a sack of Beechnut with him, and that was his dessert. I only ate with him once.

Miller: I worked with him at Climax. Viv Brink and Hy Hefley and myself used to go down to check the pump at the five hundred level, and he'd spit on everything. You'd be working on a pump and every wrench, every tool—he spit on all the handles.

Carl, you're third generation Leadville, aren't you?

Miller: Third generation. My mother's side was full-blooded Irish. My grandfather was from Dublin, Ireland. His name was Frank Walsh. He originally settled in Victor, Colorado, and then came to Leadville just before the turn of the century. My mother was born in a house located where the Penrose mine dump is right now on East Forth Street. On my father's side, both grandparents were from Sweden. They moved to Aspen from Sweden. My dad moved to Leadville when he was seventeen. On both sides, the Walsh and the Millers, they were miners—including my dad and all his uncles. I've worked in the mining industry for over thirty years; twenty-seven years of that is underground experience.

Kerrigan: There's nothing like it, is there?

Miller: When people go underground, if they aren't scared out of it immediately, they'll tell you it's very, very exciting. It's just another world. I'll never forget my first day underground—I'll never forget it. I got out of high school in 1956 and had been working at the Irene on the surface. In those days, they wouldn't let you go underground until you were eighteen. My dad always told me he didn't want me in the mines, and I told him I wouldn't go underground even though I really wanted to and to this day I love it down there. There's nothing like it. So, shortly after I turned eighteen, I took the first opportunity to go underground at the Irene shaft.

That first day I went down with Bill Hasty—a man who had been in the mines for years and knew everything there was to know about them. We went all the way down to the 1600 Level. We were going to be doing some work in the manway—the part of the shaft with ladders for men to climb—putting in some air lines. We were getting materials together when the first light I saw coming down the drift was, lo and behold, my father. He said, "What in the hell are you doing? You have absolutely no business in this mine." And I told him I was only going to work the mines for a while, and then I'd go on to school and whatever.

So, Bill Hasty and I picked up some of the tools, got in the cage, and went up to the 1200 Level. [The 1200 Level at the Irene is where the Yak Tunnel comes through and drains the water.] Bill and I were working in the manway, and I'm in awe. I can't even work because I want to look and see what is going on. It's just a couple of days past my eighteenth birthday, and I don't know what the hell I'm doing, and Hasty has been in the mines all his life, and he's barking orders at me. He's below me in the manway, and I accidentally knocked his hard-hat off. For those of you who remember him, he had a bald head. In my embarrassment I tried to help him but only succeeded in showering his head with a lot of little rocks. He screams up that shaft so loud that Dad probably heard him down on the 1600 Level, "Goddamn you, kid, your dad's right, you don't belong in the mine. You belong in some damn circus." I'll never forget it; we came up to the surface, and he had all those little bumps on his head.

You spent most of your mining years up at Climax, right?

Miller: Yes, but I started at the Irene.

Kerrigan: I did some mining up there myself. It was in the late forties and early fifties. I had come out of college and was helping my mother with the store and working in the mines, starting at the Irene. It was good money in those days, and all I wanted was $100 out of what was sometimes a $1500 paycheck. I'd take $100 dollars and, hell, I could party, drive my car, and have plenty of money. I gave the rest to my mom—she was putting the kids through college. I was living great.

This one day I was the motorman and Rivets was the whistle punk. We were down in the Garbutt tunnel, which was probably five hundred feet away from the Irene shaft; this was where we stored the powder that Rivets and I had to get when we needed dynamite from the powder magazine.

After we had been on the job for maybe three days, these miners would tell us to go get ten cases of dynamite. So Rivets and I would jump on the electric motor and head out down the drifts into the Garbutt tunnel. Mining was very dangerous, I mean, very dangerous—not only on the job but at lunch times—they were always scaring the hell out of us young guys! There were two mechanics that would slip away and when Rivets and I would go for the powder, these bastards were down the tunnel maybe three hundred feet, hiding with their lights off; as we would be coming along they would make noises like "hoo-hoo-hoo," and shit, we were already scared to death; I would put the car in reverse, and we would tear out of there. The miners would be down by the shaft laughing their asses off.

Another time—you've got to remember I had just been to college—we were pumping in the Irene shaft seven hundred gallons a minute, and five hundred feet to the surface. I knew there was an old mine down the hill that, if we could connect with a small tunnel, we could pump the water out horizontally. So I suggested to Jenkins, the boss, that maybe we should go look. We opened the drainage tunnel in a couple of weeks—the tunnel was like a rifle barrel, straight and narrow—we found a way to pump out the water. Finally the hot shot electricians wired the tunnel for electric dynamite detonators. But they put the switch in the tunnel about 50 feet from the portal.

This one day the miners (they were all in on it) started bragging me up for thinking of a better way to pump the water, and as a reward they allowed me to walk into the tunnel and pull the switch that would detonate the dynamite back in the tunnel, maybe 150 feet away. Boy, was I proud. I was enthusiastic! I was thinking I had it made as a real miner. I thought how dumb electricians were. What I didn't know was that whoever threw that switch was in a whole hell of a lot of trouble. The miners all lined up outside the portal. They knew about percussion and cocky young Irish college kids. I was going to shoot the first round! They even had bleachers outside the tunnel. They sent me in, and I threw the switch. I heard the boom and started walking out. Suddenly—Woosh! The percussion hit me and rolled me ass over teakettle. I was still rolling as I passed the bleachers!

Seppi: I went down in the Jonny Mine in 1942. I think it was to the 300 Level. I went down with a friend of mine from Boulder and Merle Roberts—he wanted to go back and see his dad and we went along with him. Mr. Roberts was working back probably five hundred feet. It wasn't a long way, but it seemed like forever because we had a stupid flashlight that wouldn't stay on. I had been down into the Jonny three or four times before, but never without a light. Off in other directions others were putting off their blasts, and I kept thinking, "Oh, my word." Anyway, we finally got to where Mr. Roberts was, and I was so grateful. There he was, up so high in a stope, in a little, tiny hole—working up there.

Kerrigan: They called those small tunnels powder boxes—tunnels usually about two feet by four feet—just big enough to get through and follow the vein. It was in those holes a miner would find a nugget occasionally. The early miners talked about "powder box raises." It's the high-grading that gave them some flexible spending. Without taking a little gold "downtown" for themselves it would have been impossible—if it weren't for high-grading they couldn't have survived. It was "quasi-legal."

Eddie, were the miner owners aware that high-grading went on?

Kerrigan: Oh, yes. But it's not like the miners were making big money at it. They'd take it to assayers like Mandy who would only give them ten percent. I got this right from Chris Kastrinas who worked the mines when he was eleven years old—they would only get ten percent, and if they complained about it he would threaten to tell the sheriff.

Kitt: Edith, I'm surprised they let women go down in the mines that long ago—wasn't it was still a superstition that women were bad luck?

Seppi: No, by then it was kind of okay for a woman to go underground. I think I might have been one of the first. I was working for Social Services, and people from the Health Department would ask me to get them into the mines. I would talk to Mr. Wilson, and he would take a few of us down—although once, he said he was going to give me a gunny sack and send me off and leave me down there looking for specimens that looked like roses. We always had to sign a paper that freed them of responsibility.

Schraeder: There were women who came down the mines back then. After I got out of high school in 1938 I worked at a few mines—the Resurrection, the Elkhorn, and others. Back in those days women were allowed down a shaft if they knew the bosses—like your Mr. Wilson. I was working as the "top man" up at the Elkhorn, and Ski Brady was running the hoist. It was my job to communicate with the man who ran the engine that raised and lowered the cage, or as we called it, "the skip." I had this handle that would make a bell ring in the building where the hoist man operated a lever that would lower the skip to the different levels down the shaft—many of the Leadville shafts were over a thousand feet deep.

Whenever a woman would come to have the experience of going down in a mine we had a little trick we would play on them. The signal I would give Ski when there were only men on the skip was three bells. Then when I could see they were all on board, I would give him two more bells and he would lower the skip down the shaft. When there was a woman on board, I would give him the three bells and then the hold down the handle to give him a tat-tat-tat-tat sound instead of a clear bell, and he would know the trick was on. He would let that skip fall down the shaft, sometimes twenty to thirty feet before slowing it down. The women back then wore jodhpurs—sort of "horse show" pants that they would tuck into their boots. You know, we must have played that trick fifty times, and I don't remember one lady getting off that skip with dry pants.

Don't you think that joke was sexist?

Miller: Well, it wasn't just women who had dirty tricks played on them. I don't know whether I should tell this story with you ladies here, but it is a true story. When I worked at Climax there were always geologists who came around to do this and that, predicting how the earth was going to be fractured and checking on the ore and taste it with their tongues. They would carry little picks with them and chip off samples from the ribs—the sides of the drift or tunnel—and ore. Well, I don't know why they did it, but the miners would get there first and urinate on ribs then just wait around for the geologists.

Kerrigan: We just tell it like it was. You know there was a lot of fooling around in the mines and in all the jobs people did back then. Joking around and also competition.

I went to work up at a job shoveling coal. It was in 1948 and I was wanting to go to school and also to build myself up, so my Uncle Jim Morrison, who ran transportation up at Climax, put me with Johnny Baldessari on a coal dump truck. Not only did we unload the cars, there was always competition to see who could load the most. And then for lunch we'd go over to where his brother Alex "Tarzan" Baldessari was, and they would practice for the mucking contests—at lunch we would shovel rock against time. I'd come home and tell my mother, "I can't take this."

Kitt: Even back in the early days there were contests. My Grandfather Tracy wasn't very tall but was heavy through the shoulders and chest. He was a phenomenal walker—particularly heel-to-toe speed walking. Mom told me of a time that he walked from Kokomo to Leadville—twenty miles—to enter a free-for-all contest against a fellow who was the contender for the world heel-to-toe championship. Grandpa walked him into the ground, had a cup of tea, and walked back to Kokomo where he had to go to work the next morning.

Magic happened that day. It was truly golden. It was as if we all looked around after listening and discovered the concept of "home." We have been connected ever since. A few weeks later Ray Kitt called and said it was one of the best afternoons he could recall. Others of us felt the same way. To all who read this book or parts thereof, thank you. Thank you from each of us who are involved in contributing to it.

Our deepest gratitude goes to our families, those who made it possible to be where we are today. Our gratitude is for their courage to migrate to a new country—many times starting from nothing. Most came with nothing but a few miserable possessions; some had trades or skills; some had families. They all had one thing in common, a dream of a better life. They were driven almost fanatically not to fail and have to go back to the life from whence they came.

Many came with no more collateral than their word and the desire to do well using strong backs, strong hands, but mostly strong hearts. Many never saw their dreams come true—taken away by illness, accidents, or other situations. Yet they kept coming, they kept on trying, and thankfully they did. They left their genetic fingerprint on each of us. We are all the products of our ancestors. Each of us has qualities and talents and have no idea why. Look back in your families, and I think you will find some answers.

If there is a common thread through our individual experiences and stories, it is our deep appreciation for the women in our lives. The women kept it all together. They took shacks and made homes. They did without so their children could eat and be warm. They bore the children and healed the sick—they were the glue and the fiber and the substance that held our lives together.

Please talk to your children. Make sure they know their "roots." If possible, write or record the history and stories of your families. One day your children and grandchildren will want to know about their ancestors.

It is their heritage.

29

You Might as Well Dance

If the wheel is fixed
I would still take a chance.
If you have to walk on thin ice,
you might as well dance.
    —Found on a restroom wall in Leadville

When we were little kids, we had no television, and the radio wasn't too good either. So, on Friday nights, after dinner we would often gather around the kitchen table. Clyde, my mom's younger brother, would walk up Leiter Avenue from Chestnut Street, and sometimes John, my dad's brother, would come over from West Seventh. When they came to our house, my parents, my brothers and sister, and these two uncles would all play games. Sometimes Mom would make fudge or taffy. Often we would play mumblety-peg. We played that game so frequently that the center board on the kitchen table eventually had to be replaced. The oil cloth Mom put out during meals covered the jackknife gouges, but they got so deep they caused the noodle soup to list precariously.

On different occasions other aunts and uncles on both sides of the family would drop by. On these evenings, games would be replaced by stories. They'd tell baseball stories, snowstorm stories, and outlaw stories, but the best were Pioneer Bar stories about my granddad, who knew Wyatt Earp, Doc Holliday, Horace Tabor, and Marshal Duggan. Whenever the tales got around to Duggan, the next story was always about Edie and Mindy.

Dad was a great story teller. Also, he loved to recite poetry, particularly poems that told a tale such as those by Robert Service. Dan McGrew and the gal called Lou and the Malamute Saloon all took on a reality of their own when he brought those words alive. Sometimes he would quiet the room with a sentimental rendition of the maudlin masterpiece, "The Face on the Barroom Floor." We'd all listen so closely as he spoke the tragic tale, and then, right at the end of the poem:

> *Another drink, . . . with chalk in hand, the vagabond began*
> *To sketch a face that well might buy the soul of any man.*
> *Then, as he placed another lock upon the shapely head,*
> *With fearful shriek, he leaped, and fell across the picture . . . dead.*

When the artist, with one last stroke, leaped and fell across the picture dead, Dad would likewise leap and sprawl on the kitchen floor. He'd lie there for a dramatic pause and then turn to the kids and say, "drunk!"

Now that I think of it, it seems my dad knew that true art is never wholly sad or wholly humorous—the same sort of realization that distinguishes jazz from country music.

Dad didn't tell the Mindy story very often, but it's not the kind of tale you ever forget. It was about her trip to Denver following the death of Marshal Duggan. This was a family story. In most of the books written about Leadville and in the magazine articles about its gunfighters in general and Marshal Duggan in particular, there is mention of my great-aunt Mindy and the dance she did in front of the Texas House. That was public knowledge, witnessed by a large crowd and reported in the *Herald Democrat*. The whole story, the story of the fulfillment of Mindy's oath has never been told outside the realm of family kitchens.

When Dad told the Mindy story, it was a dramatic production with narrative and dialogue—the essence of an event rather than the recollection of an event. I want you to know Aunt Mindy as well as I did when my father told us of the opening of her heart.

John Minor Larsh had taken Mindy to the D&RG Depot on Poplar Street at noon on April 23, 1888. When he picked her up in a borrowed buggy that morning, he was surprised to find she was still wearing a black dress. Also, he had no idea what business Mindy had to conduct in Denver. He had asked her once, and she had tersely replied that it was something she had to do, and nothing else was said. That was the way Mindy was, and John didn't bother pressing her when he knew it would be in vain.

John had thought the entire eight-year tragedy was finally over. It had been two weeks since the town's most notorious bully, ex-Marshal Duggan, was found shot on the sidewalk in front of the Texas House. He was shot at close range just behind the right ear, and his blood was still in evidence the next day. Though he hung on for a few more hours, he finally died. Not many were surprised by the violent nature of his demise, nor were many saddened by his loss.

It was there on that board sidewalk that Mindy had made good on the promise of eight years earlier. Arriving in a bright red dress and carrying a bundle under her left arm, she stood in the street before the tavern door for at least ten minutes before she began, long enough for a crowd to assemble—patrons of the infamous gambling saloon and various others who had heeded the fast traveling word that Leadville's "lady in the black dress" was ready to dance. Her brother Johnny stood across the street. He had walked her there and then stepped away from her scene. With a toss of her wrist, she brushed back the mob and stepped to the sidewalk. At her glance, all fell silent, and she spoke.

"In this bundle," she declared, and her voice was strong though trembling with emotion, "is the tattered clothing I have worn for eight years of mourning, eight years of sorrow—my widow's weeds. I no longer need them. When I leave here I will deliver this dress to Mrs. Duggan, for now it is her time to grieve. It's her time to suffer the spilled blood of her man as it was mine eight years ago when Duggan murdered my husband, Lewis Lamb.

"Some of you were there that day and heard the promises I made. Some of you were there to see the stain of my husband's warm blood upon my blouse where I had cradled him in death. You know that I have lived that oath daily in the wearing of the weeds. Well, now also recall that I swore to Duggan, 'As God and you are my witness, I will dance at your death.'"

With those words of horror, she dropped the bundle and began a series of graceful though pain-wrenched pirouettes choreographed by years of mental anticipation, turning and turning upon the dark, stained boards as the mute crowd stood in awe. Abruptly she stopped. She picked up the dress, Johnny joined her, and they walked away.

"How old was Aunt Mindy in 1888?" my brother Donald asked.

"Well," my dad began, "she was born in a farm house near Eldorado, Ohio, in 1844. That would have made her forty-four. Mindy used to claim she was four years younger than she really was. She wouldn't give her age in years, but rather in summers. No one ever challenged her because in Leadville it was easy to understand how someone might lose track of a few summers. I remember one year when summer was on a Thursday about a week after the Fourth of July."

"What happened after your dad took Mindy up to the depot to catch the train for Denver?" someone would ask. Dad then, as if on cue, went on with the telling of this amazing family legend.

Leadville had about two feet of snow on April 28 that year. John Minor had no choice but to walk up to the depot to meet Mindy's returning train. You couldn't chain-up a horse to get through such deep and wet snow like you can a truck. Even allowing for the standard delay, he ended up waiting at the railroad station for a couple of hours before he heard the steam whistle blowing as the D&RG passenger train made its way up from Malta. It was 11:00 P.M. as he stood out on the platform listening to the magnificent sounds of the iron horse as it rumbled and screeched to a stop. The hissing hot steam penetrated the icy air and created a billowy fog. Emerging from the mist, as if in a motion picture, was Mindy.

She was not dressed in black. Traces of a new orange dress were visible beyond the fringe of her heavy coat. She was carrying a small satchel. It was as if the metamorphosis was still in process— Mindy wearing orange in transition from mourning black. Standing in the cloud of smoke and fog she cast an image John Minor was never to forget.

"It snowed. We'll have to walk," he told her.

"First we have to talk."

Without another word they walked along Poplar Street toward town. At Tenth Street they entered an all-night cafe. It was in the building that later became Frank E. Brown's Grocery Store.

They took a booth in a corner near the coal stove, ordered coffee, and Mindy said, "Johnny, don't interrupt me. I might not be able to start again once I stop."

"I'm supposed to be dealing cards down at the Pioneer at midnight."

"You may be late."

Mindy had never been one to talk much, but when she did she had a way of really getting your attention. John just signaled for the waitress to bring them two coffees and sat back to listen. She waited for the coffee to arrive and then she started.

"What I'm going to tell you tonight I'll never tell again, so please pay attention."

"I will," he said raising his cup.

"When we met you in Deadwood over ten years ago, it was the first time Edie and I had ever left Mama's kitchen. Since then I have been to Redcliff and out to Evergreen Lakes, but never anywhere by myself. When you brought me up to the station the other day, I had no idea what to expect—a lady traveling alone on a train to Denver.

"I knew what I was going to do but not knowing for sure why, or, particularly, how. Johnny, I've never been so scared. I sat in my green velvet seat watching the moon shine on the Arkansas until the light of early morning. By then we were in this incredibly deep canyon—the conductor announced it as the Royal Gorge. I'd never even heard of half the towns where the train stopped.

"Finally, after more than eighteen hours, we pulled into Union Station. It was about dusk, and I found myself standing there in the middle of a crowd of strangers and more alone than I had ever been in my life. I think it was right then, out on the sidewalk in front of the station in the flurry of people coming and going, that I was confronted with how futile my life had become. I was in the middle and, yet, touching nothing. I was there to act out a commitment I had made, and nobody in the world except me would even know what I had done. Is this making any sense?"

John was wise enough not to say much, but he did say he knew what a big city Denver was and, for that matter, what a big world it was and how natural it was to be frightened by it all.

"No, Johnny. By then I wasn't feeling fear—it was despair. But I also knew it wasn't a matter of debate whether to continue on or not. I had been eight years getting there, and there was no turning back. It was as if I was in control of not being in control."

John sensed the importance of Mindy's need. He knew, as anyone would who had been witness to the major events of his sister's life of dramatic and tragic changes, whatever it was she was telling him needed to be said. He remembered burying his first wife Emma at the graveyard in Georgetown. He remembered the guilt, the sense of his own inadequacy, and the difficulty of trying to express his feelings to Rachel. Mindy was now doing the same thing. John had been there for most of it. He had been there back in Illinois when Edie was born, and their mother had charged Mindy with watching out for her— "helping Edie find her way." He had encouraged and supported Mamie, Mindy, and Edie on their way west to Deadwood and into Leadville—as they had supported him. He was there to give his sister away on the day she married Lewis. He was also there on the terrible November day when Duggan killed Lewis and there when Mindy swore an oath. Over the eight years he had been there to see the daily sorrow of her black dress and had seen her dance on the killer's blood. He had put her on the train just days before—she had been wearing a new black dress, telling him her mourning was not yet over—and now he sat listening not only with his ears but with his heart as well.

He had no idea what Mindy had done in Denver. He was curious but also patient. That night he was her brother, but he was also her friend, and he would listen to her story. He sought her eyes. John knew how to read eyes—years of shuffling fate about the felt of a gaming table had given him that skill—a credential that separated professional gamblers from those who merely played games of chance. He saw something in Mindy's blue-gray eyes he had never seen before. In that instant he saw more deeply into her heart than ever before in all the years of his life. He knew his dear and troubled sister was about to reveal aspects of the fulfillment of her "pledge" about which he had no knowledge.

She had stopped to add sugar to her second cup of coffee, and John thought about that damn dress she had been wearing all those years—the one she had delivered to Mrs. Duggan a couple of weeks earlier. John, Rachel, and Edie had often discussed Mindy's unbending resolution. They would ask, as people all over the town must have: Why? Why not get on with her life? What did it really mean? Years and years passing, and what would it prove? Who cared? And, "For God's sakes," they would tell her, "the thing is in tatters." He thought to himself that now that she had at last cast off her black threads, she would once again be faced with a woman's daily dilemma of deciding what to wear. He smiled at that. Mindy's voice penetrated his whimsical silence. "John, are you paying attention to what I'm saying?"

There was no doubt John was paying attention.

She went on. "From the station I walked across Market Street to a hotel. Fortunately there were others waiting in line to register for a room. I was the only single woman and I didn't want to stand out any more than I had to. I told the clerk I was there to attend a funeral and would be needing a single room for two nights. The black dress helped. My room was on the third floor."

For someone as taciturn as Mindy to be giving such detail, it was almost as if some great force inside her was driving her to tell her story.

"I was hungry but didn't dare leave my room until morning. I sat by the window and looked down on Wazee Street. There was a young girl there who looked to be in her teens. She was standing under a gas light trying to sell herself. I thought of Edie back in Leadville and, Johnny, I just sat there and cried.

"I must have eventually fallen asleep because I awakened with the sun coming in across the unused bed. It was time to venture forth. I put on my red dress and then covered as much of it as I could with my overcoat. I walked down to the sidewalk. I was hopeful one of those strangers could direct me to the Riverside Cemetery. Johnny, did you know they shipped Duggan's body down to Denver for burial?"

"Yes. I guess I knew that. I never asked why, though."

"He had family living in Denver, a brother I think. And there was plot of ground for him with his parents at the Riverside Cemetery. It's hard to imagine a man that wicked having a mother—I always thought of him as being some orphan from Hell. Well, anyway, I had no idea how difficult it would be to find—it's not like going from West Second to the Evergreen Cemetery.

"I was hungry and went into a restaurant and sat at a small table. The waitress was waiting on about fifteen people at the same time and was in a terrible hurry. I wanted to ask her the way to the cemetery, but she fled as soon as I finished giving her my order. After a short time a gentleman came in and sat nearby, and I asked him if he knew how I might get to the Riverside Cemetery. "Before he could answer the waitress who was flying by at the time said, 'Hang on a moment, Dearie, I'll tell you how to get out there,' and then dashed on in a run from the fry cook to the customers while simultaneously carrying on four separate conversations.

After a while she stopped and asked me, 'You going out there for a funeral?' I gave her an answer that must have sounded strange. I told her that in a way it was a funeral but in another it was going to be a dance. She told me to go back to the Union Station and ask about a horse cart that went out to the cemetery. And then, just as she was about to take off again, she said as she glanced down at the red ruffle of my dress hanging below my coat, 'And another thing, Dearie. You'd better make up your mind, funeral or dance—there's one hell of a difference.'

"Out on the sidewalk, I looked at the reflection of myself in the window, and I saw this lonely, confused, old-looking lady. This fossil. This fool who after eight years was prepared to dance at a funeral. I thought of how right the waitress had been. I had better make up my mind because, indeed, there was one hell of a difference.

"It must have taken a couple of hours, but I did manage to find the right car and find the cemetery. Once there, with the instructions of the gatekeeper, I was able to find the fresh dirt marking Duggan's grave. Then I walked over to the far side of the cemetery to a point that looked down on the river and sat down on a stone bench and waited for the dance—so much for the funeral."

John had to interrupt. "Wait a second. I thought you had already done your dance. It seems like fifteen people a day have told me they were at the Texas House when my sister did her twirl. Now you're telling me you went all the way to Denver to try your two-step on grass?"

"Yes, but Johnny. I didn't just go to Denver to do a dance." For the first time in many a moon John saw a twinkle in his sister's eye. "I also had to urinate."

With that, John, looking at his sister with some degree of incredulity, said, "So do I," and got up to leave the table. "Order me a shot of whiskey. I need something stronger than coffee if I'm going to hear the rest of this adventure."

A shot and a beer were waiting John upon his return. "Well, go on with it," he said. "Don't leave me sitting here."

"Johnny, you were there on Purdy's porch that November day. You heard me swear to wear black until Duggan died and then to dance on his grave—all while I held my husband's bleeding head in my lap. Vows are sacred to me. The next day, as you well know, I delivered the same message to Mrs. Duggan. What no one knew then was that I made another vow that afternoon.

"You remember, it was one of those early November, wintry days of chill and light snow. Duggan was home when I knocked on the door, but I didn't see him right away. Mrs. Duggan answered, and I told her about the widow's weeds and about how I was going to dance when he died and, finally, that I would bring her the mourning dress. She looked at me with a blank stare and didn't say a word.

"I was about to leave when Duggan came crashing into the front room enraged beyond belief. Had I been a man, I know he would have killed me. He called me horrible names, and he called you and Rachel and our sisters and even our mother horrible names, too. I never told you about this because I knew you'd get yourself killed calling him for it. He kept up this blasphemy for a good five minutes as I slowly backed out of the door. His wrath sputtered out, and it was quiet for a moment.

"With courage that could only have come from a combination of righteousness and terror, I said to him in a very calm voice, 'Marshal Duggan, not only do I swear I will dance on your grave, I'm also going to piss on it. Good day.'

"You said that right to the face of Leadville's most ferocious gunman? You told him you were going to piss on his grave?"

"Yes. And don't forget the dance."

". . . And you did?" John asked tentatively.

"Dance?"

"No. The other."

With a smile she said, "You bet I did."

(At this point in the story, a couple of us kids would usually burst out giggling and my dad would give us all a stern look. He'd tell us how serious it all was and that we better take it as such. Then he'd have to smile. "Now there's 'just pissing,' and then there's 'principled pissing,'" he'd say.)

Mindy went on. "It was a day like no other I had ever lived—a day of reflection, a day of looking at my whole life and seeing all its years and times and memories. It had led to an afternoon on a stone bench at the edge of a cemetery. How many people have seen such a clear boundary between their past and their future as I did there while waiting to finish that which had been, so as to begin what was to come?

"As the sun made its way across the Denver sky that afternoon, I realized it was time to look to the future. God knows I hadn't thought it would take eight years. I know now how much easier it is to say something than to do it—to get into a situation than to get out of it.

"There is quite a view from the cemetery—it can give you a sense of the whole continent. Looking east you see the plains stretching back a thousand miles to Illinois. The people of Colorado refer to the entire eastern part of the United States as being 'back.' You go back east. To the west are the foothills, and beyond them, rising up are the snow peaks of the Rocky Mountains. No one thinks of going back west—we go out west.

"The Riverside Cemetery, for me, was the border between the past and the future of the country and of my life as well. I had gone back east to fulfill an obligation tied to my past. As I waited for the sun to set beyond the magnificent mountains, I faced the west and toward the future. I thought of my family. You, Johnny, and Rachel. I thought of Mamie and her school yard filling with happy Leadville children, but mostly I thought of Edith.

"I felt the chill and realized it was dusk. The mountains were silhouetted by the promising glow of sunset, and I was alone in the dimming light of the graveyard. I gathered up my satchel and walked across the grounds toward the plot of ground under which Duggan lay. I had found his grave by the fresh dirt and by an identification tag attached to a stake driven into the ground. There was a raised pile of dirt and a card that read:

Martin Duggan
Born: County Limerick, Ireland, November 10, 1848
Died: Leadville, Colorado, April 9, 1888

"I stepped to the grave. I thought of the years, of Duggan's short and vicious forty years of violent desperation. I thought of the years, the terrible, mournful eight years I had given to grief. And I thought of the tears.

"Then I did it. I turned a somber step or two, the dance; and then I raised my dress and completed the execution of my oath. Vengeance wasn't mine, only sorrow. I thought of the years and felt the tears that burned my face.

"Grabbing my suitcase, I walked through the wrought iron gateway, out to the street, and made my way to the hotel. That's it, Johnny. I bought this dress the next day and left my dancing clothes in an alleyway. Then I waited for the six o'clock train, and here I am. I hope you don't think me awful—I just did what I felt I had to do."

"Mindy, we all do what we have to do," said John, "But you seem to do it with a hell of a lot of flair. Let's go home."

"Yes, Johnny, but I have to make a stop along the way."

John wanted to ask where, but decided he would no doubt find out—along the way. They walked along Poplar Street with Mindy holding John's arm. With his free hand he carried Mindy's traveling bag. At the corner of Ninth and Poplar was Mamie's school yard. They turned west toward Harrison Avenue. Turning south at Harrison, they walked past the *Herald Democrat* and then the Tabor Grand Hotel on the corner of Seventh. They continued on past the court house between Sixth and Fifth, then past the Silver Dollar Saloon with the Tabor Opera House across the street. At Second, they turned right at the Bucket of Blood Saloon and headed down the infamous State Street.

John stopped and said, "Mindy, the only place you and I can stop on this street is at the Pioneer, and you've said you'd never go in there. What are we doing?"

"Johnny, this is the first full day of my new life in this town without that dreadful black dress. I've kept all the promises of my grief; now its time to start keeping another promise I made long before."

John and Mindy entered the swinging doors of the Pioneer Bar. The place was packed, and everyone was listening as Edie finished her medley of saloon songs up on the stage. She was singing the last verse of "Those Gambler's Blues":

> *. . . and now you've heard my story*
> *I'll take another shot of booze;*
> *If anybody happens to ask you,*
> *Then I've got those gambler's blues.*

Mindy had worked her way through the crowd to the piano. The applause was loud, and the raucous miners were continuing their nefarious pleasures. Edie was climbing down from the stage when she saw her sister.

"Get your coat on," Mindy said as she hugged Edie. "I think when Mama asked me to take care of you and to help you find your way, she was talking about tonight. The 'way,' sister, is out those swinging doors."

Afterword: Reflections
Robert Nichols

My parents were born and spent their youths in the coal country
of Appalachia—my mother in eastern Kentucky and my father in
West Virginia. I have uncles and cousins who spent their whole
working lives in the labyrinthine depths burrowed beneath the
hardwood forests and huckleberry patches of the great eastern
mountains. I never knew two of my uncles because they were lost
to the sudden hazards of the mines before I was born. Others knew
the slower hazard of "black lung." I remember my Uncle Paul
walking up the gravel driveway of my grandmother's house and
the smile he would give me through the mask of coal dust that
coated his face as he headed down the cellar steps to the shower.

When Ed proposed that we combine efforts in the creation of
a work about his hometown of Leadville, the idea immediately
appealed to me as one who had missed the mines by one generation and as one who had known the mountains of Colorado for a
score of years.

For a subject to be worthy of the effort required in the production of a book, it should be unique enough to be interesting and,
yet, universal enough to have wide empathetic basis in the experiences of readers. Leadville was ideal. Historically, geographically,
and economically the town has a singularity of identity that makes it
unlike any other place in the world. Regarding the presence of elements that are universal to the human condition, just read the

personal stories we have gathered here and you will know the values that are basic to the survival of decent communities anywhere in the world. Recurring themes—perseverance in the face of adversity, the rewards of hard and honest labor, the joys of a close and supportive family, the courage that is born of necessity—are common to any cluster of humanity determined not to be lost to despair.

A sweet sadness entwines the tales told by the keepers of Leadville's oral history. When each told the stories of grandparents and parents and of the town as known in the ephemeral epoch of youth, though the recollections were almost always humorous and the spirit universally positive, there was the presence of an under-lying sense of mortal loss to it all. Don Kerzon, grandson of Frank Zaitz, spent an hour or so telling me of his childhood in the Aus-trian neighborhood of the west side of Leadville. He told of a com-munity where people took care of one another. There was always a neighbor, a friend, a relative there to share the best and worst of life's burdens and gifts. He described wonderful festivals where lambs from his grandfather's farm would be roasted and wine drunk, songs sung, and the entire west-side Austrian community would celebrate life together. I asked if those times were over, and he assured me that such days were surely past.

Stories of youth are as temporal as they are beautiful. Many of the people I talked with viewed their personal experiences and those of their families as being uniquely valuable and forever van-quished by the persistence of change. ("With cable television and Nintendo, it will never be the same again.")

Such is mortality. To find more than transient wealth to these tales, we must know them to be more than just golden moments of a single generation. Ed found the quotation by Voltaire that we used in the book, to the effect that history doesn't repeat itself, but people do. When this wisdom is applied to the recurring environ-mental, socio-economic, and political blunders of our species, it is tragic. But when it is seen as an assurance that the beauty of the human condition might also find replication in succeeding gen-erations, it has less of a devastating effect on the spirit. In each life can be the joy of carefully choosing a flat stone and skipping it across the mirror-still surface of a pond; of exploring the often awkward and always blissfully unreasonable instincts and rituals of love; of knowing the delirious pride and tactile bond of cradling the warmth and vulnerability of a baby in our arms. Unless there is an unprecedented and radical development in human consciousness, we will likely continue to elect self-serving fools to run our societies; we will likely continue to sacrifice the majority of our creative and spiritual essences to the narcotics of comfort and ease; and we will likely not rise above the cruelty and ignorance that have dominated the past. But each of us has the opportunity to know the good feelings that come from active compassion, the return of friendship given, and the marvel of seeking the answer to questions unanswerable.

You certainly don't have to be from Leadville to know the wondrous pleasures of good family, good friends, and the allure of the mysteries of existence; but, somehow distilling this mixture of history and tradition has brought such priorities into a clearer focus for me. It has been a very worthwhile creative process for me.

I had many memorable "Leadville" experiences while working on this book. Much of the spirit of what I had encountered in the libraries, the barrooms, and the parlors of this fine town was crystallized in an unforgettable incident that occurred while seeking a couple of hours of a "miner's" view of the world.

I was 1,100 feet down the Black Cloud Shaft of the Asarco Mining Company up in Iowa Gulch having my first go at drilling in a dank and eerie stope. I was being treated as a privileged character that day with geologist Ben Arndt providing me with a personal tour. I had never been "underground" before and was hoping I wouldn't make a fool of myself. A miner named Randy had graciously allowed me to man his pneumatic drill and have at the lead-rich rock with a four-foot bit. I was determined to do right by my mining heritage and stayed with it all the way in. Randy tapped me on the shoulder and shouted for me to pull back a lever and let the pressure off. I did so and, with a geyser-like belch, a spray of rock particles and water blasted from the hole and covered me with the gritty mix. I removed my safety glasses, spat out some of the residue, and began picking the rubble from my beard. Randy said, "I guess I should have told you to stand back when you let the pressure off."

I put a hand on his muscular shoulder and said that if I hadn't seen the ease with which he threw a 130-pound drill around we might have had a real problem. Then we all laughed—the geologist who knew what was coming, the novice driller who took a bath, and the miner who honored me with a rite of initiation kindred to mining traditions that probably go back as far as King Solomon's mines.

"How about another go?" I asked.

"Sure."

And the next time I was standing the hell out of the way when I released the pressure.

Leadville, in spirit and tradition, is yet alive.

Nostalgia is sentimental recollection of mortal interaction with the infinite. In Leadville are the mines and winters and the incredible mountains to constantly remind people of both their mortality and the presence of the infinite. It is not surprising that people still find religious inspiration in Mount Massive. The Native Americans who inhabited this land long before the lure of mineral wealth brought white prospectors to the banks of the Arkansas River knew of the holiness of the great mountains. Somewhere in the stretch between the humbling powers of the gods and the defiant spirit of Leadville's people, there is much we can all learn about survival.

I hope you readers have enjoyed this visit to Ed Larsh's hometown as much as I have.

Massive Magic

There is but one magic mountain
for Leadville folk.
I was aware of its presence at a tender age.
The family would go 'round the loop
and drink its mineral-laden soda water.
My mother later gazed at the sunsets
trying to understand the connection with WWII,
silently seeking solace somewhere
west of the Sawatch Range.

I can't explain the magic that penetrates
the crystal clear air-waves between
Mount Massive and the old mining town,
and yet can I feel it,
as do most of my Leadville friends—
ragged-ass miners
not excepted—
poets all.

—ED B. LARSH

Afterword: Reflections on Home
Ed B. Larsh

Carl Miller, who spent nearly thirty years underground in the mines of Leadville and who brought his knowledge and experience to the Leadville Mining Museum, contributed to our book by sharing his ideas and memories. When I asked him for a statement of his personal beliefs about Leadville, he said, "I personally think that the free press in America, believing literally in the Bill of Rights, especially as witnessed in small towns, has made the difference between the theory of democracy and its practice."

Carl brought to my attention something that Carlyle Channing Davis, an early newspaper editor in Leadville, once said. Davis paraphrased a statement by the English novelist, William Makepeace Thackeray, and applied it to Leadville. It pretty much sums up what I believe also. "There has been but one Leadville. Never will there be another. Leadville has ambassadors in every quarter of the world—her courtiers upon every road. Her officers march along with armies, and her envoys walk into statesmen's cabinets. Leadville's ambassadors are ubiquitous."

I do, in fact, feel as if I am a Leadville ambassador; I haven't walked into many statesmen's cabinets, but I have connected with a great number of people who understand the concept of "home." I also have learned that you can find such people in every walk of life.

People such as Carl Miller can fool you, for example. I knew of only two people in Leadville who had ever heard of William

Makepeace Thackeray—one was a plumber, and the other was Don Griswold, a Latin teacher. Now I know of a third, an eloquent, ex-miner named Carl Miller.

We were well into the intimate stories of *Leadville U.S.A.* before we discovered the main vein. As we excavated the past, both personal and collective (what you might call autobiography and history), we eventually discovered that our central theme was the literary mode called *Romance.* The story of "going home after having left it" was being told to us over and over. It wasn't until Jane and I visited the farms around Preble County, Ohio, that we began asking, "Why? Why in 1875 did five of fourteen children leave home for the lure of the West? Why go against the continental and psychic grain—over the Rocky Mountains into the unknown?"

We learned a simple truth: what Homer was saying through Odysseus was that you must leave home to fulfill the promise that we can all be free, that we can be successful on our own. The lure of the West in 1875 offered a new start, a fresh new opportunity, a chance to overcome failure.

Going to these farmlands of the Midwest in 1992 was, in fact, looking backward. There are very few new frontiers in the last decade of the twentieth century. That may account for why so many of us seem forced to die on the hills of our heritage. We are seeking home on the eighth floor of the Genealogical Library in Salt Lake City, Utah.

The five Larshes that came to Leadville in 1878 were fugitives. They were searching for El Dorado in one sense of the word, and they were searching for a sanctuary where they could be themselves in another. Those who stayed in the mountains through a winter or two—or fifty—at ten-thousand feet discovered both. El Dorado wasn't the quick fix of gold but the truth of universal values. In finding that out, they could be themselves—a man working so that he could have some leisure to enjoy his family, a mother who feels she is very fortunate because her kids are coming home to dinner. Some people of Leadville found the temporary comforts of social intercourse in the enclaves of ethnic identity, but that wasn't enough. They still had to struggle; the world was bigger than Frank

Zaitz or the Elk's Club, or even working at the Little Jonny Mine.

Researching and writing an intimate oral history of your home-town does, in fact, lead you into every quarter of the world. It can also send you back to the connections that, at the time, seemed formed for other purposes. I didn't understand the word "home" until I picked up A. Bartlett Giamatti's beautiful book, *Take Time for Paradise.* I now understand *Leadville U.S.A.*

I took the liberty of writing to Dr. Giamatti when he was president of Yale University. It was during the great "Moral Majority" epidemic of this country's not so distant past. I had read in the *New York Times* of Dr. Giamatti's courageous stand in the face of the religious fanaticism sweeping the nation. He had addressed a letter to the prospective members of the incoming freshman class at Yale that has implications far beyond the occasion for which it was written.

In essence, his letter said that if they, as future Yale students, believed in the bigotry and prejudicial divisiveness that was being promulgated by the propaganda merchants of the Moral Majority, Yale was not the place for them to come.

I wrote a letter in support of his stand. I had never met him, but I so strongly supported his view I felt obligated to let him know. Here was a scholar, a leader of one of America's Ivy League citadels who stood up to be counted as a majority of one against the euphemistic babble of the Moral Majority. The least I could do was to send him a "bravo" and let him know he was not entirely alone. To my amazement, he wrote back, not a form letter, but a two-page personal letter expressing sincere gratitude for my understanding and support of his courage.

A few years later I wrote him again, this time to congratulate him on his appointment as Commissioner of Major League Baseball. Again, he wrote to thank me and told me of a book he was writing on baseball and the concept of "home." A few weeks after he took office, Pete Rose was found guilty of betting on the outcome of baseball games, and Commissioner Giamatti took another courageous stand and suspended Rose from the sport for life. A short time later, I was addressing a rather large meeting of educators on the importance of values in our bankrupt society, and somehow the question came up as to whether I believed Pete Rose should be admitted to the Baseball Hall of Fame. My reply was—no, Pete Rose didn't belong in the Hall of Fame, but A. Bartlett Giamatti did.

The book he mentioned was published after his death. He died on April 1, 1989. The book was aptly titled, *Take Time for Paradise.* When he died, America lost more than a college president and a baseball commissioner; it lost a hero, a scholarly philosopher, and a daring poet. Only a poet could use the concept of "home," relate it to America's national pastime, and simultaneously catch the essence of life as a struggle in which freedom is the fulfillment of the promise of an energetic, complex system. Giamatti believed that we cherish baseball because it is a game where reunion and freedom are both possible. He said that we work so that we can have time to enjoy leisure, to play, to appreciate art and beauty, to listen for a distant rhythm, and to see the drama of life with a creative eye.

Going home is where restoration occurs because that is where it matters most. Stability, origins, a sense of oneness, the first clearing in the woods—to go home may be impossible but it is often a driving necessity, or at least a compelling dream. As the heroes of romance beginning with Odysseus know, the route is full of turnings, wanderings, danger. To attempt to go home is to go the long way around, to stray and separate in the hope of finding completeness in reunion, freedom in reintegration with those left behind. In baseball, the journey begins at home, negotiates the twists and turns at first, and often founders far out at the edges of the ordered world at rocky second—the farthest point from home. Whoever remains out there is said to "die" on base. Home is finally beyond reach in a hostile world full of quirks and tricks and hostile folks. There are no dragons in baseball, only shortstops, but they can emerge from nowhere to cut one down.

I believe there were unique circumstances that created a Leadville character. They were those conditions, those phenomena that brought thousands of people into an isolated, two-mile high, experience of discovery at a special time in the development of the West, both economically and historically, and then said to them: "It ain't gonna get any better than this . . . now what?"

Americans went west beyond the wide Missouri because they were adventurers, but also because they were fugitives searching for a new beginning where they could be free from the oppression of the economic past. It is little wonder that many of them were unable to feel "safe at home" in the cold and isolated mountains, among the cold suspicions of cultural differences. Not everyone was as strong as Augusta Tabor or Rachel Larsh.

What happened was that most of them, even after they arrived and had settled into their own particular ghetto, eventually picked up and moved on, looking for El Dorado some place else, trying another geographical solution, attempting to find themselves, escaping what they perceived as failure. Most of the 1880 fugitives didn't find what they needed in Leadville, but some did. *It is really in honor of those heroes and heroines that we have written this book:* those few hundred who stayed and risked seeking, and making, home, hoping for a reunion. In this lies the theme of *Leadville U.S.A.*

Acknowledgments

A partial list of those who shared—we couldn't possibly list them all—but the book is because of their love for Leadville, as are their stories.

Julia Beurman
Iona Brink
Alberta Mangold Coble
J. J. Coble
Jimmy Connors
Michael Donovan
Terry Fitzsimmons
Evelyn Furman
Fred Geis
Don Griswold
K. Jean Harvey Griswold
Jerry Harrold
Walt Jackson
Bill Kerrigan
Ed Kerrigan
Wallace Kerzon
Ann Kitt
Ray Kitt
Ed Kutzleb
A. J. ("Jack") Laing
Don Larsh
Jack Larsh
Carol Brink Luoma
Jack Luoma

Gerald McMillin
Thelma Larsh McMillin
Michael McNierney
Don Moffett
Rose Peschel Montaro
Tut Montaro
Ginny Myers
Bad Pete #5
Frank Pacheco
Jimmy Raine
Neil Reynolds
Doc ("Billy") Rose
Bernard ("Bun") Ryan
Johanna Jacopiz Schaeffer
Ted Schaeffer
Harry ("Squint") Schraeder
George ("Ginger") Schrieber
Edith Seppi
Bill Skala
Jean McDonald Steffan
Francys Stolcar
John Swenson
Vivian Swenson

Index

294   *Leadville U.S.A.*